IMAGES
of America

ERWIN AND PAINTED POST

On the Cover: Following World War I, militaries worldwide recognized that they had to modernize. This truck at Dresser-Rand was one of many experiments in that direction. (Courtesy of Corning–Painted Post Historical Society.)

IMAGES
of America

ERWIN AND PAINTED POST

Kirk W. House

ARCADIA
PUBLISHING

ISBN 978-1-4671-2090-6

Published by Arcadia Publishing
Charleston, South Carolina

Printed in the United States of America

Library of Congress Control Number: 2013946601

For all general information, please contact Arcadia Publishing:
Telephone 843-853-2070
Fax 843-853-0044
E-mail sales@arcadiapublishing.com
For customer service and orders:
Toll-Free 1-888-313-2665

Visit us on the Internet at www.arcadiapublishing.com

Contents

ACKNOWLEDGMENTS

Over the years, I have had the privilege of ransacking the photograph collections of the Corning–Painted Post Historical Society (C-PPHS) while composing three books. I have been in "back rooms" in the shivering winter and the sweltering summer, but it has always been a pleasure. Since this pleasure has continued even as personnel have changed, it is clear that this welcome is part of the institutional personality at the society, both at the Benjamin Patterson Inn Museum complex and at the Painted Post–Erwin Museum in the Delaware, Lackawanna & Western (DL&W) depot. Indeed, C-PPHS director Sheri Golder is the one who first suggested that I take on this project. Unless otherwise noted, images in this book are from the Corning–Painted Post Historical Society.

Numerous images come from the Steuben County Historian's office (SCH), where we need to thank Historian Twila O'Dell and her able colleague, Eleanor Silliman. Others came from the Steuben County Historical Society (SCHS), where Nedra McElroy in particular has been assiduous in building up the photograph collection. Kris Gable and the good folks at Corning Incorporated (CI) have once again been helpful. Richard Price (RP) sent in two key images as soon as he learned that this project was under way. Mike Connor made some photographs available from the Erie Lackawanna Historical Society (ELHS). The Glenn H. Curtiss Museum (GHCM) provided several aviation photographs. Several contemporary photographs were taken by myself (KWH), and another comes from the Finger Lakes Trail Conference (FLTC).

For those who want to further explore this area of New York State, we should mention three Images of America books: my own *The 1972 Flood in New York's Southern Tier*; *Corning*, which I did in collaboration with Charles R. Mitchell; and *Painted Post*, by Jamie Bosket. All historians of the area owe a debt of gratitude to Tom Dimitroff and Lois Janes for *History of the Corning–Painted Post Area: 200 Years in Painted Post Country.*

And I owe a personal debt of gratitude to Sheri Golder, helpful and hospitable director of the Corning–Painted Post Historical Society, and to my wife, Joyce House, who helped me sort through photographs and sped up the process considerably by recording words while I scanned pictures. Thanks to them, and to all who have helped.

INTRODUCTION

Until the American Revolution, this territory was under Seneca rule, as something of a military frontier. Most of the major Iroquois towns and cities were farther north, but there was a good-sized town where the rivers joined, at what is now called Erwin. This was a strategic point. The rivers themselves were highways, and the nexus of rivers here form the Chemung, which farther east joins the Susquehanna, which runs all the way down to Chesapeake Bay. The Susquehanna and Chemung formed a promising route for friend and foe alike. The town at the junction kept ward on that system and on the tributaries that join it. On top of that, three major land routes came together here: one along the Chemung and Conhocton Rivers; one along the Canisteo River; and a third running along the Tioga River, down into (or from) what is now called Pennsylvania. The town with the painted post watched them all.

The Iroquois, or Haudenosaunne, as they called themselves, maintained their independence by adaptation (some attended college in Europe), military might, and highly skilled diplomacy. But that independence came to an end following a devastating invasion during the Revolutionary War, and a series of harsh treaties afterward. The United States took land title for itself, then sold it off for revenue or gave it away in payment for obligations. The first white resident was William Harris, who arrived in 1786.

Col. Arthur Erwin had done well in the Revolutionary War, and in the real estate game. Among other things, he owned eight or nine miles of the Delaware River. In 1789, he was driving a herd of cattle from Pennsylvania for sale in Niagara Falls when he passed through the stretch of country where the Canisteo River joins the Tioga River, and where the Tioga joins the Conhocton River to form the Chemung River. After studying the prospect (and the prospects), he drove his herd to Canandaigua and cut a deal at the land office, using his cattle as a down payment. The trip to Niagara would not be needed, after all, and for $1,500, Arthur Erwin owned a large swath of what is now Steuben County—today's Town of Erwin, and more. Steuben County was created from Ontario County in 1796.

Not that it did him much good in the long run. In 1792, Erwin visited again, leaving sons Francis and Samuel behind to manage the estate. On his way home to Bucks County, Pennsylvania, Arthur Erwin was shot dead in a dispute with an alleged squatter. Land speculation on the 18th-century frontier required steel nerves and an iron constitution, not to mention knowing when to duck.

The Town of Painted Post was established in 1793. The "supertown" was eventually partitioned into the current towns of Hornby, Campbell, Erwin, Lindley, Corning, and Caton, plus the City of Corning. The Erwin family stayed with the town formed in 1826 and named for their cattle-driving patriarch. They were not thinking of future historians, though, for the men recycled their given names several times in each generation, in the meantime running through numerous military ranks.

In 1833, Capt. Samuel Erwin laid out what is now the Village of Painted Post within the Town of Erwin. A plank school existed on the site before the village itself. As the Civil War approached,

Erwin residents showed a high percentage of literacy, not unusual in the North. Learning continues to be important; in 2013, Sriram Hathwar of Painted Post took third place in the Scripps-Howard National Spelling Bee. There are two public schools, Erwin Valley Elementary and Corning-Painted Post West High. The latter is scheduled for conversion to a middle school in 2014.

Though overwhelmingly a rural community, Erwin was carried along on the currents of national life. Some 250 Erwin men went to the Civil War, and a couple of dozen died, not counting those who were discharged and gave up the ghost at home. This total also excludes those men who lost a limb or suffered other disabilities.

The Great Depression brought a Civilian Conservation Corps camp. During World War II, the hamlet of Coopers Plains had its own dedicated air-raid siren. But, with strategic targets in short supply, it never got put to a practical test.

In the second half of the 20th century, Erwin kept pace with the nation at large. The one-room schools were gone by 1957. A man in Gang Mills was the first local victim of the 1972 Hurricane Agnes flood. Another 17 people died in the event. As the century waned, dairy farms were converted into space for hotels and retail establishments. The town, comprising 29.16 square miles, now has two post offices, in Painted Post and in Coopers Plains. The 2010 population was 8,037 people.

In Seneca times, the waterways were highways. The Conhocton, Tioga, Canisteo, and Tuscarora Rivers come together in Erwin, forming the Chemung River. Later, railroads and interstate highways used Erwin as a meeting place. Industry thrived in the Gang Mills–Painted Post area, while the rest of the town remained cheerfully rural, the haunt of game lands, dairy farms, and hiking trails.

The Erie Railroad pushed through in the 1850s, followed by competitors and feeders. Today, there are major rail yards (Norfolk Southern) and major industries (Dresser-Rand, Corning Incorporated). There is also a foot trail that runs from Erwin to Alabama. High-tech research and production facilities for the 21st century overshadow 18th-century burial grounds. Welcome to Erwin.

One

The Village

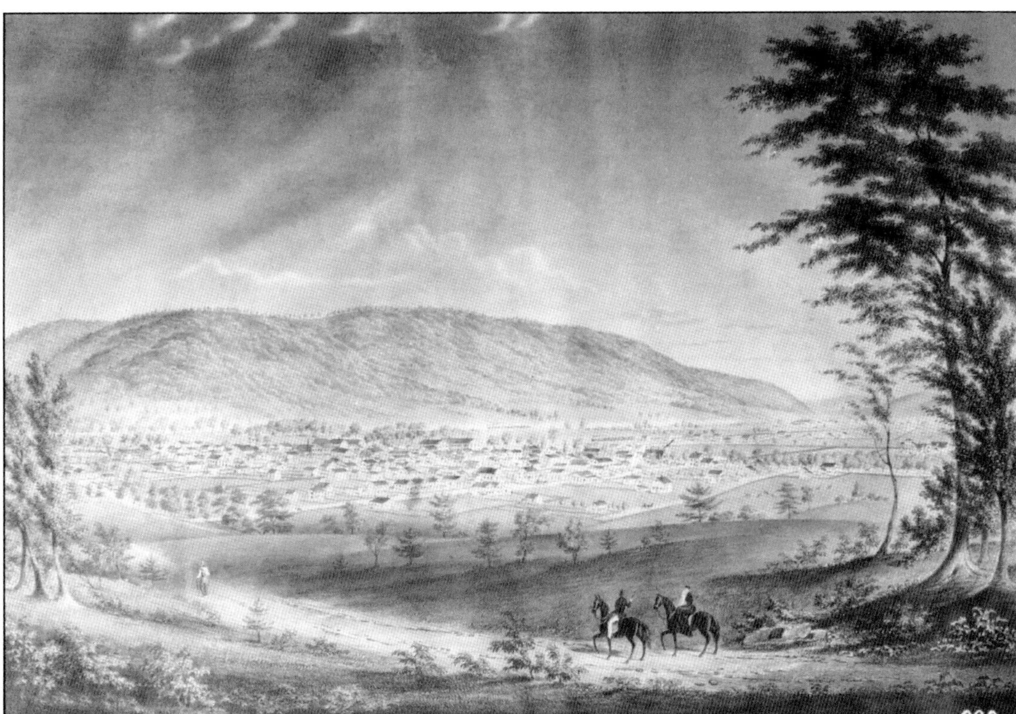

A village in New York constitutes an additional layer of government, rather than a separate incorporation. Since 1893, Painted Post has had a village government with its own board, taxes, zoning, and services, including police, water, and sewage. It remains part of the larger, mostly rural Town of Erwin. In 2013, after a hard-fought campaign, voters elected to retain the village incorporation, rather than dissolve entirely into the township.

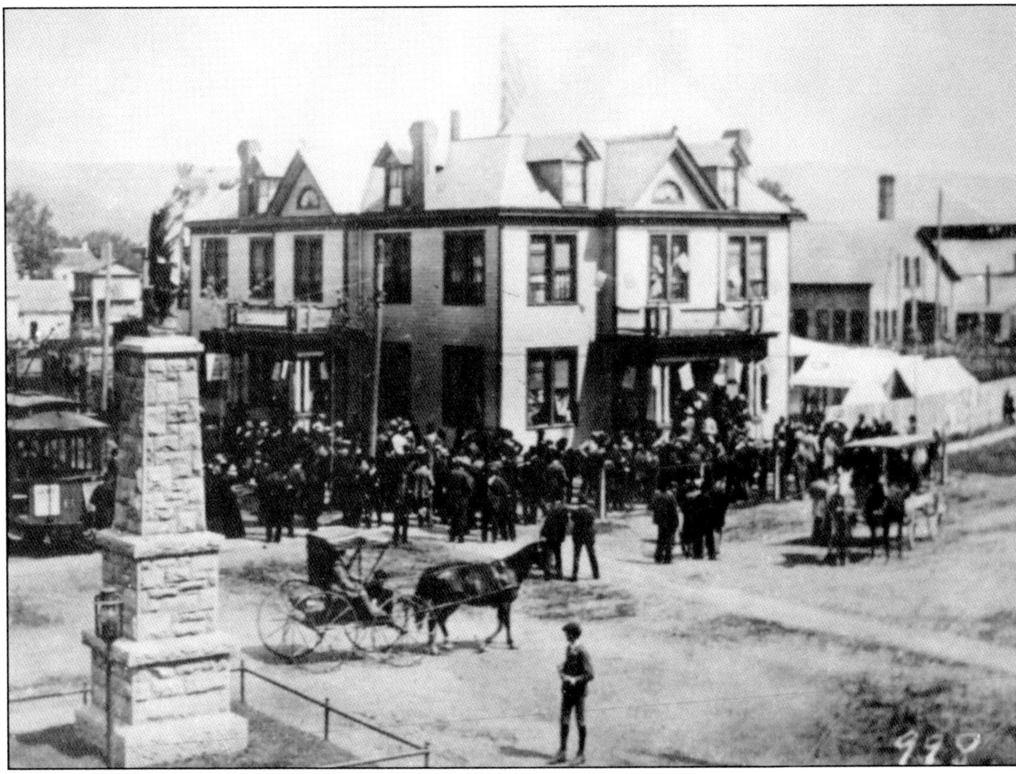

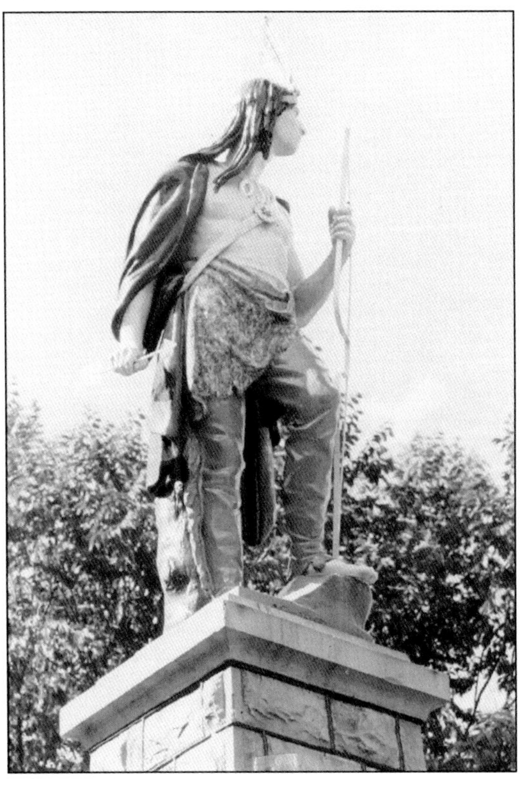

The "Painted Post" country got its name from a huge tree elaborately decorated by the Iroquois. After the tree's demise, local whites mounted a series of metal Indians in its memory. Note the electric streetcar on the left. A trolley line joined Painted Post with Corning, Elmira, and Watkins Glen.

This metal statue, the third in the series, was blown down in a 1948 windstorm. Compared to the first two sheet-metal versions, it was a realistic depiction of an Indian, or at least a realistic depiction of what someone in a factory thought an Indian looked like. All three of these figures now stand in the Erwin–Painted Post Museum at the old DL&W depot. This photograph was taken in 1913.

Col. H. W. BOSTWICK, Major DANIEL GORTON, Capt. THOMAS M'BURNEY, J. P. MALLORY, WM. G. GILBERT,	Painted Post.
BENJAMIN FARWELL, D. H. BONHAM, URIAH BALCOM,	Campbell.
Col. F. E. ERWIN, Lieut. Col. A. ERWIN, Jr. WASHINGTON BARNES,	Erwin.
Major TIMOTHY WHITING, HENRY S. WILLIAMS, S. H. ARNOLD,	Tyrone.

An 1837 invitation to the Military and Civic Ball in the county seat of Bath (see page 87) listed two colonels, a lieutenant colonel, a major, and a captain in the militia of Erwin and Painted Post. The towns covered much more territory than they do today, but they still had a combined population of only 2,708, almost half of whom were women while many of the remainder were overage or underage. Two of the field-grade officers were Erwins, of course. (SCHS.)

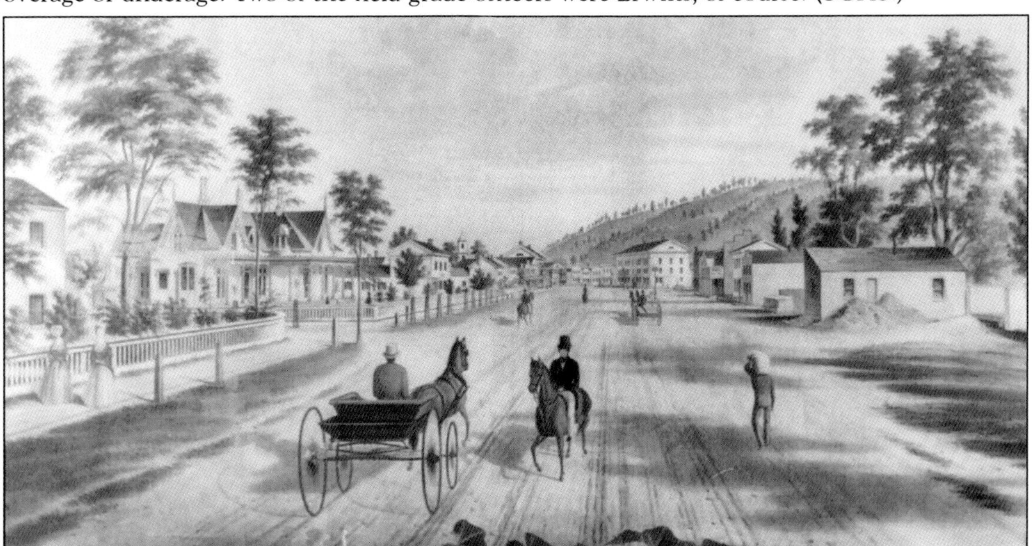

"I have fallen in love with American names," wrote poet Stephen Vincent Benét, and Painted Post was one of them. That vanished town name was revived in 1893 for the village. Water Street in the village, shown here, must have been quite an elegant place in the 1800s.

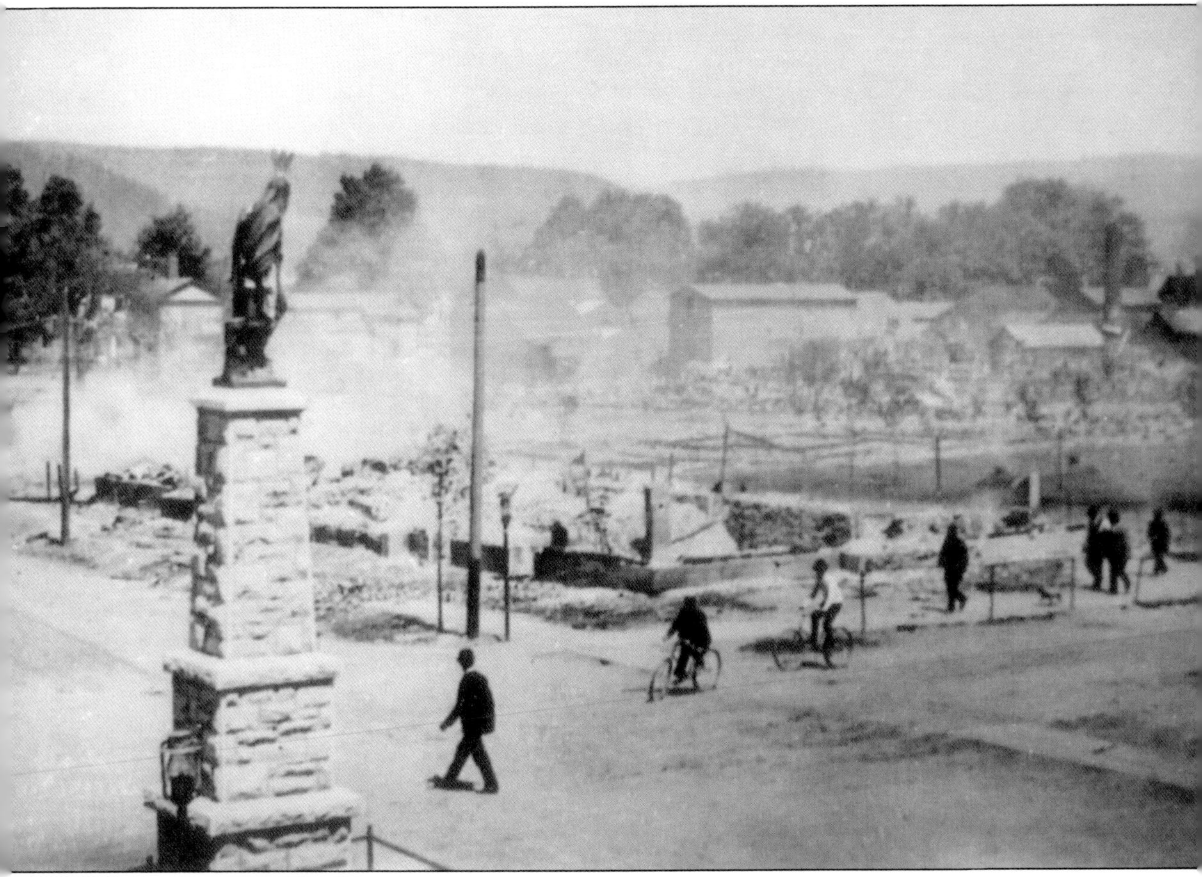

Village buildings were commonly constructed of wood frame. This, combined with the prevalence of fire for cooking, heating, lighting, and power generation, meant that fires were at once inevitable, frequent, and devastating. On May 16, 1896, a fire in downtown Painted Post destroyed a hotel, a livery stable, three homes, and Weston Engineering. In this photograph, the statue appears to be surveying the smoldering ruins. (SCH.)

Even in the wake of the 1896 blaze, the trolley continued to roll through town.

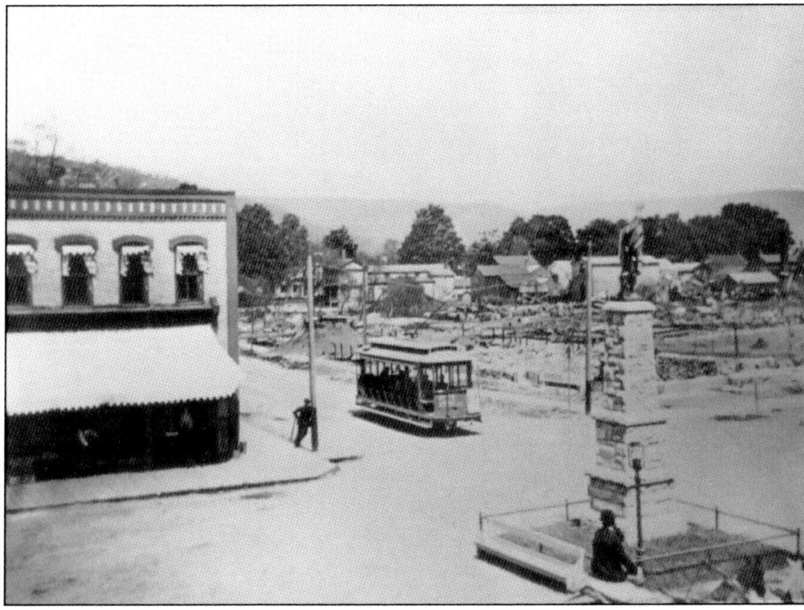

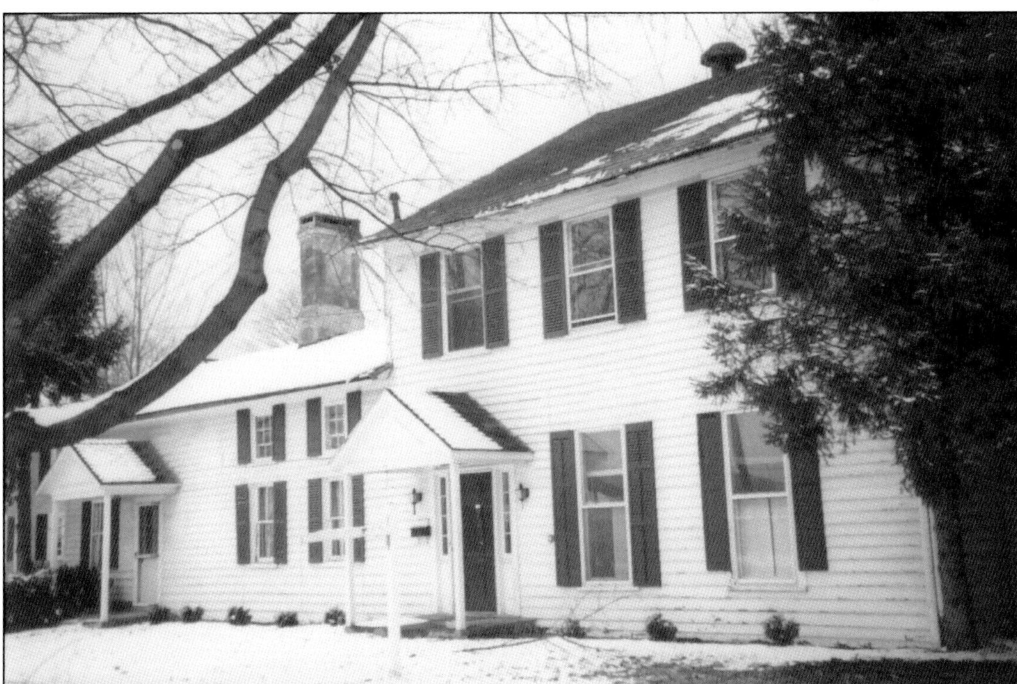

Samuel E. and Rachel Erwin built the first frame home in Painted Post in 1822, at what is now the corner of West Water and Steuben Streets. According to the 1879 W.W. Clayton *History of Steuben County*, "Capt. Erwin was the ideal settler and pioneer, his height being nearly six and a half feet, and his frame erect and powerful. It is said that for physical vigor and endurance he had no equal in the county, if in Western New York." (SCH.)

This fine 19th-century photograph shows Hamilton Street coming up from the south, across the bridge on the left, and Water Street leading away to the west. Note the spiderweb of utility wires, and the Baptist church to the right. Just visible in the lower right-hand corner is the railing that surrounds the Indian statue. J.R. Jones Grocer has the storefront at center. Mr. Jones has his delivery wagon parked directly in front of the store, very likely in anticipation of the photographer.

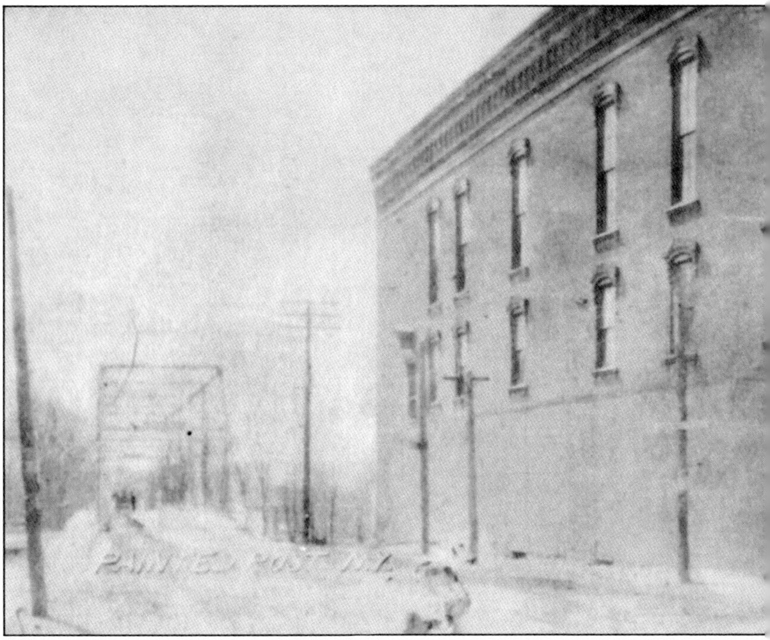

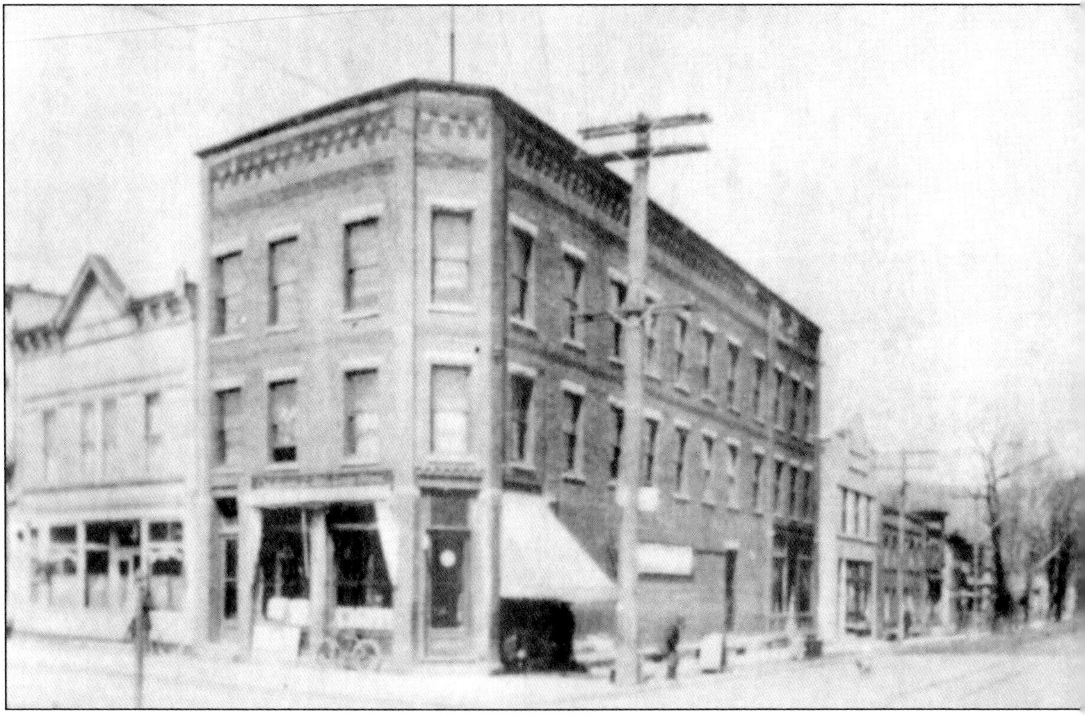

In this companion photograph to the one above, Hamilton Street heads off to the north, and Water Street leads eastward at far right. The bicycle on the sidewalk places this photograph as not before the 1890s, and the railing for the statue dates it as no earlier than 1894. A motorcar is shown on Water Street, further dating the photograph as probably no earlier than 1900. The

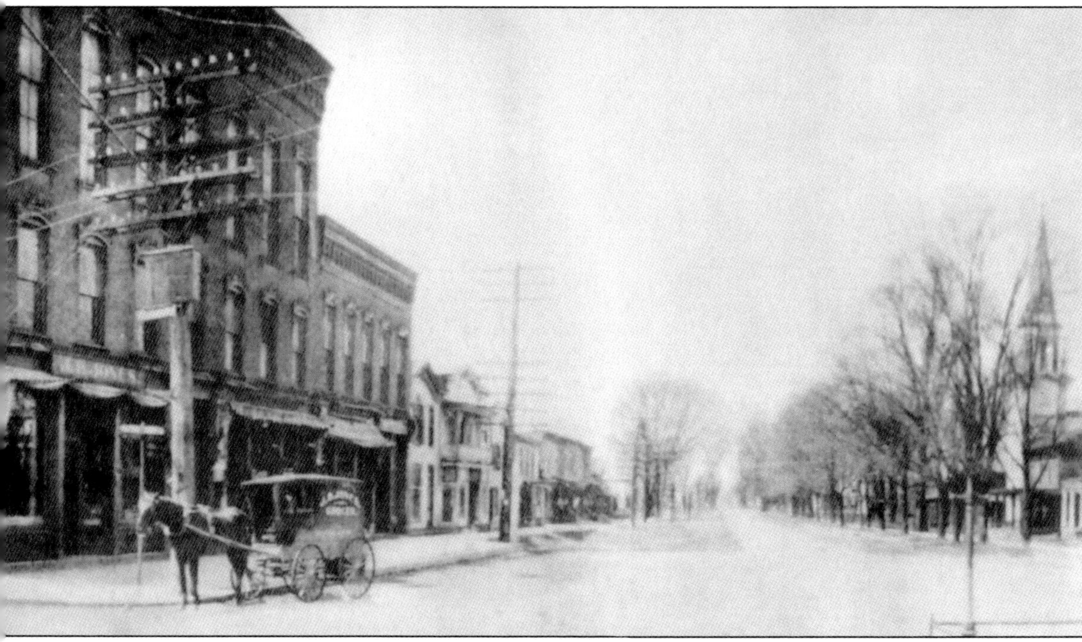

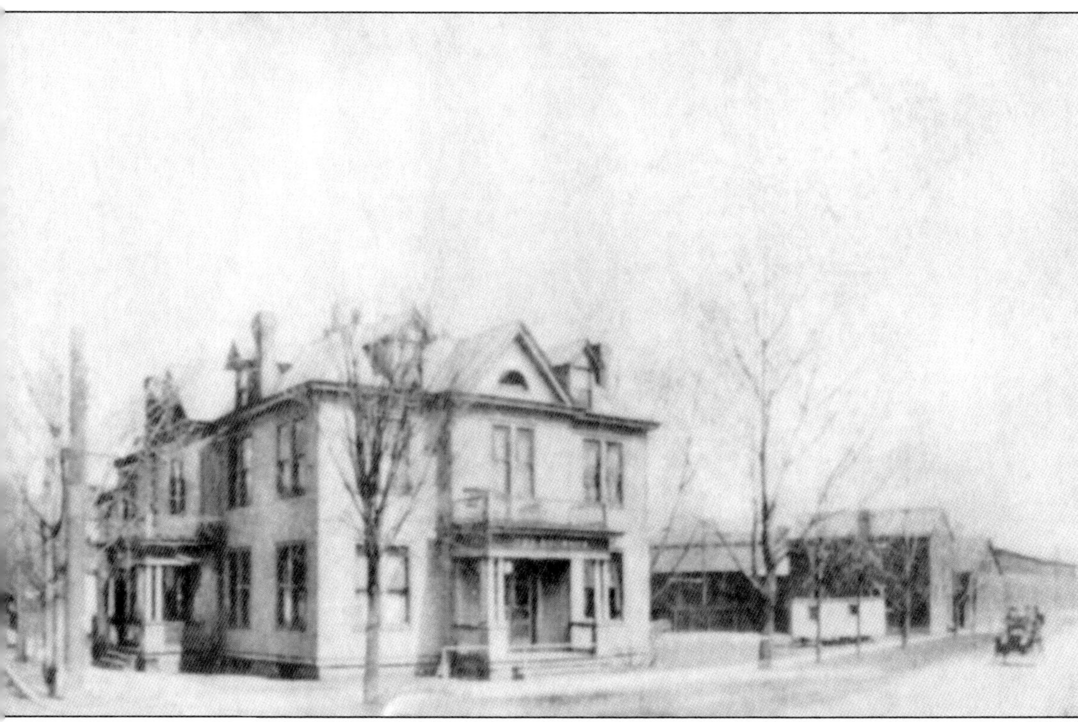

industrial facilities along Water Street had several identities after the 1896 fire, and in 1905, they became Ingersoll-Rand. For this and the previous image, the photographer set up near the statue but kept it out of the field of view.

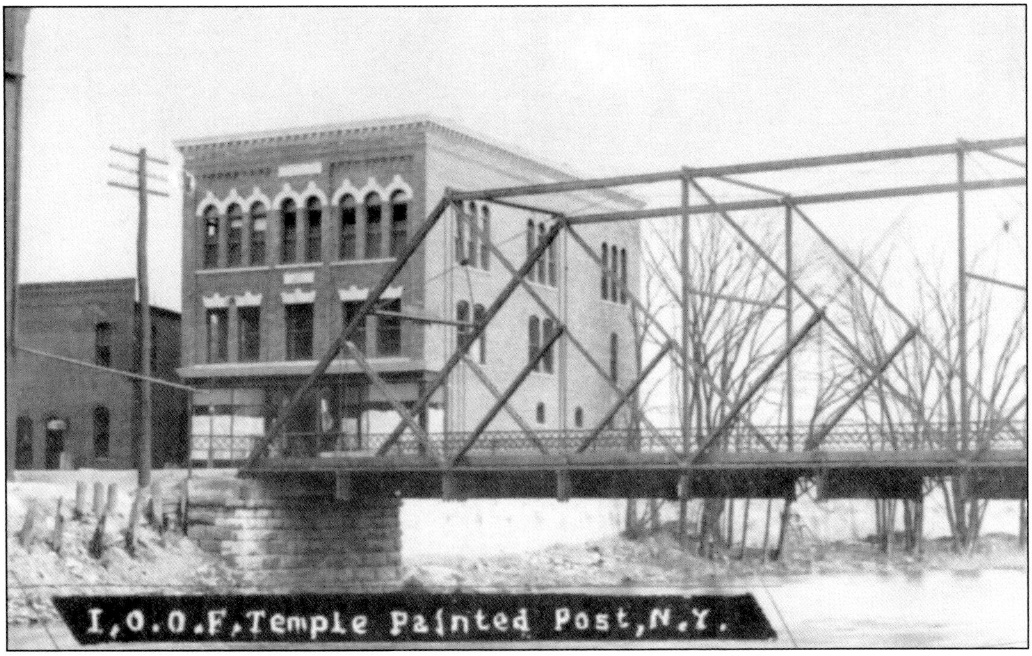

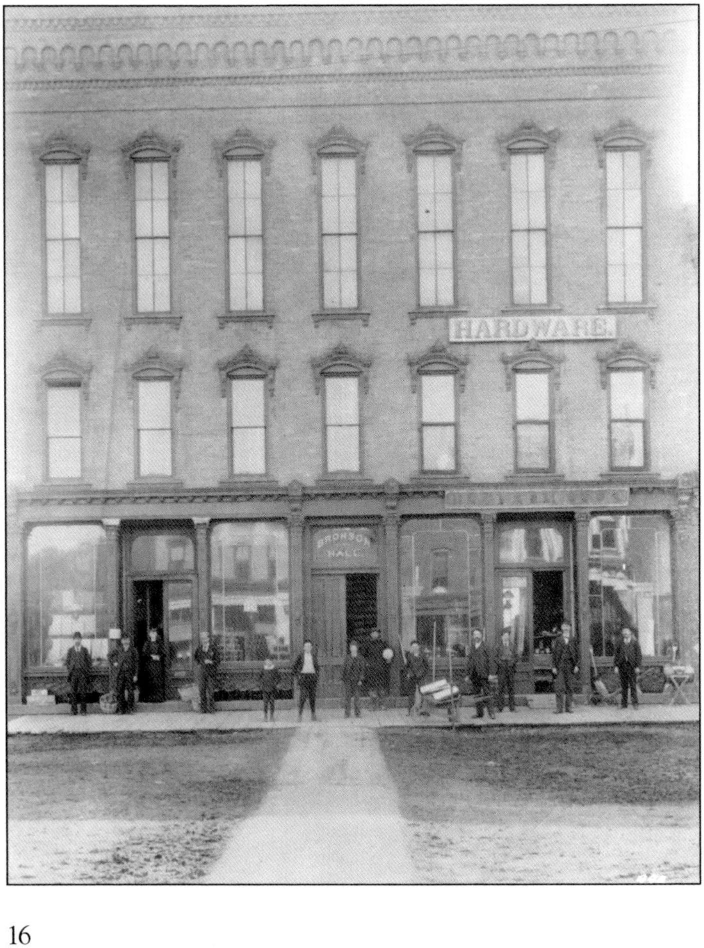

Like most towns from about 1840 to 1970, Erwin had its share of lodges and social clubs. As this postcard shows, the International Order of Odd Fellows (IOOF) had its home right by the Hamilton Street bridge.

Bronson Hall at various times held Bronson Bank, Masonic rooms, a public hall, offices, a hardware store, and what appears to be a grocery store in this photograph. The truly assiduous scholar could study reflections in the lower window to obtain a (reversed) image of the building across the street.

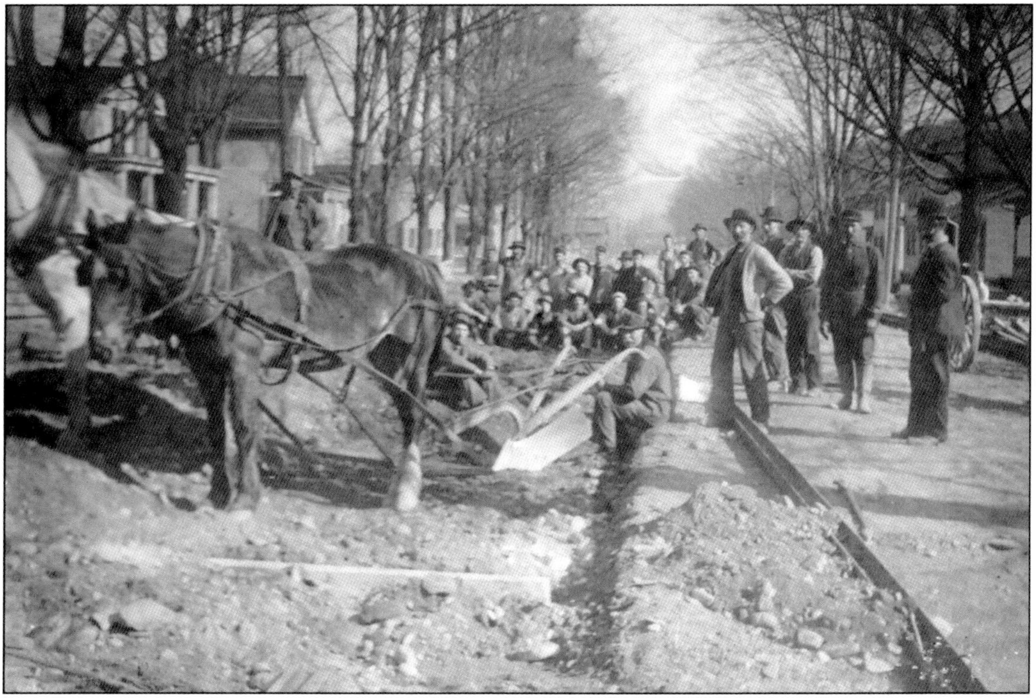

Streetcar tracks are being installed around 1894 or 1895 at what was then Hamilton and High Streets. The men and horses on the job seem to be outnumbered by sidewalk superintendents.

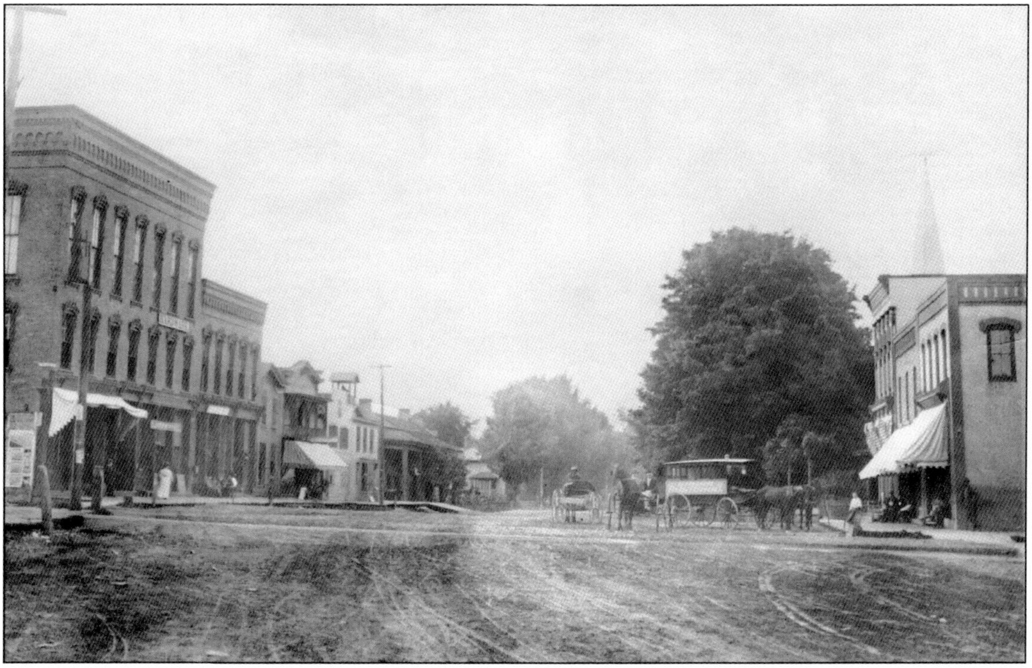

This photograph of Water and Hamilton Streets shows the steeple of the old Baptist church on the right. The tower of the old firehouse is visible just left of the utility pole in the distance, left of center. The horse-drawn omnibus on the right displaying the words "Corning Painted Post" dates this photograph to before the electric streetcar.

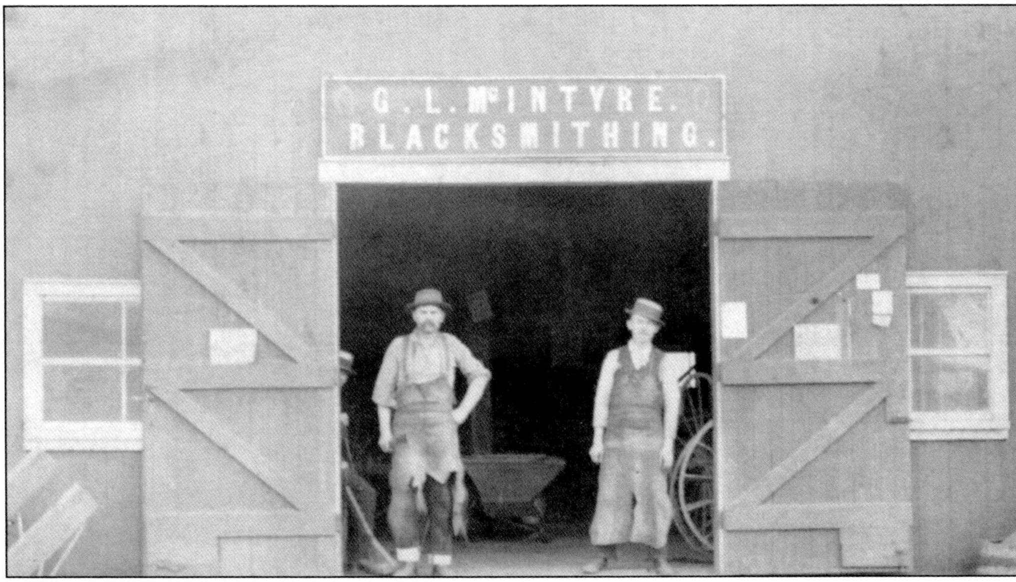

Before firms such as Rand, Imperial, and Weston, there were smiths. These workers were vital in the age of the horse, but their work extended far beyond that. Blacksmiths fabricating new parts from the pattern of a broken part kept America's machinery humming.

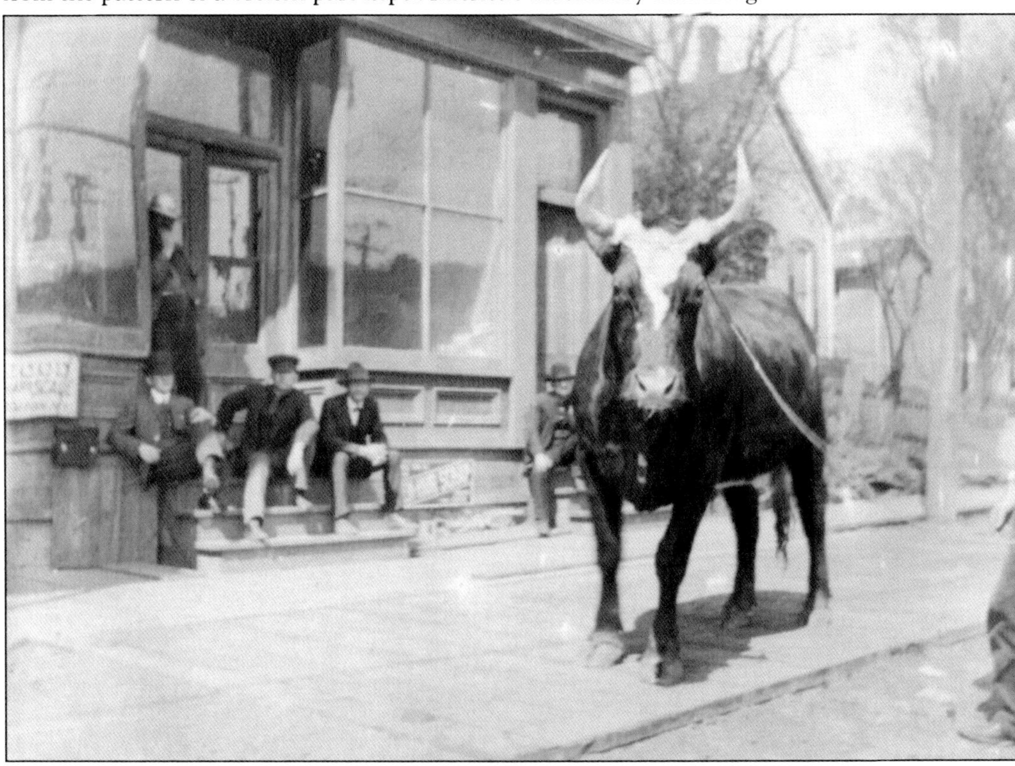

It is not known why this bull (or steer, or heifer) is on the sidewalk. Wild West shows visited from time to time, and this may be connected with one of those. The men in the background are trying to look unconcerned, but note that they also seem acutely alert, poised to make a quick break for it if necessary.

The current Indian statue, erected in 1950 and designed by art teacher Norman Phelps of Painted Post High School, is arriving at its destination.

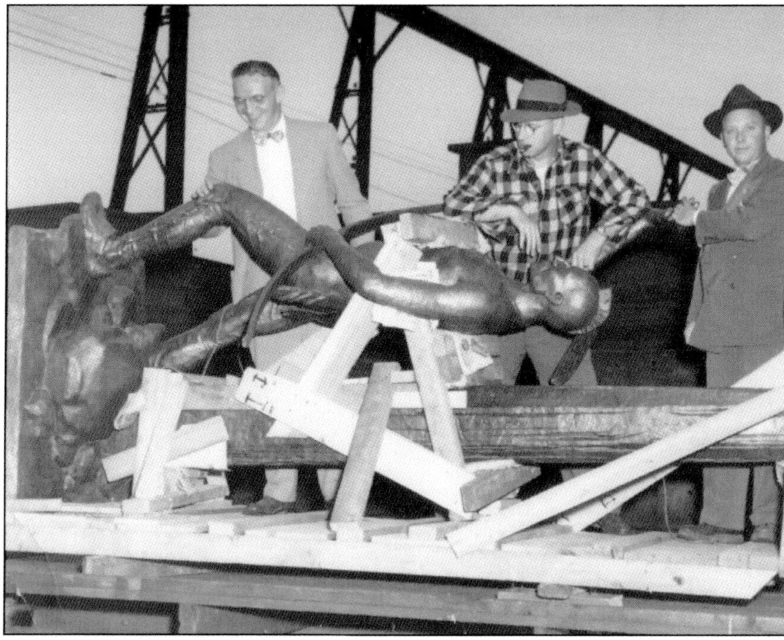

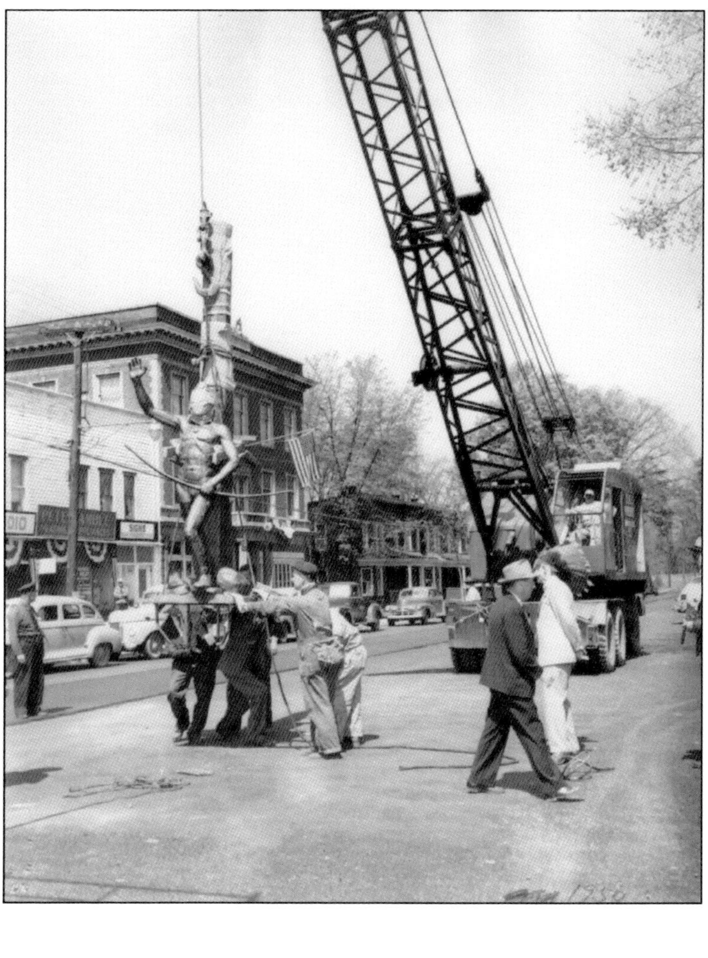

The statue is being "walked" into place. The back support suggests the original painted "post," though of course that shaped and decorated tree trunk would have been much larger. Besides following in the stream of earlier monuments, this statue represents Franco-Seneca Chief Montour, whose family is also remembered in the nearby community of Montour Falls.

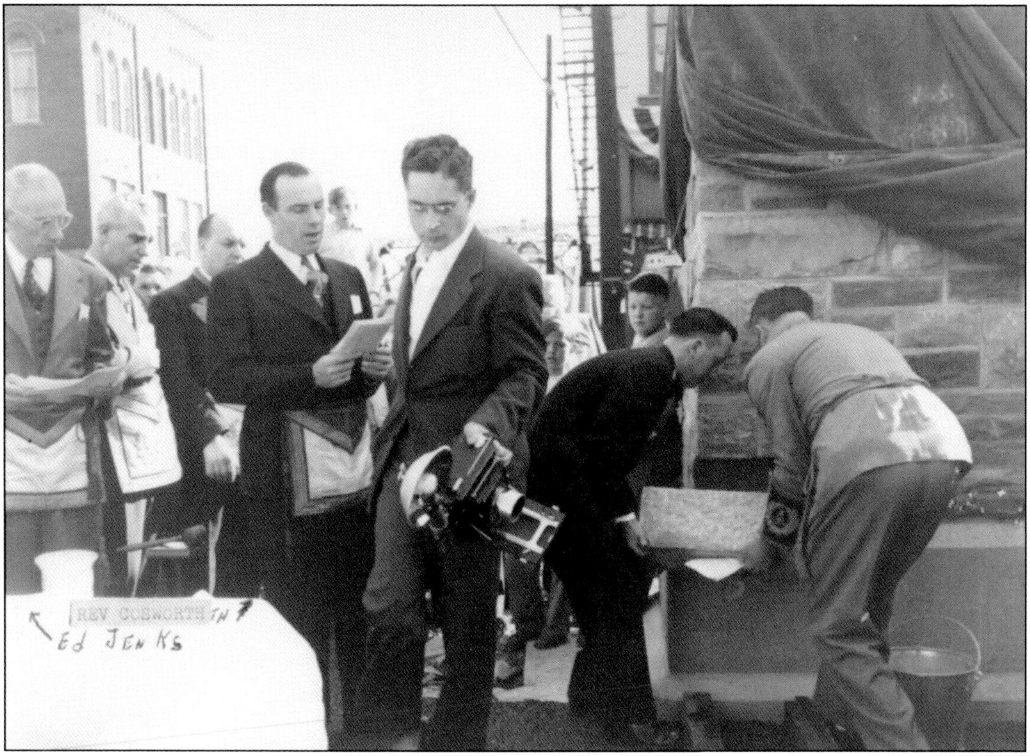

Here, the cornerstone is being laid, accompanied by Masonic rituals.

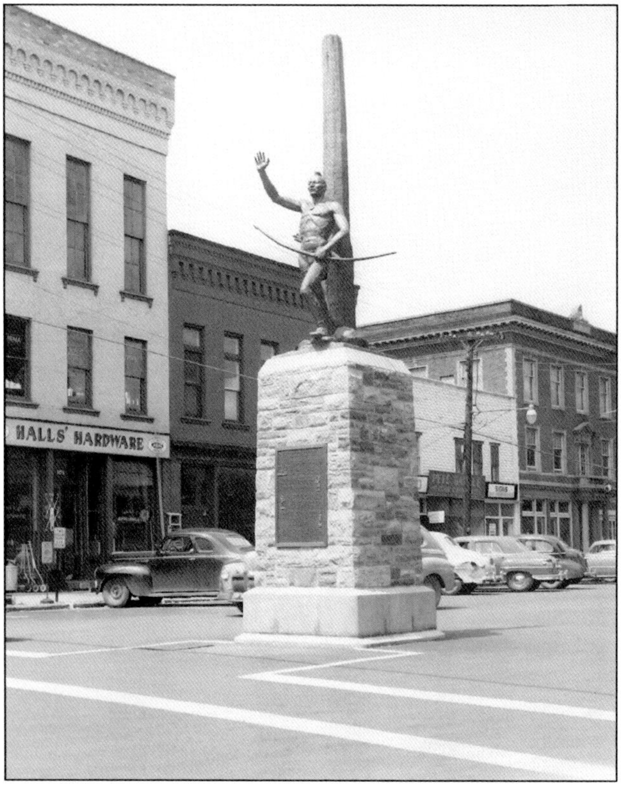

The statue is in place at last. After the 1972 flood, it was moved a few yards, to the site of Village Square Shopping Center, across from the Erwin Municipal Building, to get it out of traffic. Not surprisingly, it has become the symbol of the village. (SCHS.)

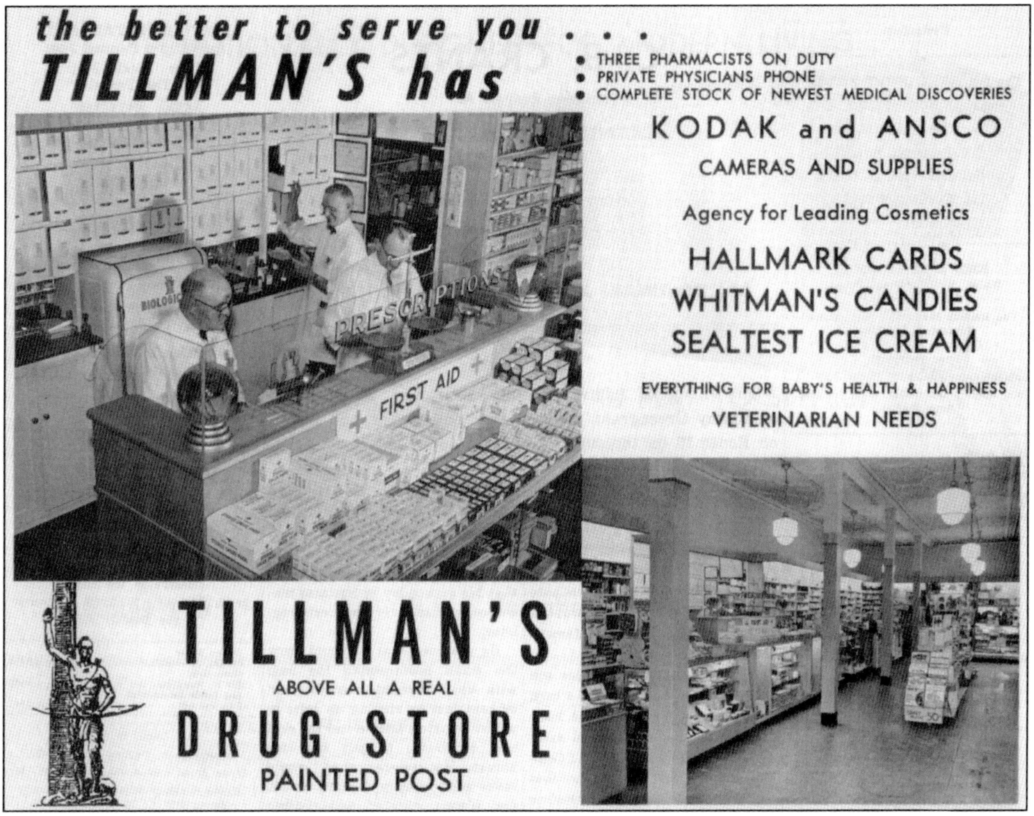

Tillman's Drugs, within sight of the statue, was flooded with the rest of the village in 1972. Here it is in happier times, 16 years earlier. (SCHS.)

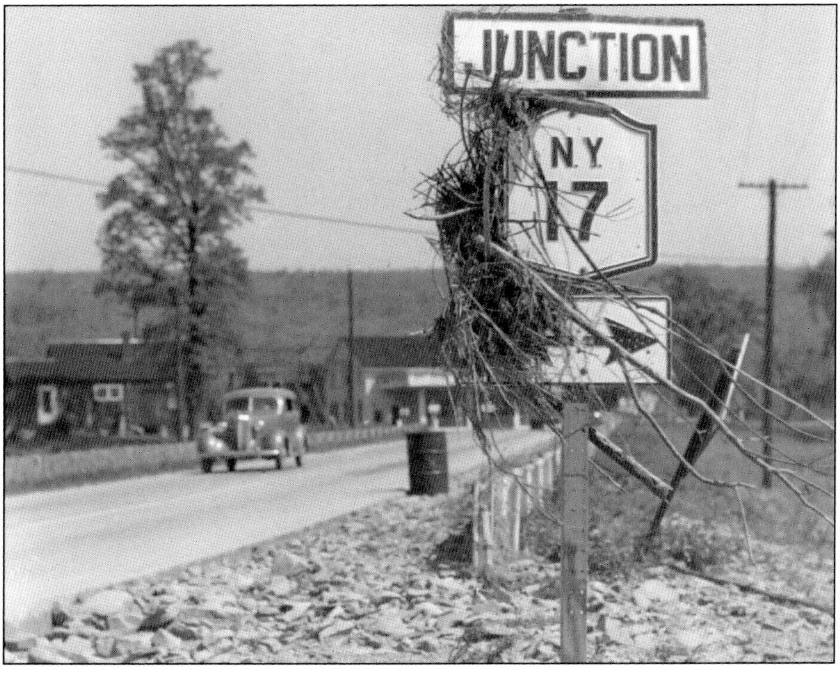

The river gave, and the river took away. Sometimes, the river rose mighty high. The flood of July 1935, the aftermath of which is seen here, was particularly destructive. But it was only one in a long series of such events.

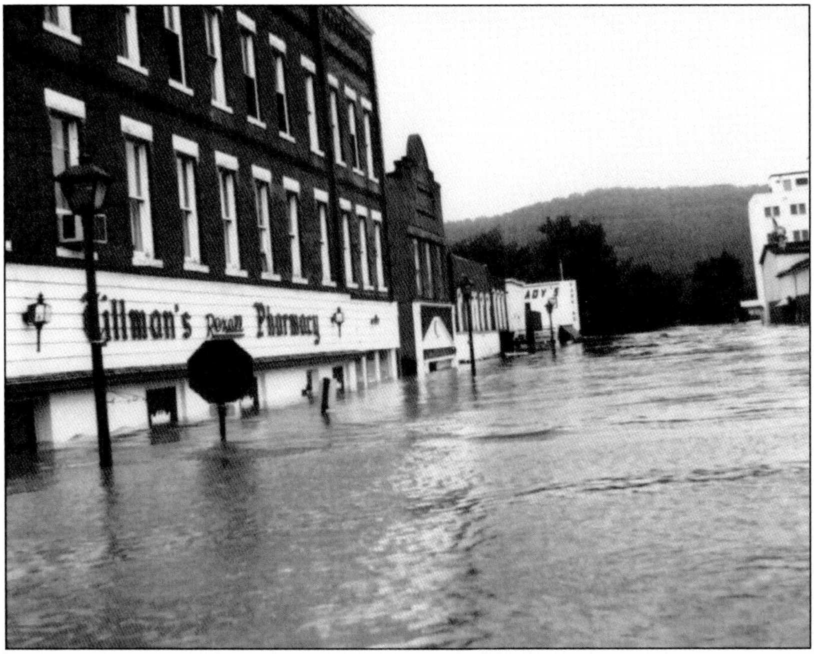

The worst disaster was the Hurricane Agnes flood of June 1972, which killed 18 people in the immediate Corning–Painted Post–Gang Mills area alone. The downtown business district in Painted Post was devastated.

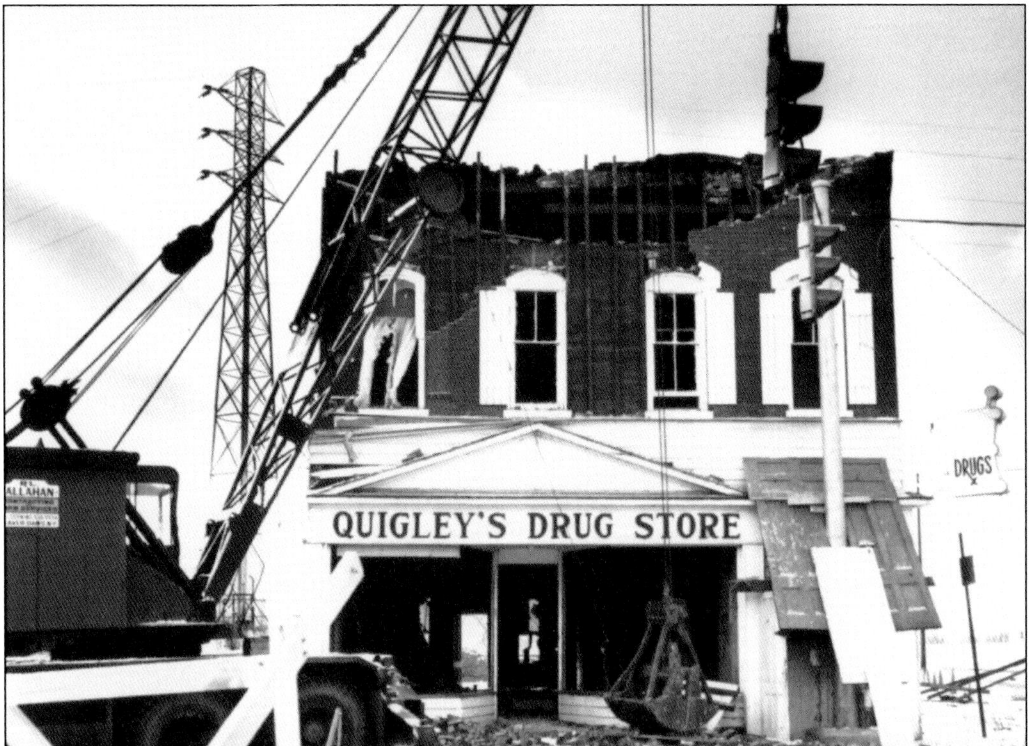

Quigley's Drug Store in Painted Post, along with many other homes and businesses, had to be condemned following the June 1972 flood. Considering the village alone, 80 percent of the space was flooded, 60 percent of the homes were damaged, and half of the residents were displaced.

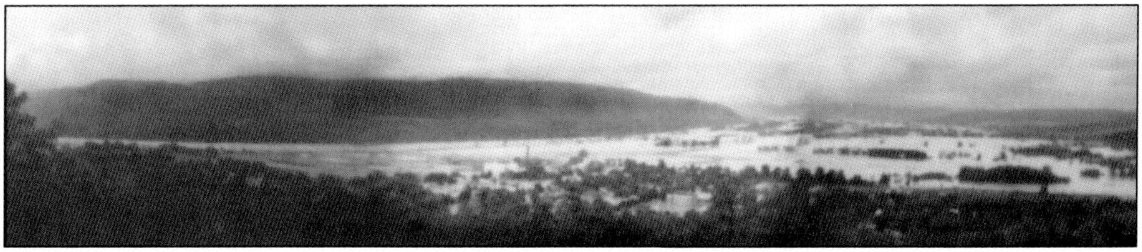

Believe it or not, the worst was over by 2:30 p.m. on the day of the Hurricane Agnes flood, when Bruce W. Moran took this panoramic photograph from the top of Fairview Avenue and Davis Street.

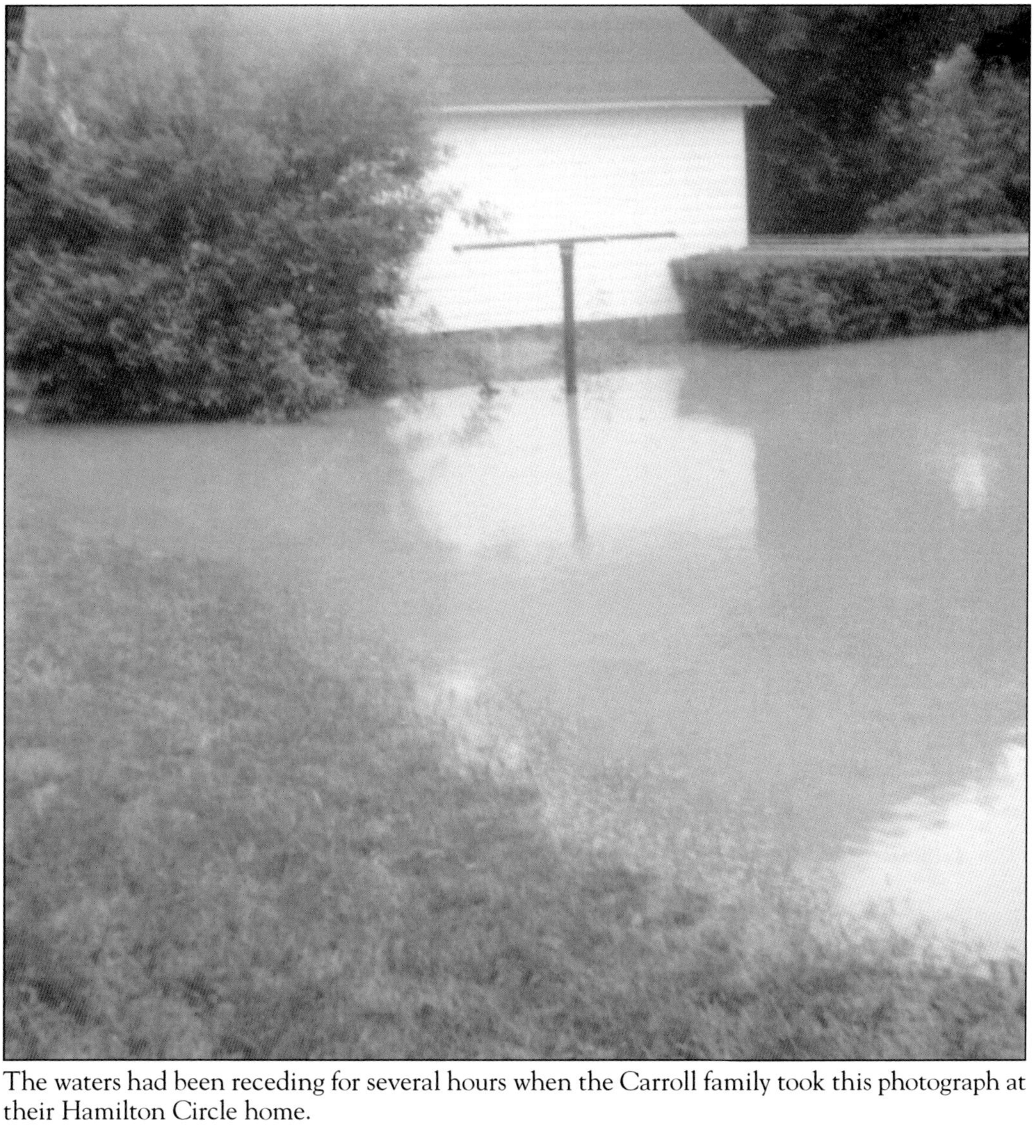

The waters had been receding for several hours when the Carroll family took this photograph at their Hamilton Circle home.

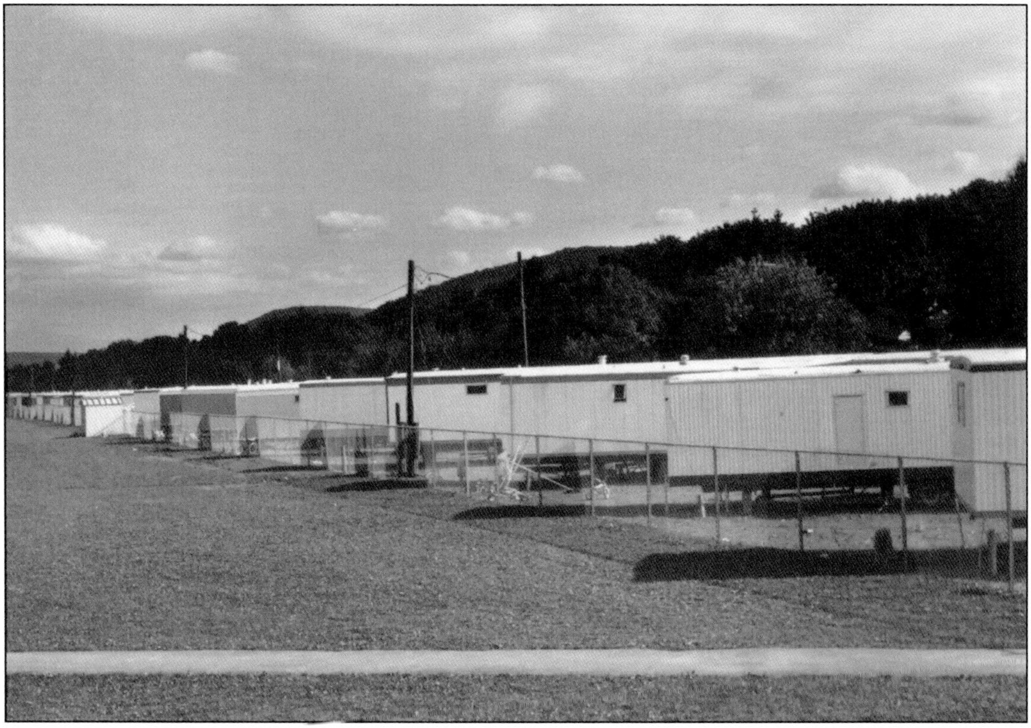

Many homes were lost altogether. Of those that survived, many took a year or more to be made habitable again. The US Department of Housing and Urban Development brought in hundreds of trailers and set them up at Craig Park in Painted Post.

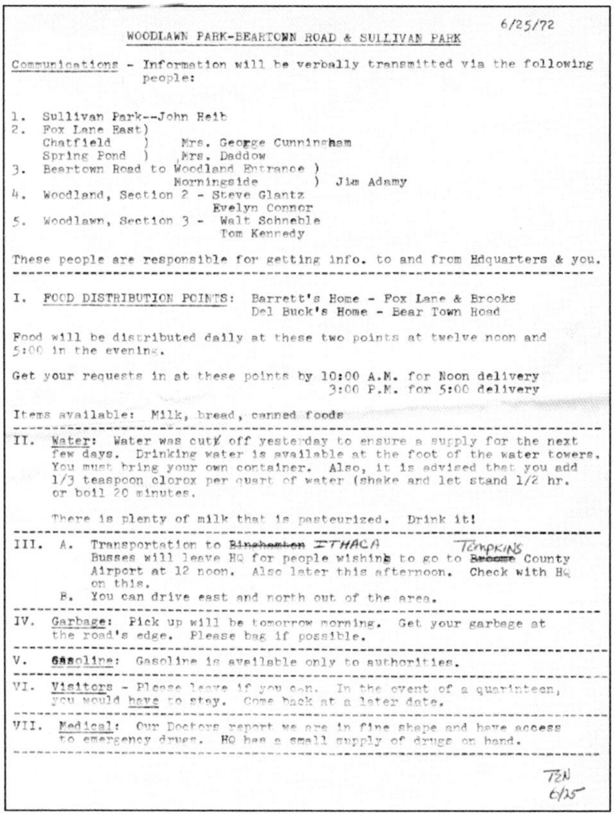

6/25/72

WOODLAWN PARK-BEARTOWN ROAD & SULLIVAN PARK

Communications - Information will be verbally transmitted via the following people:

1. Sullivan Park--John Heib
2. Fox Lane East)
   Chatfield) Mrs. George Cunningham
   Spring Pond) Mrs. Daddow
3. Beartown Road to Woodland Entrance)
   Morningside) Jim Adamy
4. Woodland, Section 2 - Steve Glantz
   Evelyn Connor
5. Woodlawn, Section 3 - Walt Schneble
   Tom Kennedy

These people are responsible for getting info. to and from Hdquarters & you.

I. FOOD DISTRIBUTION POINTS: Barrett's Home - Fox Lane & Brooks
Del Buck's Home - Bear Town Road

Food will be distributed daily at these two points at twelve noon and 5:00 in the evening.

Get your requests in at these points by 10:00 A.M. for Noon delivery
3:00 P.M. for 5:00 delivery

Items available: Milk, bread, canned foods

II. Water: Water was cut off yesterday to ensure a supply for the next few days. Drinking water is available at the foot of the water towers. You must bring your own container. Also, it is advised that you add 1/3 teaspoon clorox per quart of water (shake and let stand 1/2 hr. or boil 20 minutes.

There is plenty of milk that is pasteurized. Drink it!

III. A. Transportation to ~~Binghamton~~ ITHACA
Busses will leave HQ for people wishing to go to ~~Broome~~ TOMPKINS County Airport at 12 noon. Also later this afternoon. Check with HQ on this.
B. You can drive east and north out of the area.

IV. Garbage: Pick up will be tomorrow morning. Get your garbage at the road's edge. Please bag if possible.

V. Gasoline: Gasoline is available only to authorities.

VI. Visitors - Please leave if you can. In the event of a quarinteen, you would have to stay. Come back at a later date.

VII. Medical: Our Doctors report we are in fine shape and have access to emergency drugs. HQ has a small supply of drugs on hand.

TZN
6/25

This typed memorandum on water, food, distribution, and other vital news was reproduced by hand-cranked mimeograph machine. The previous day's original copy was written out in longhand and copied by spirit duplicator. These sheets were vital conduits of communication in the days following the flood. It often took days for family members just to find each other. (SCHS.)

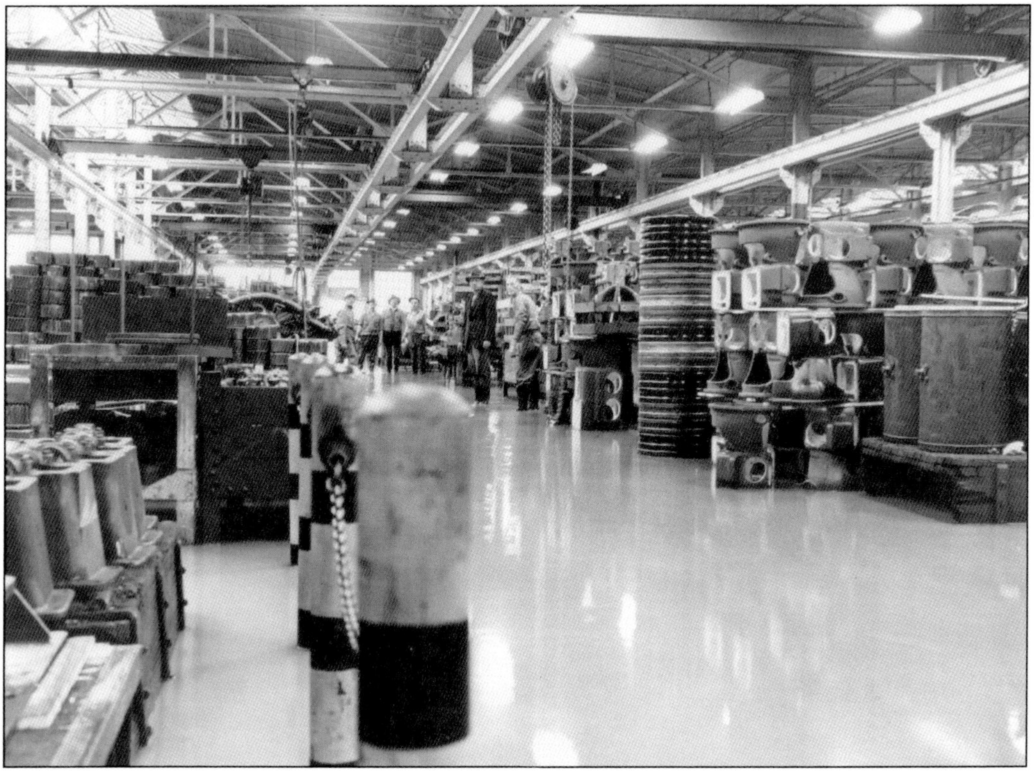

It is not known which flood caused the damage shown here, but the clothing indicates it might be the major inundations of 1935 or 1946. Ingersoll-Rand suffered along with its community when the rivers rose.

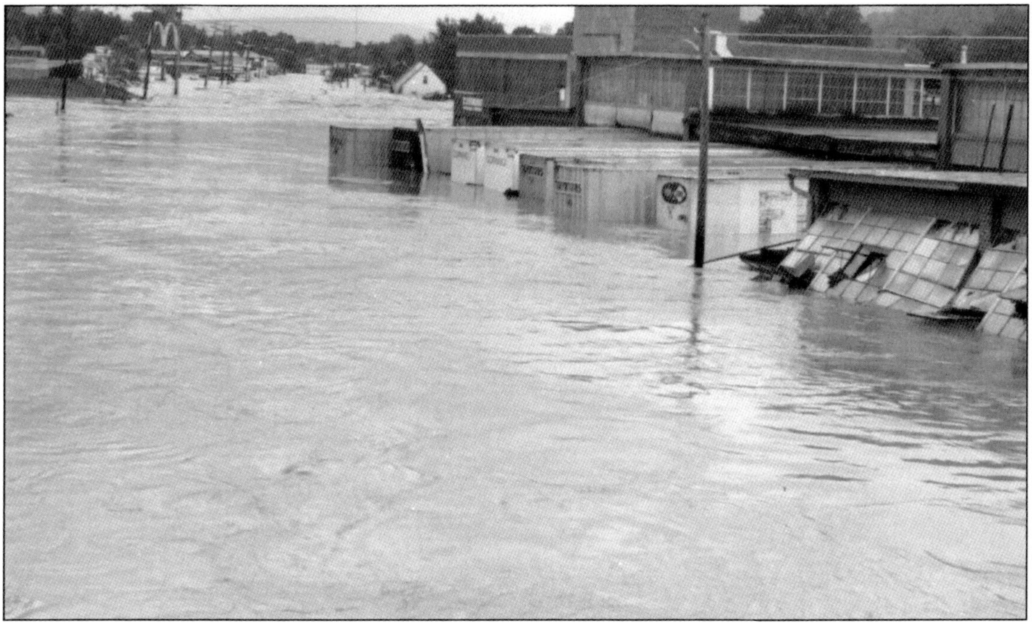

The Corning Fibre Box Company, among other firms, did not survive being flooded during Tropical Storm Agnes in 1972.

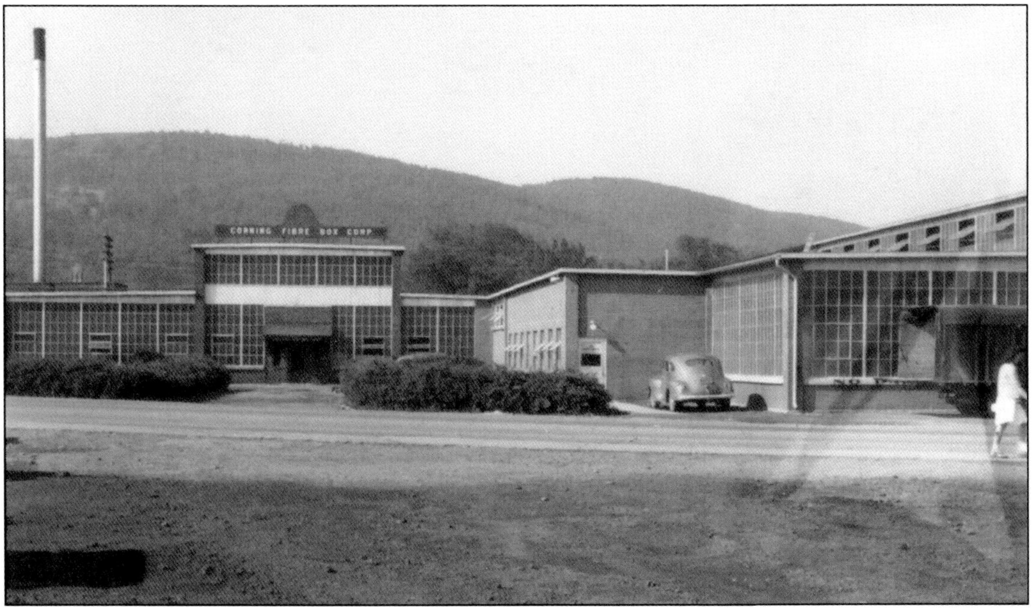

The Corning Fibre Box Company, irreparably damaged in the 1972 flood, is seen here in happier times, 30 years earlier.

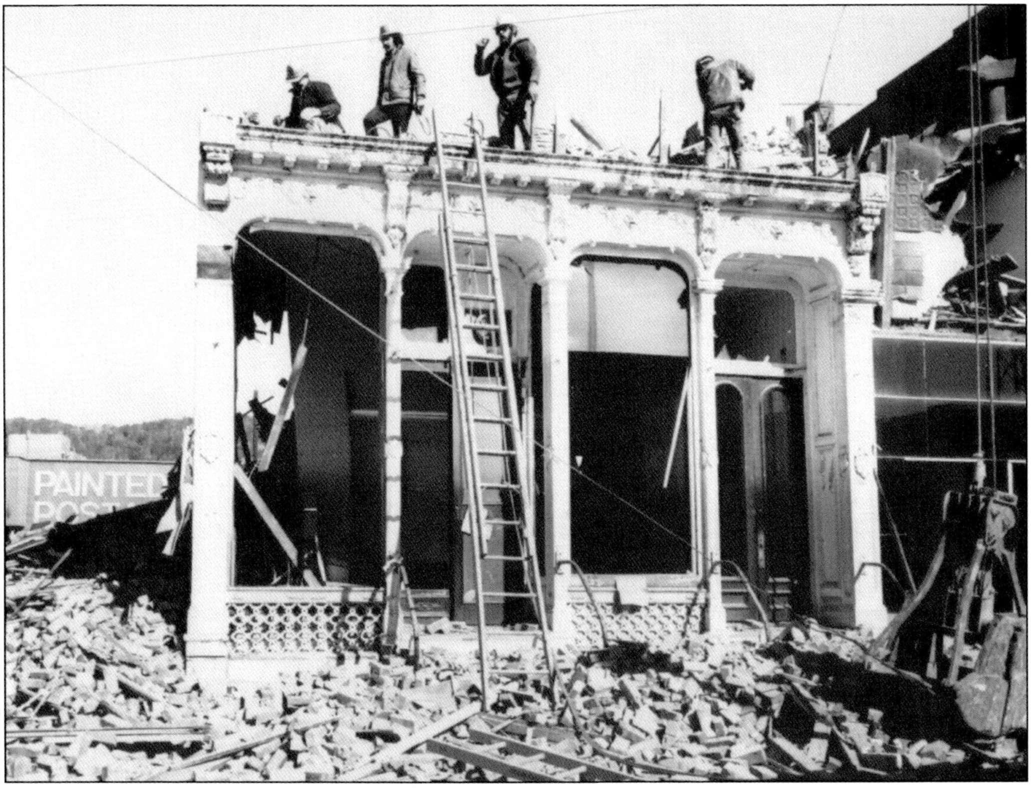

Visible behind the demolition work is the post-Agnes urban renewal project—a new shopping center—that replaced these lost commercial buildings, some a century old. The Masonic building, with its cast-iron front, was one of the casualties. The space at lower left was once a barbershop.

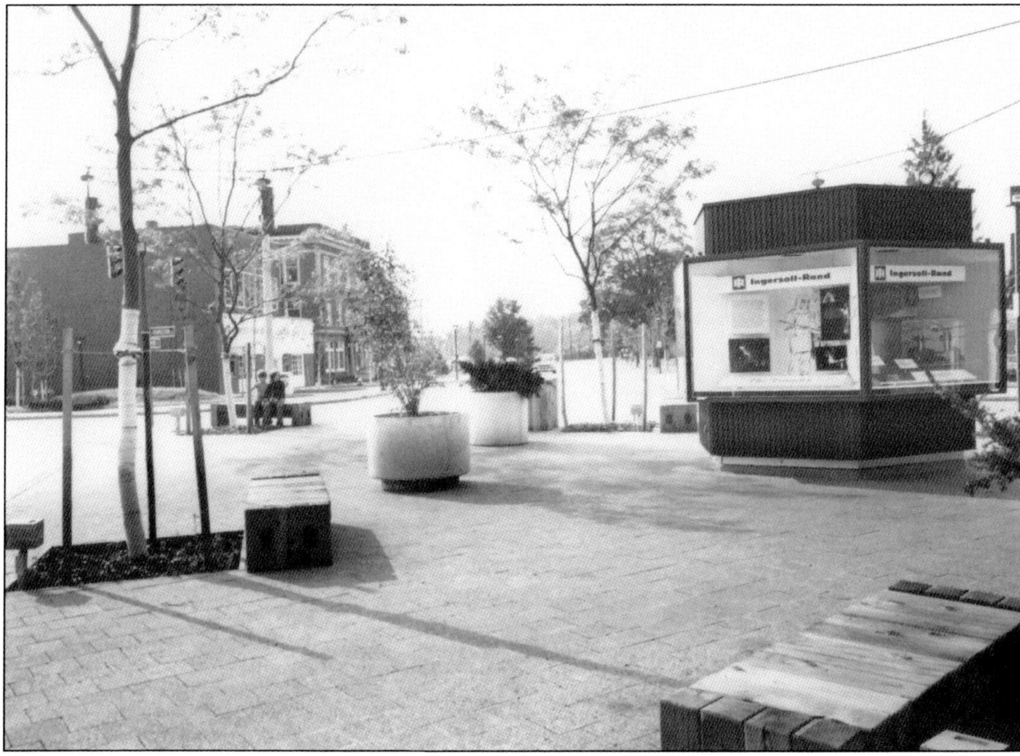

The angular, industrial (if not antiseptic) look shown here was typical of the 1970s. Village Square is still a very busy shopping center.

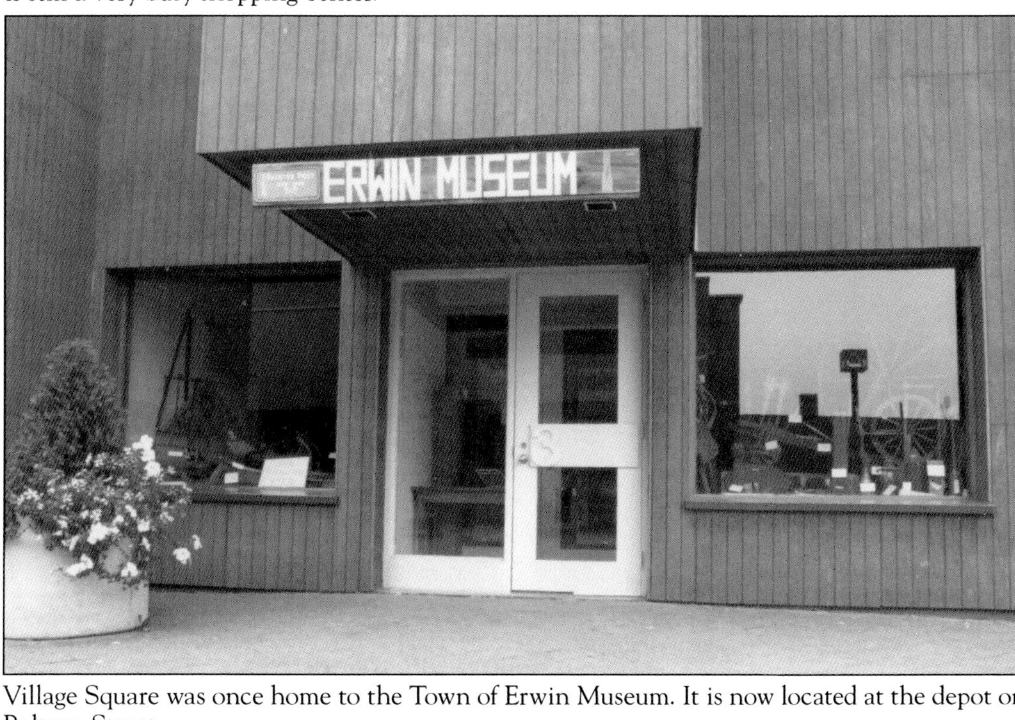

Village Square was once home to the Town of Erwin Museum. It is now located at the depot on Pultney Street.

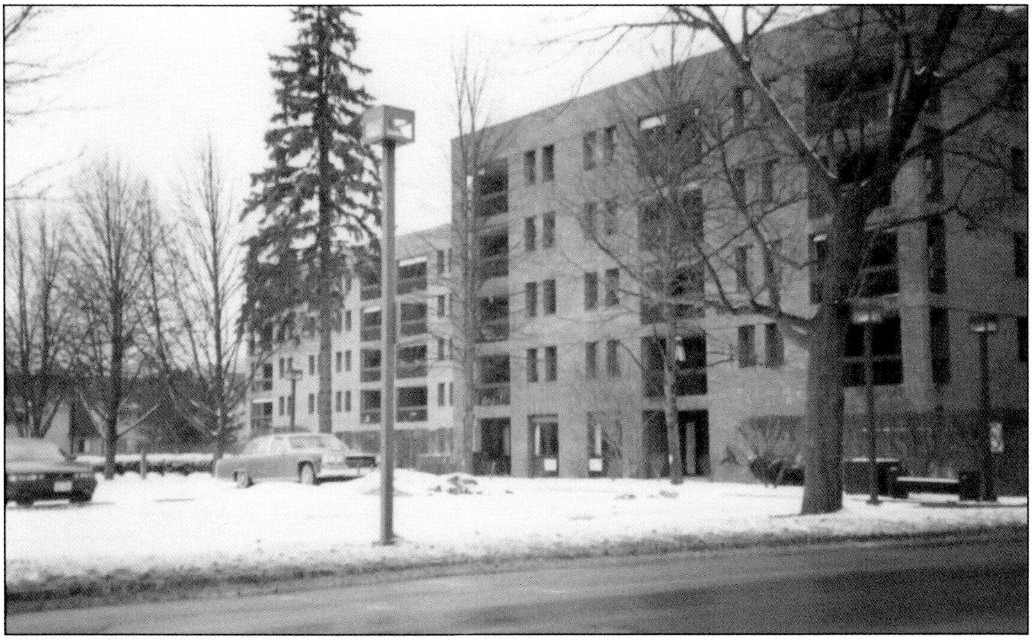

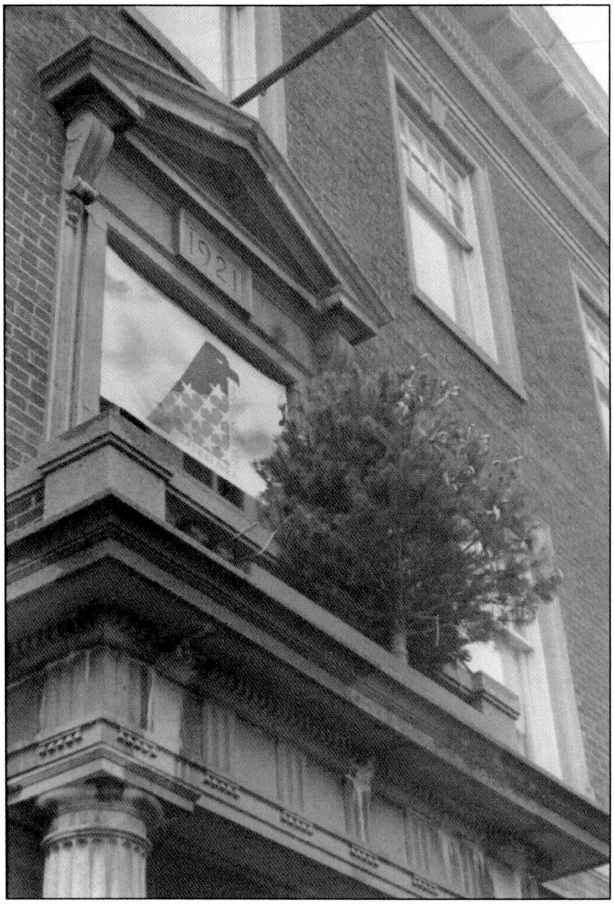

The Village Square Apartments, at 25 North Hamilton Street, were one of the post-Agnes urban renewal projects. (SCH.)

Erwin's fine municipal building, which survived the 1972 flood, still stands in Painted Post. Presumably, this photograph was taken during the Christmas season. Today, a monument just east of this building commemorates the 1791 Treaty of Painted Post.

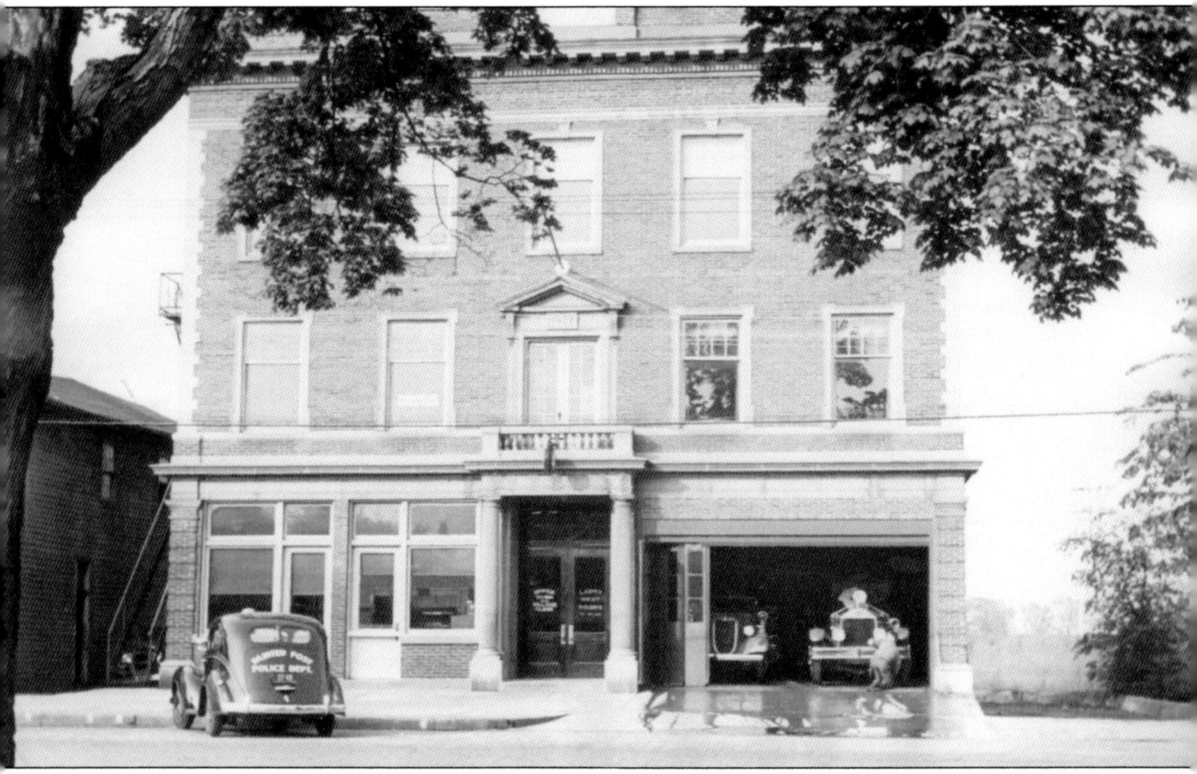

The firefighters at the municipal building have either been washing their equipment or draining their hoses. It is most likely the former, to judge from the fellow crouched in front of the bumper. The police car is quite elegant.

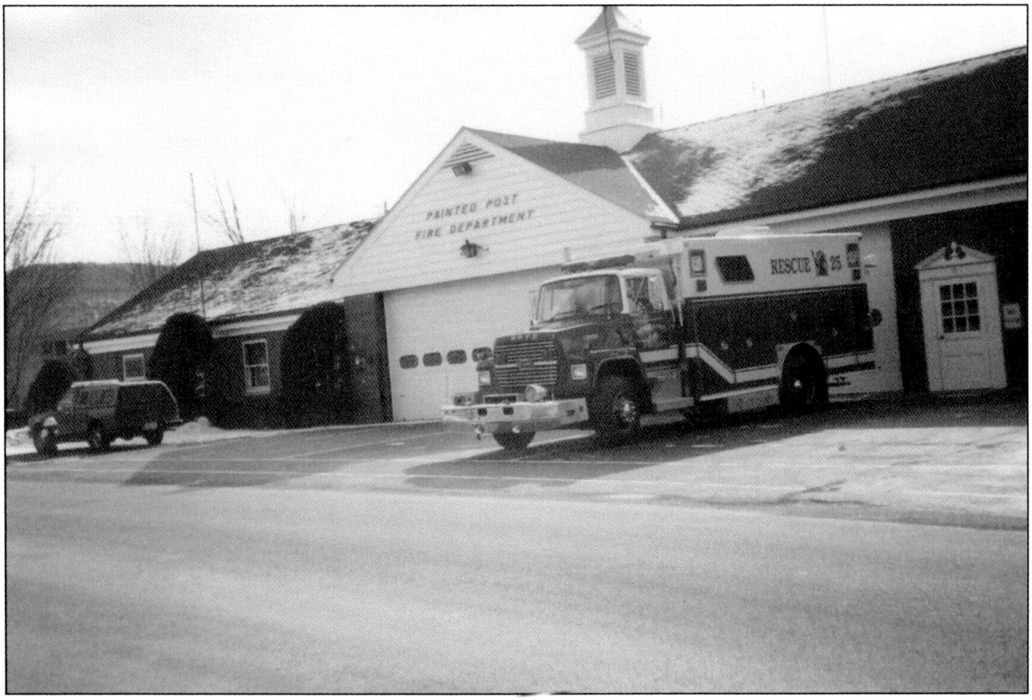

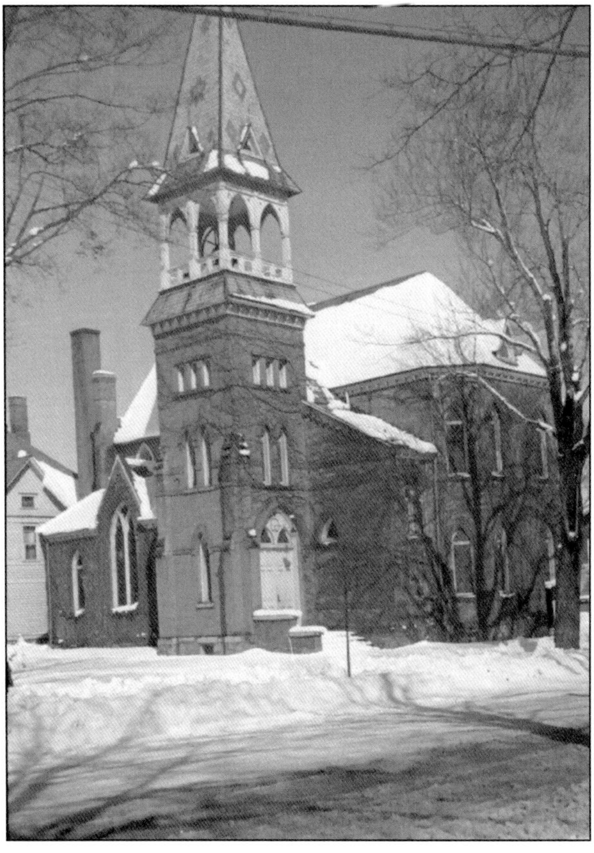

The village fire department was organized on April 21, 1886. When a new village municipal building went up in 1952, the fire department went with it. (SCH.)

The Presbyterian congregation, which incorporated in 1839, created this impressive edifice in 1881–1883. It cost $5,200 to erect. When it was devastated in the 1972 flood, the Presbyterians joined with the nearby Methodist Church to create a new facility, shared by both congregations. The old parsonage is visible in the background at left.

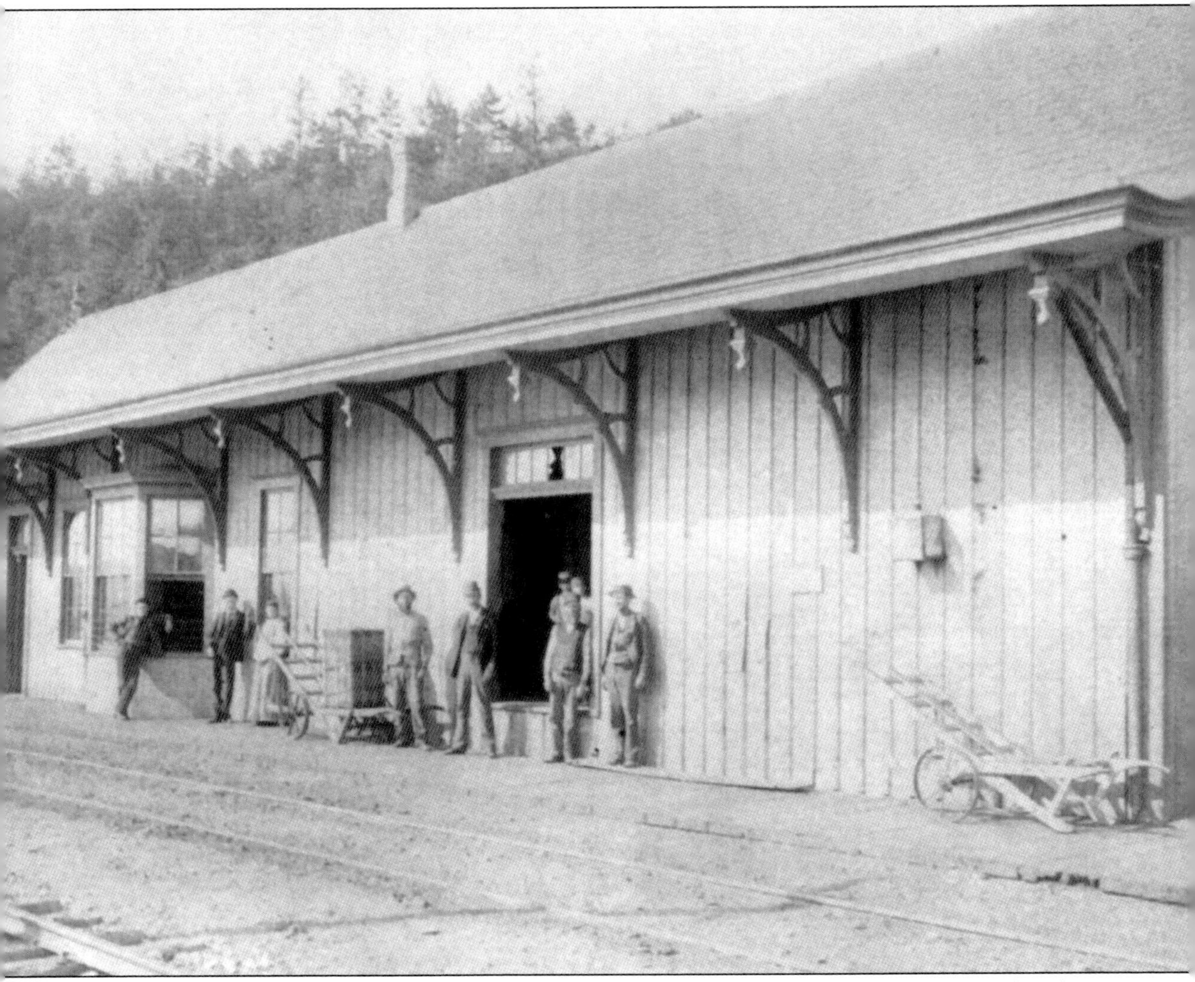

For years, the town municipal building also housed a town and village museum, now located at the old Delaware, Lackawanna & Western depot. That museum is operated by the Corning–Painted Post Historical Society. (RP.)

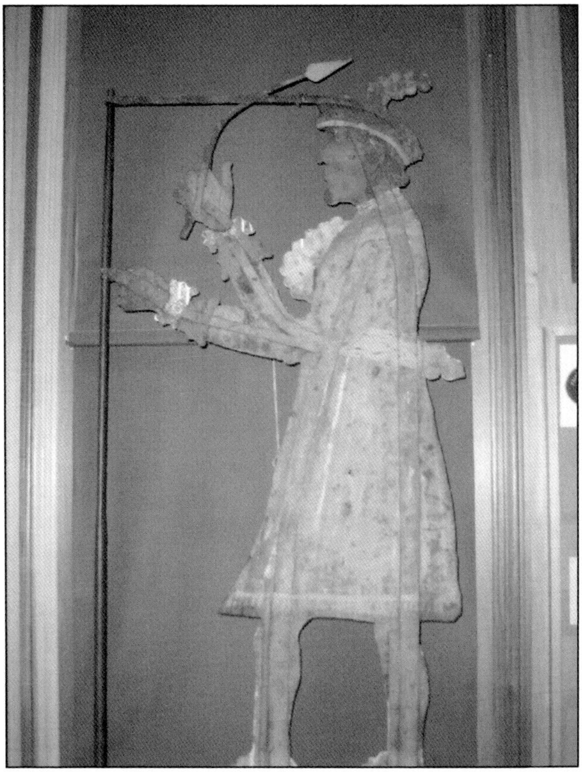

After the original painted post deteriorated, as well as an 1803 replacement, the community erected a series of Indian figures to keep its memory alive. The current statue is the fourth such figure, and all three predecessors are at the museum in the depot. This sheet-metal figure, installed in 1824, was the first. The artist was paid one cow. (KWH.)

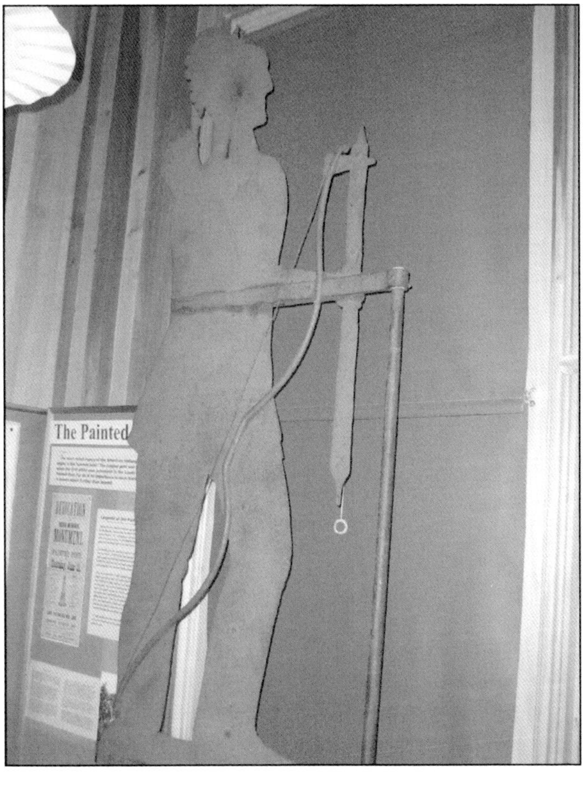

The second figure, installed in 1880, was also a flat metal silhouette. For some years, this figure and its successor faced each other across the square. (KWH.)

The third Indian depiction was a fully rounded figure that stood from 1894 until it was blown down and broken in a 1948 wind storm. See also page 10. (KWH.)

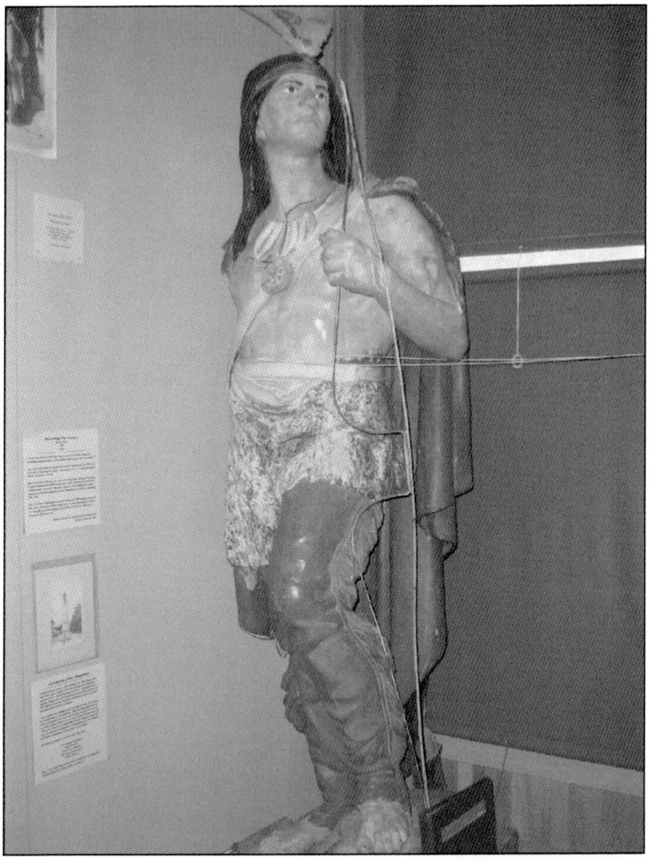

Flags and an orator added to the festivities when Painted Post dedicated its Civil War statue (obscured by the trees). Most of the Labor Day 1913 crowd is intent on the ceremony, but one man is carefully studying the exciting new motorcar.

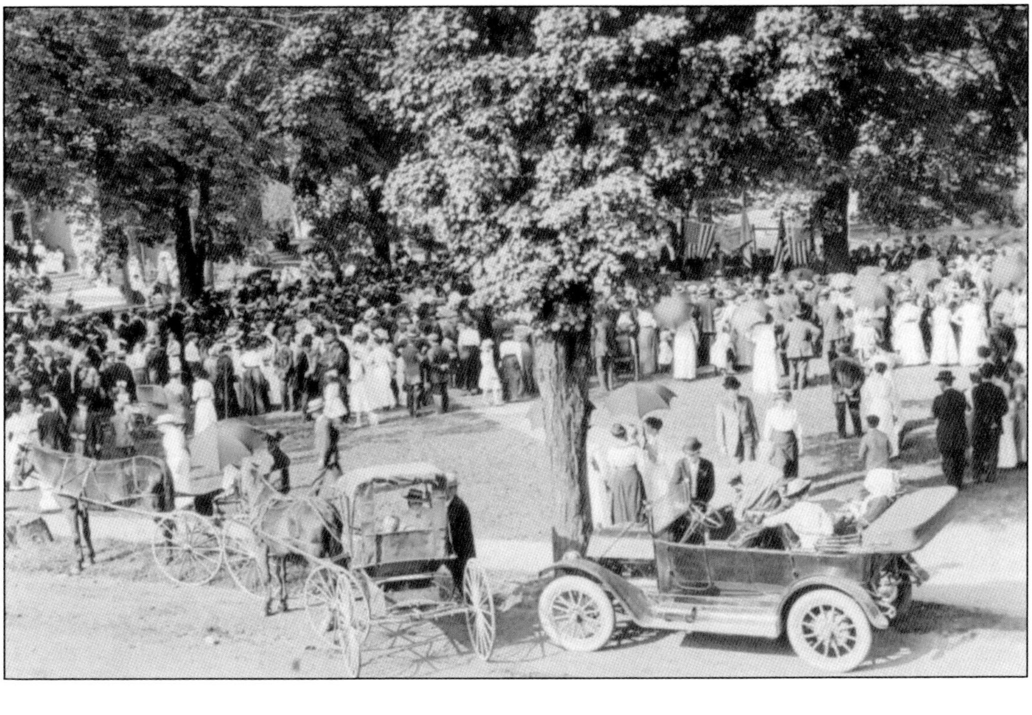

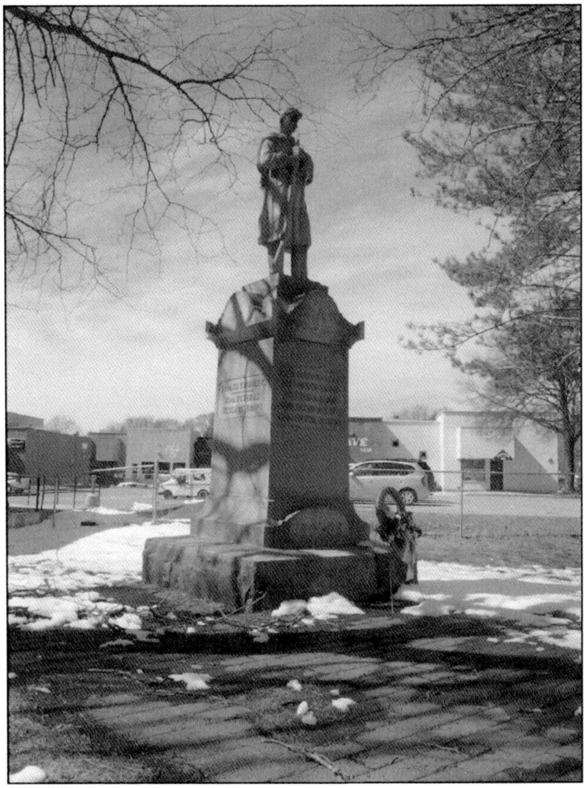

The life-size statue, like the rest of the monument, is made of Barre granite from Vermont. (Photograph by Joshua House; SCHS.)

The town's post office, located next to the Civil War statue, was a New Deal project. It is still in service after three-quarters of a century. The building was inundated in the 1972 Hurricane Agnes flood, which damaged the Federal Art Project mural in the lobby.

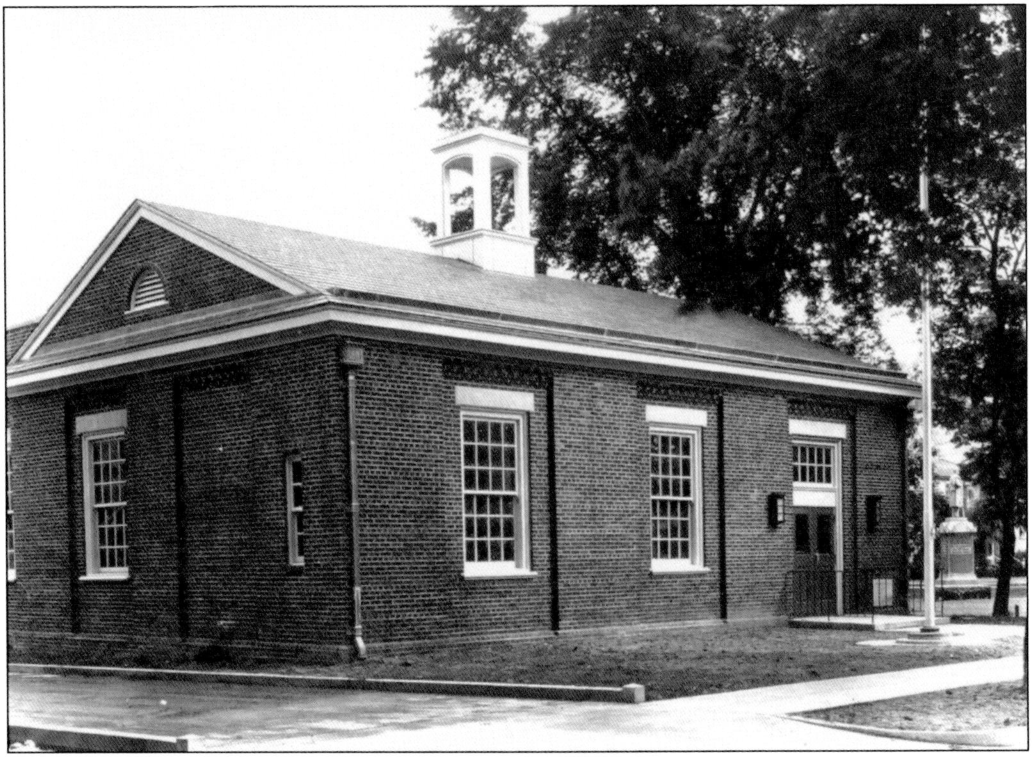

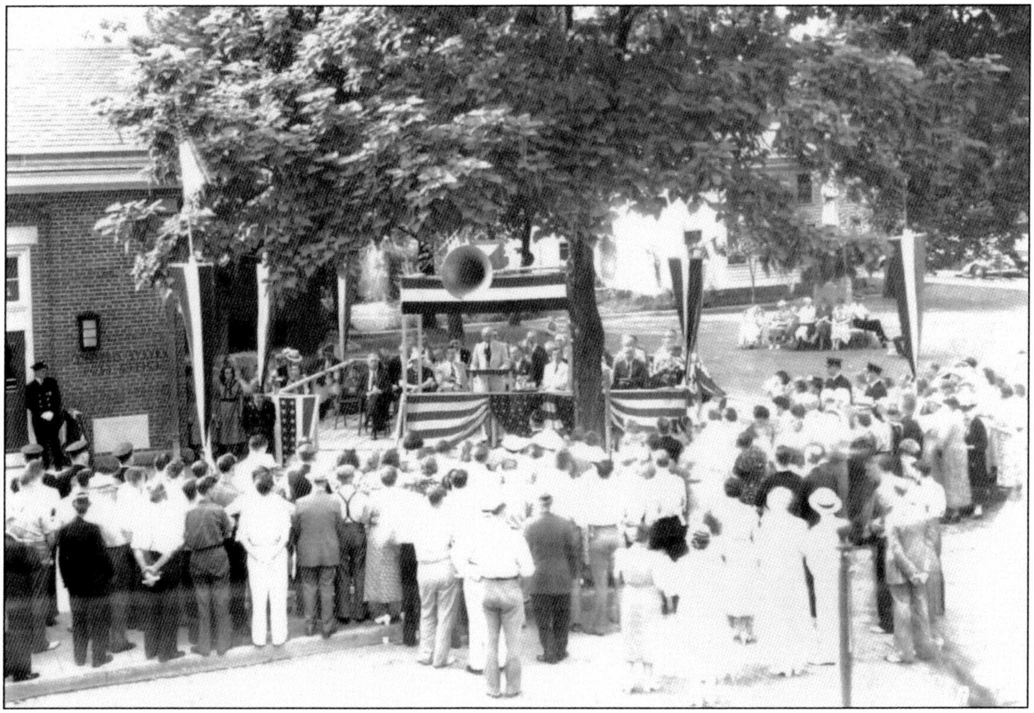

This photograph shows the post office dedication in 1938. Note the people at right rear, seated around the Civil War statue. That appears to be a Girl Scout at left, between the building and the stand.

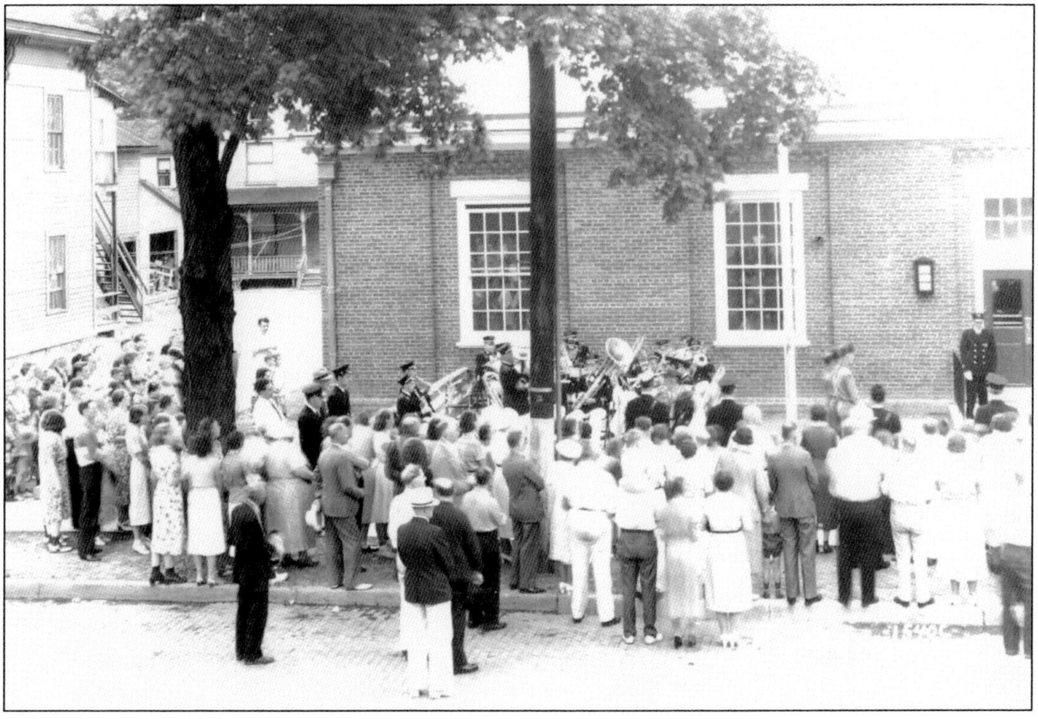

A band performed during the festivities.

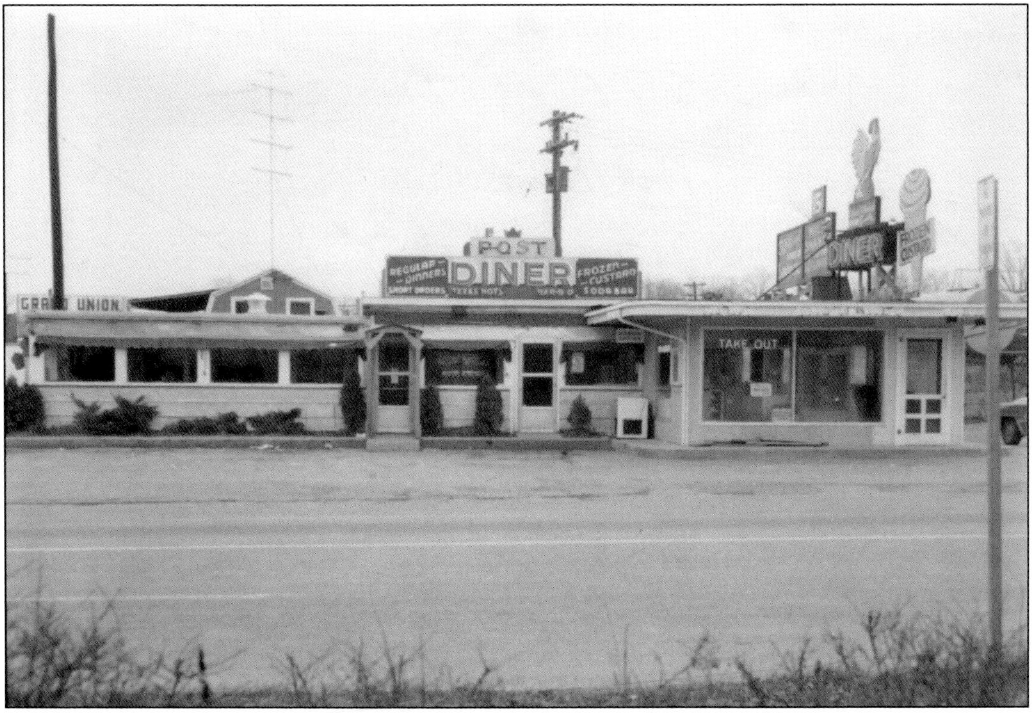

The Post Diner, like many other diners, started out as a manufactured building (left). Additions were later constructed to make it a more permanent structure. (SCH.)

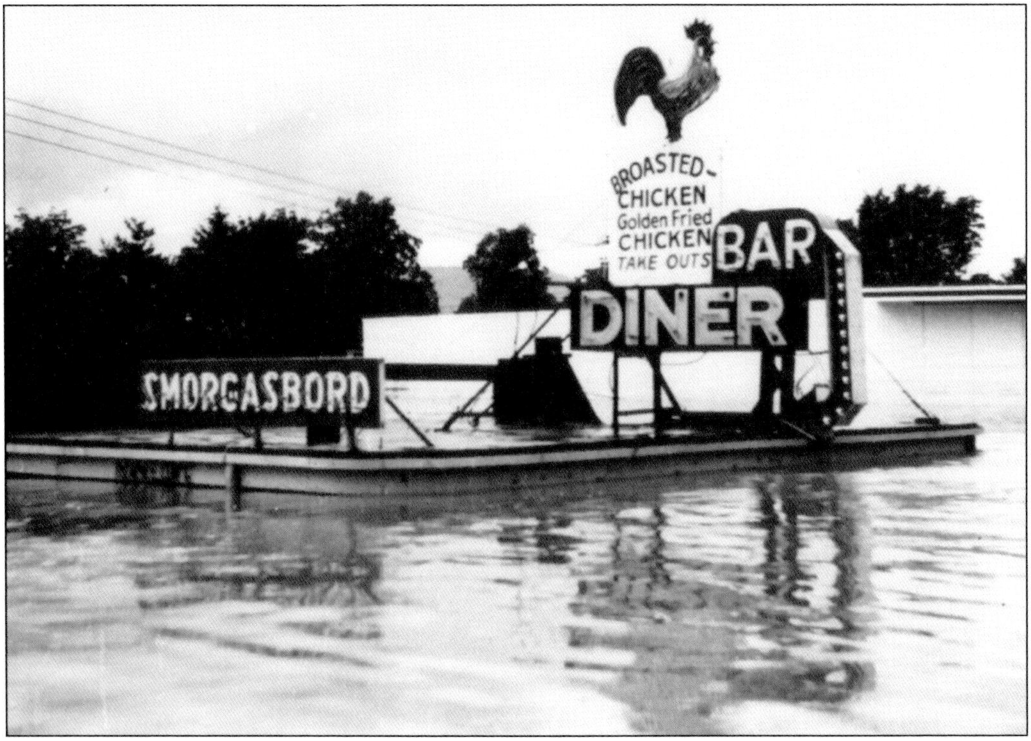

The 1972 floodwaters rose above the roof of the diner, leaving only the signs exposed.

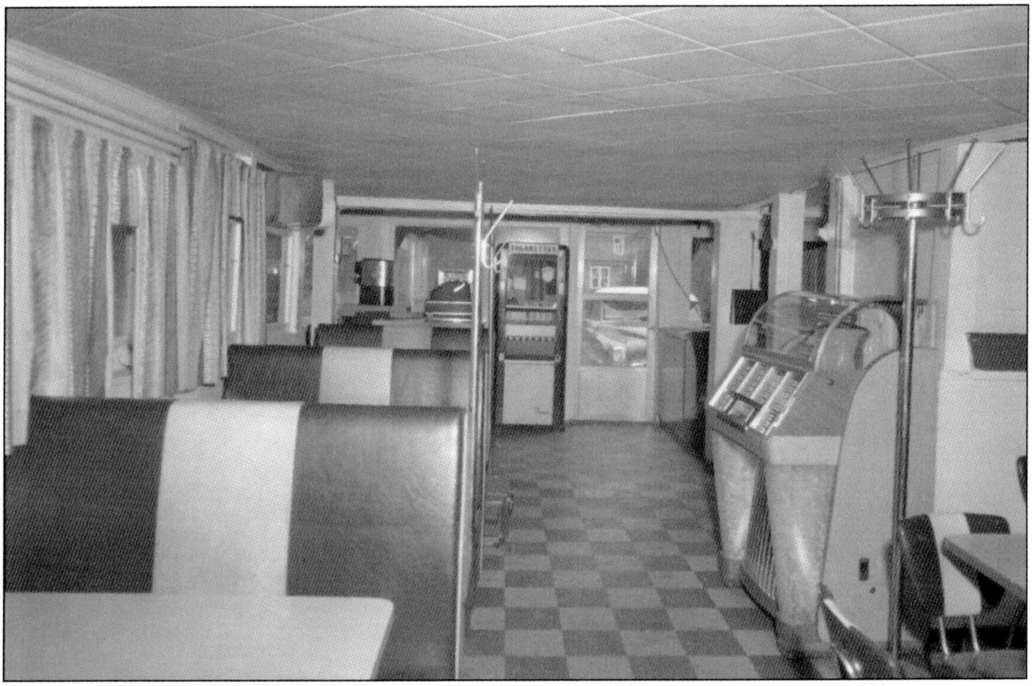

In an earlier age, the jukebox and cigarette machine were necessities for a place like the Post Diner. Visible through the doorway at the rear is a classic car with a white top. The Post stood at 117 East High Street. These photographs of the diner were taken in 1957. (SCH.)

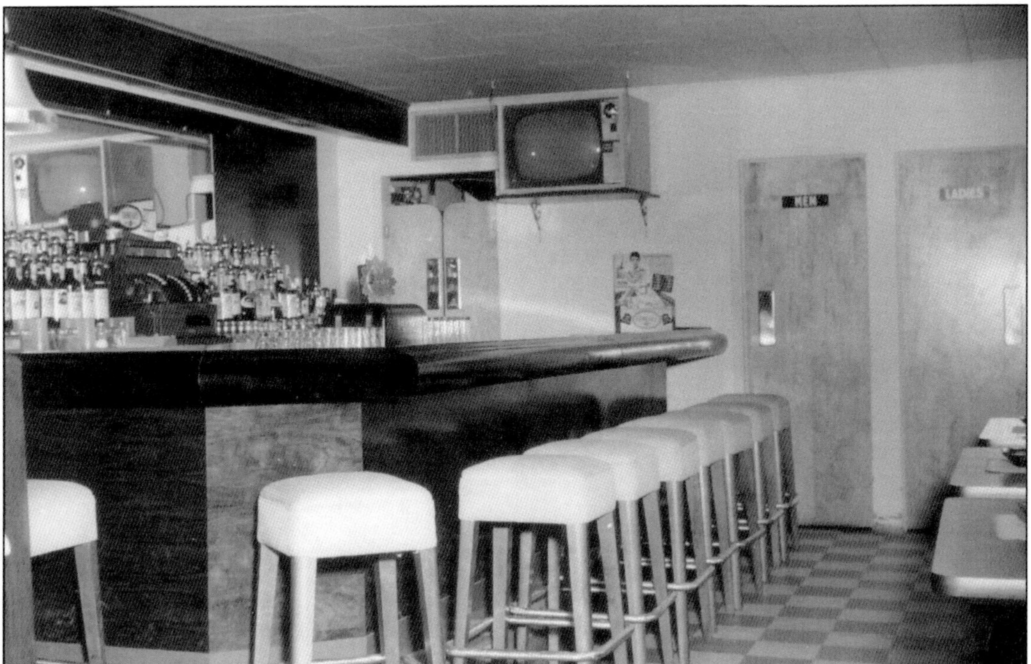

The Post also featured a bar, a television set, and Western New York's Genesee Beer. Genesee remembered its friends in the area, rushing thousands of gallons of distilled water to Corning–Painted Post during the flood disaster of 1972, most of it in Genesee Beer bottles. (SCH.)

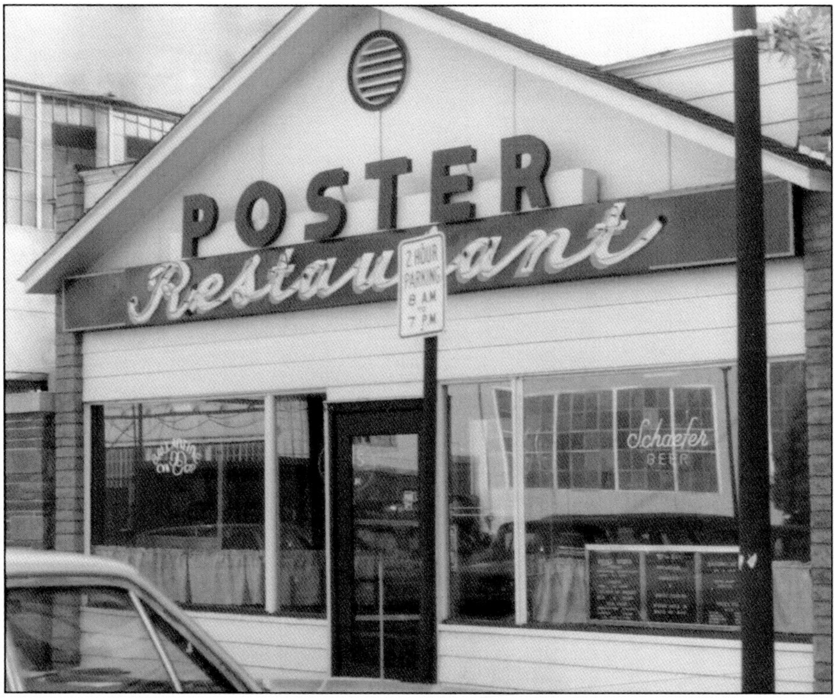

The Poster Restaurant, on 102 East Water Street, was well located to serve office, retail, and factory workers on their lunch breaks. (SCH.)

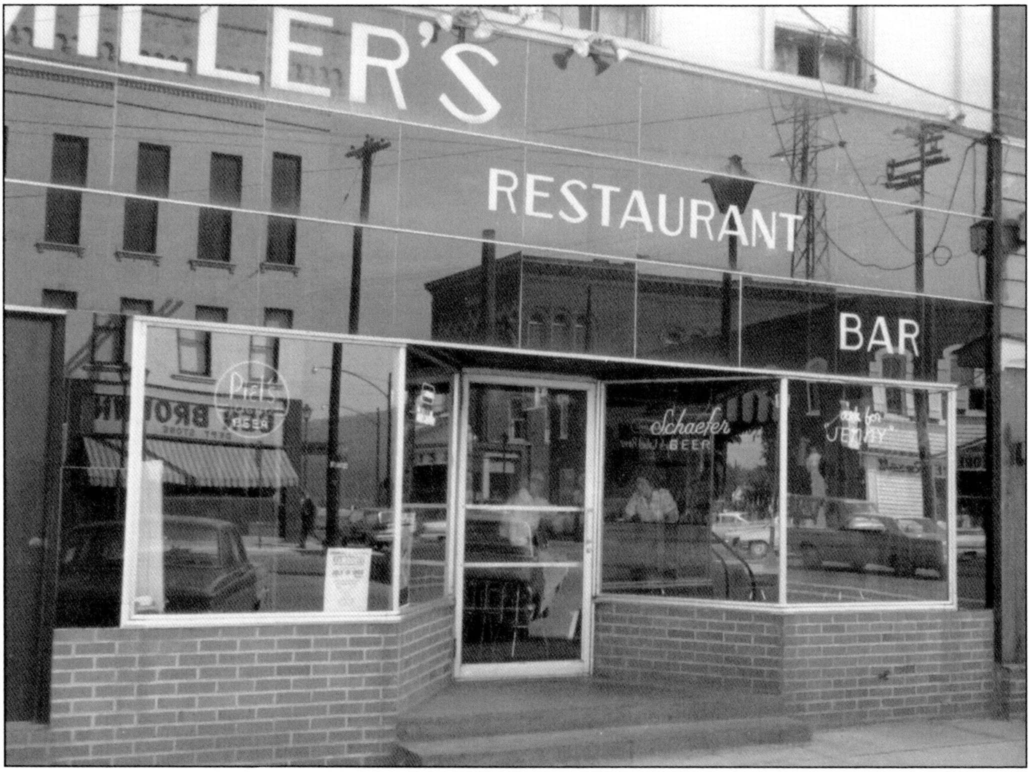

Note how the windows of Miller's Restaurant catch the reflection of businesses across the street. The eatery, on Water Street, is seen here in 1966. (SCH.)

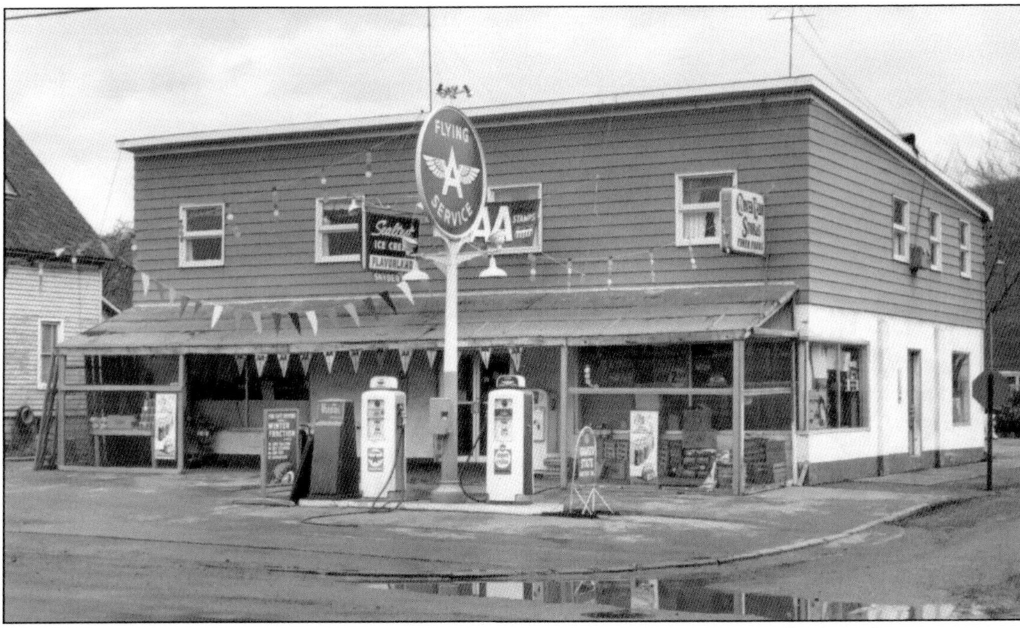

Snyder's Grocery, at 523 East High Street, had its own gas station. Among the brands seen on signs in this photograph, Canada Dry, Quaker State, and Sealtest still exist today. Flying A, Veedol, and Clover Farm are either gone or are hard to find, at least in the Erwin region. (SCH.)

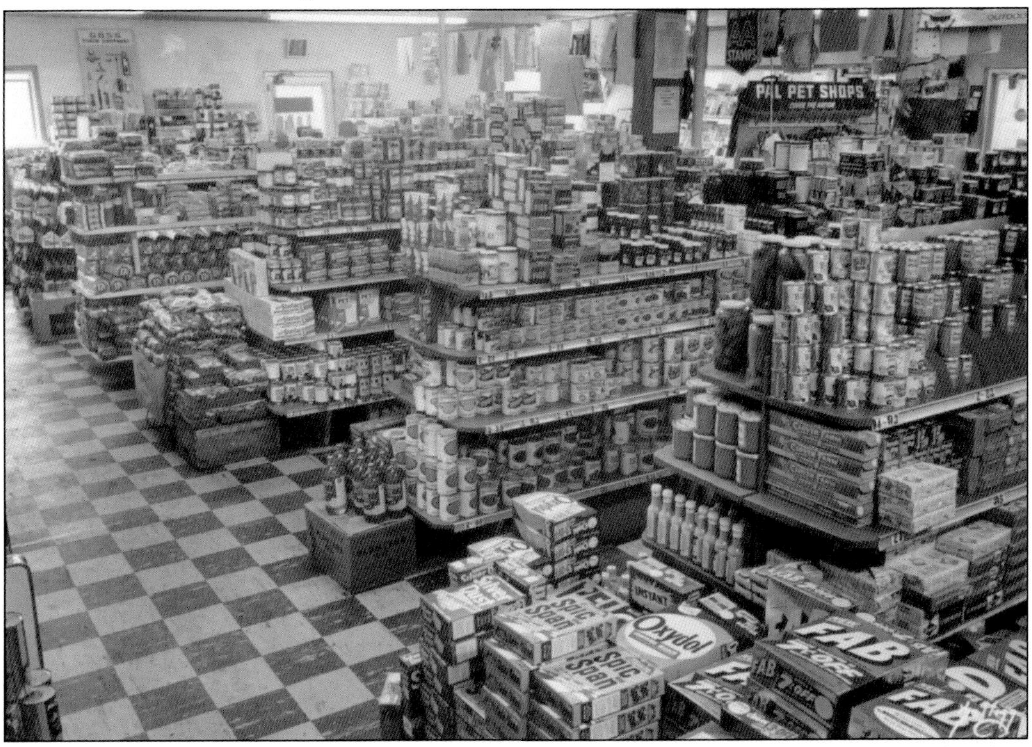

Shown here is the interior of the Snyder's/Clover Farm store. Among familiar, or once-familiar, brands are Fab, Silver Dust, Pal, Spic and Span, Oxydol, Tetley, Starlac, Boss, and Ray-O-Vac. Snyder's apparently was not taking any risk of running short on stock. (SCH.)

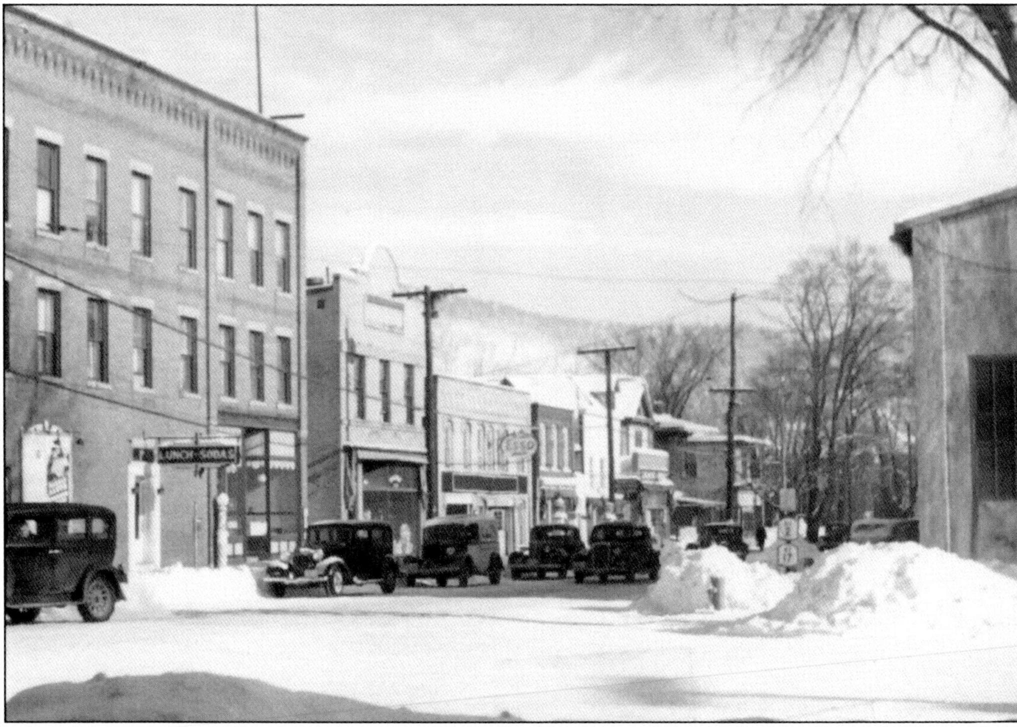

Yes, it has been known to snow occasionally in Western New York. Note the sign for Esso (now Exxon) and the tall barber's pole, just under the sign for lunch and sodas.

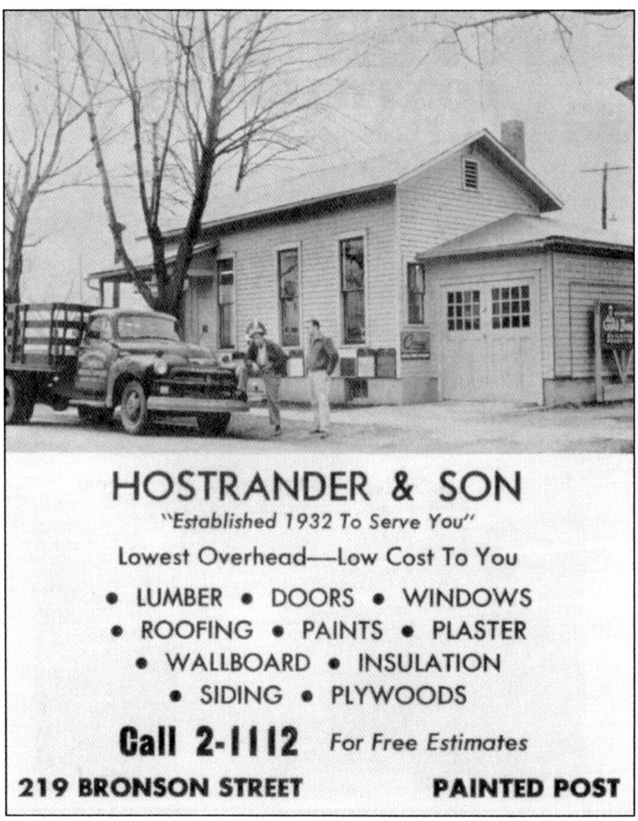

Hostrander & Son, on Bronson Street, dealt in lumber, doors, and windows. (SCHS.)

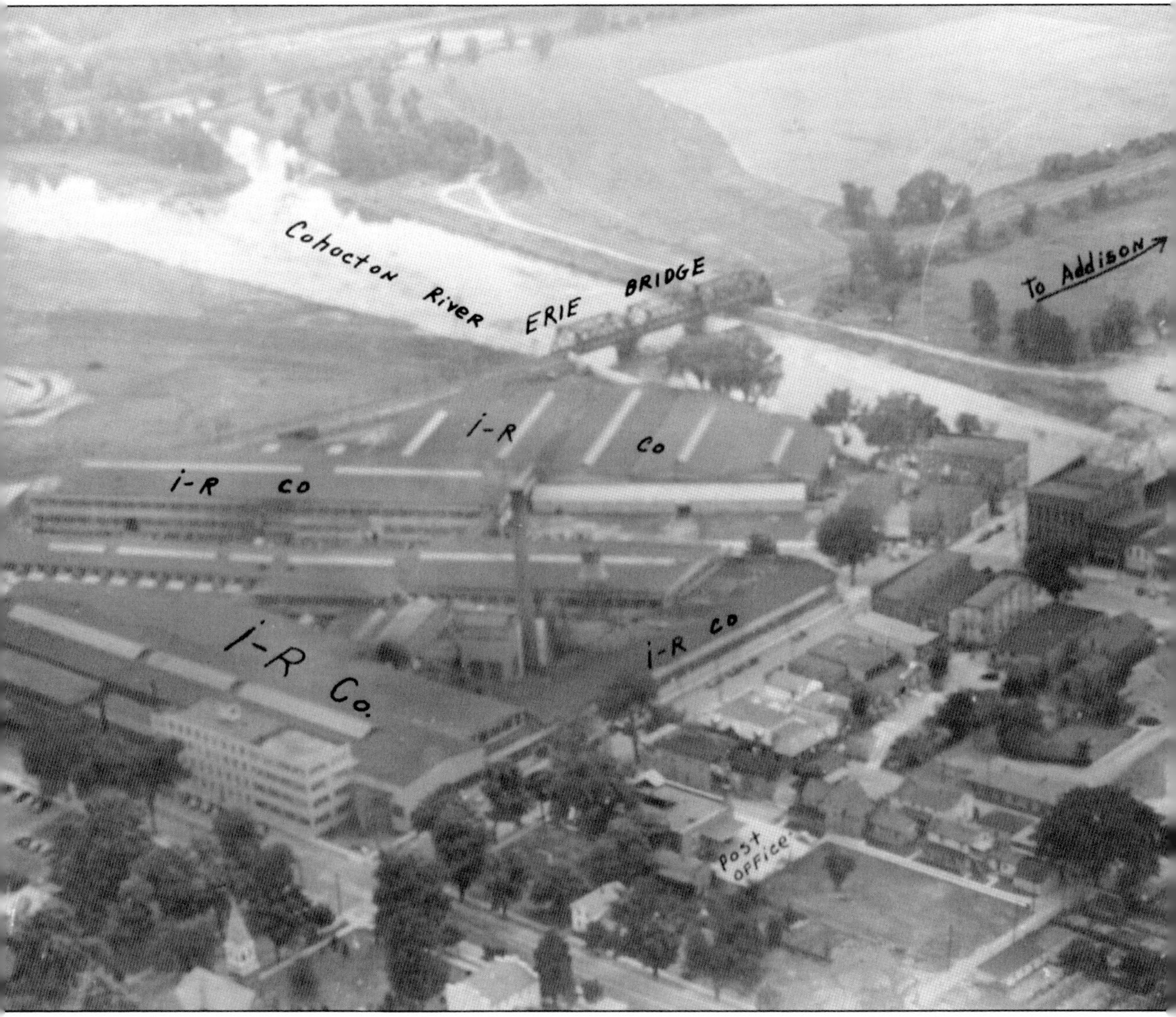

Ingersoll-Rand, now Dresser-Rand, has long been a major employer. Its facilities dominate the center of the photograph. The Odd Fellows temple (see page 16) is unlabeled but clearly identifiable near the river, just to the left of the highway bridge. The New Deal post office is at lower center. The space across the street and to the right of the post office, leading toward the temple, became Village Square after Hurricane Agnes. The Presbyterian Church (steeple at lower left) became the site of the joint Methodist-Presbyterian edifice after both facilities were flooded in 1972.

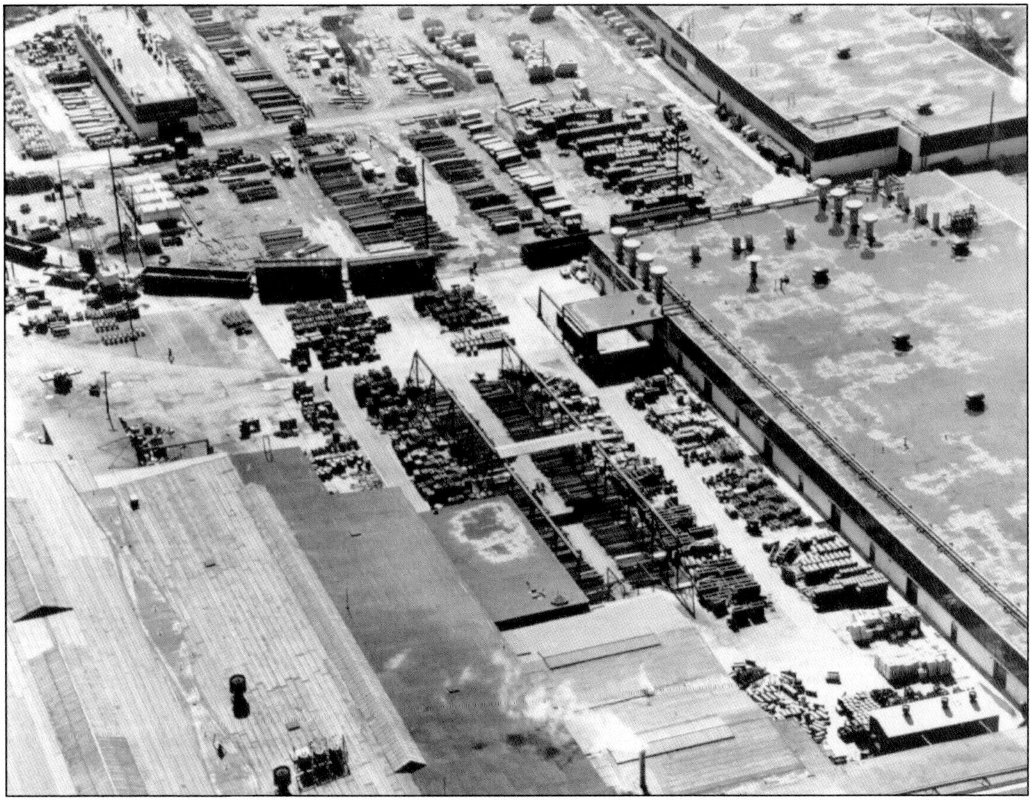

This 1958 photograph suggests the importance of the rail lines to "the Rand." Even today, trains still run down the middle of Chemung Street, visible at lower left in the previous photograph.

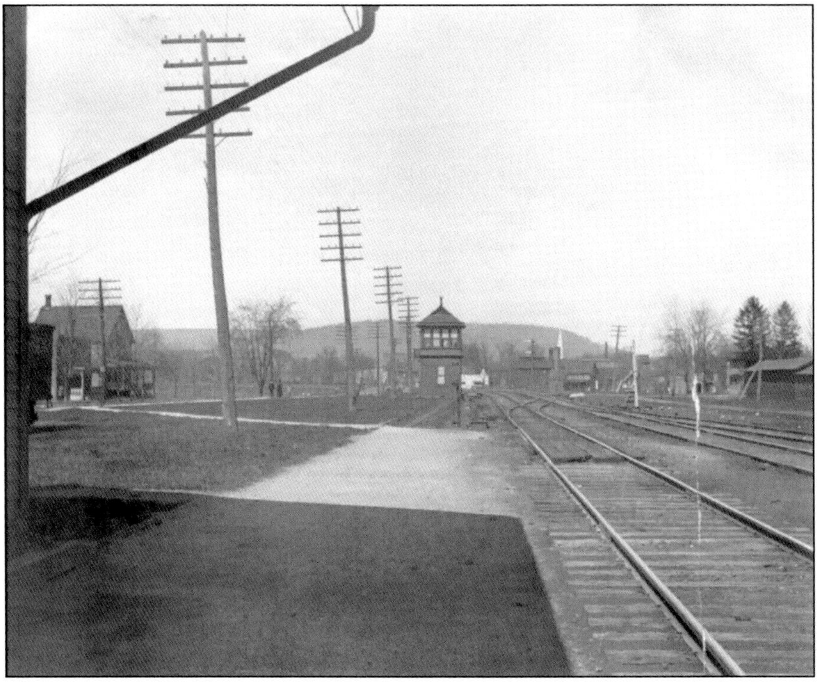

In the foreground of this 1908 photograph is the edge of the Erie Railroad passenger platform at East Water Street.

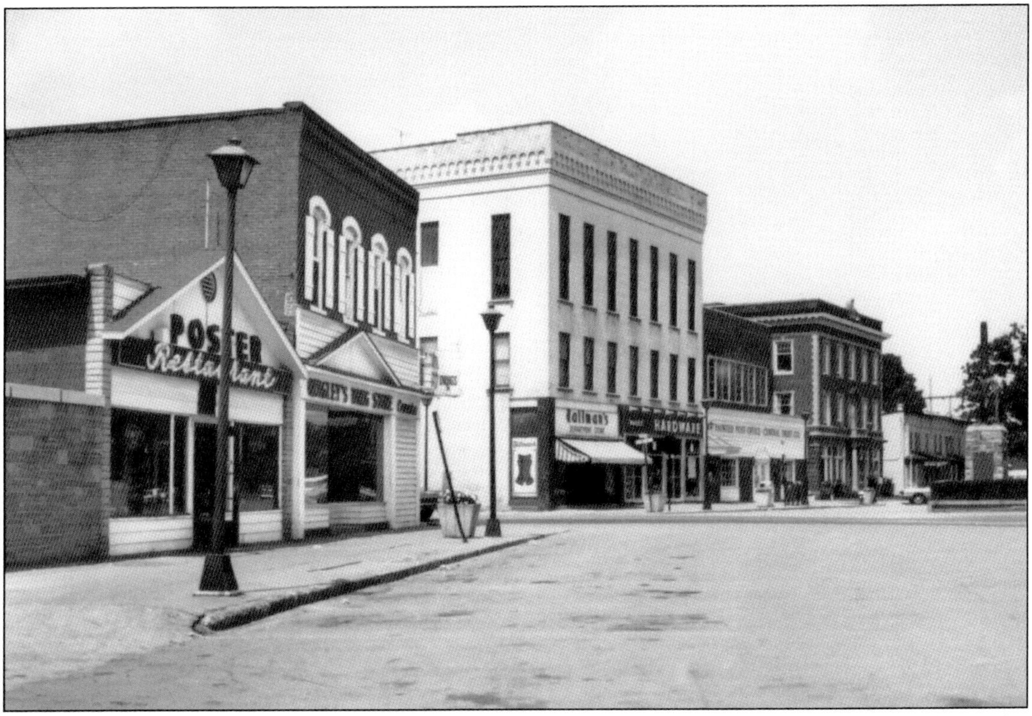

The three-story, red-brick municipal building stands near the end of this row, across from the statue. Most of the structures to the left of that building were swept away by urban renewal after the 1972 flood. Tallman's was relocated to the new Village Square Shopping Center.

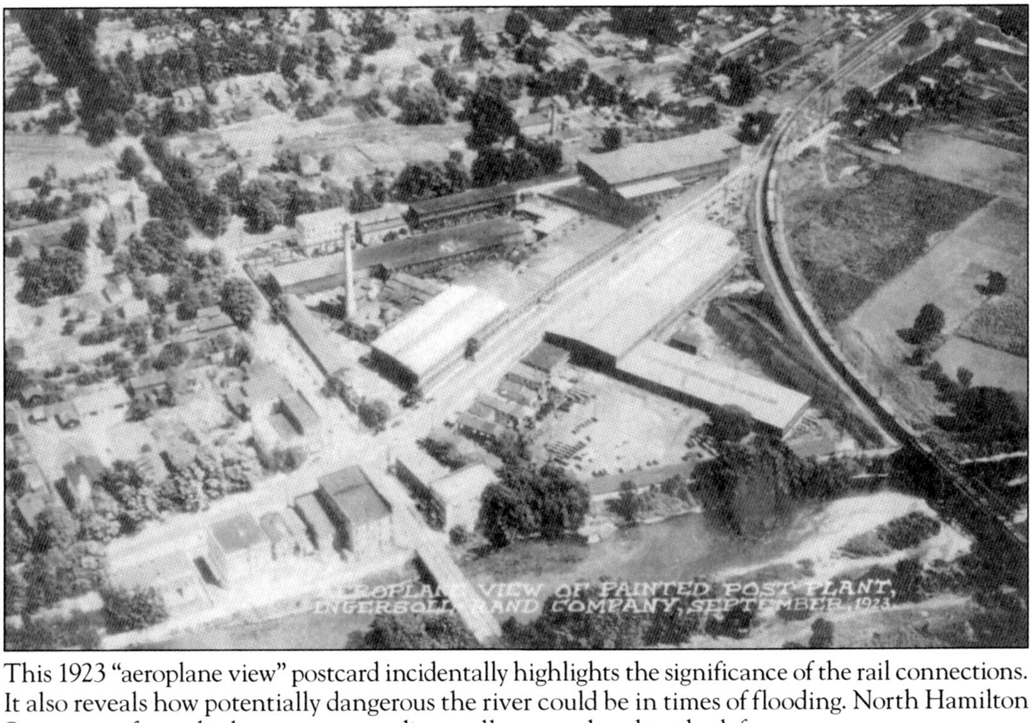

This 1923 "aeroplane view" postcard incidentally highlights the significance of the rail connections. It also reveals how potentially dangerous the river could be in times of flooding. North Hamilton Street runs from the bottom center, diagonally upward and to the left.

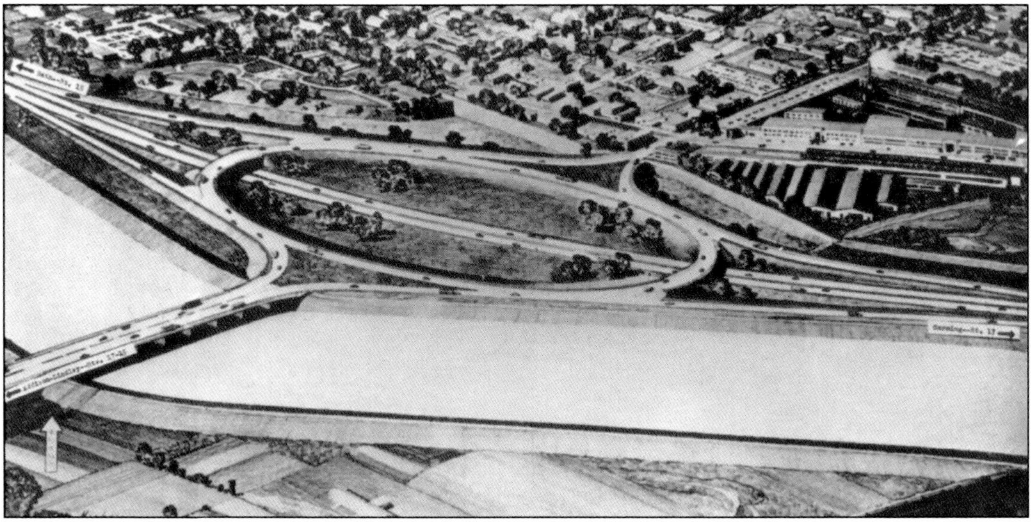

In 1959, the New York State Department of Public Works envisioned a new interchange for Routes 15 and 17, along with added flood control. It took a half-century and a new design, but the current interchange still reflects the original concept. The Rand is on the right. Today, the south (lower) side is no longer covered in farm fields.

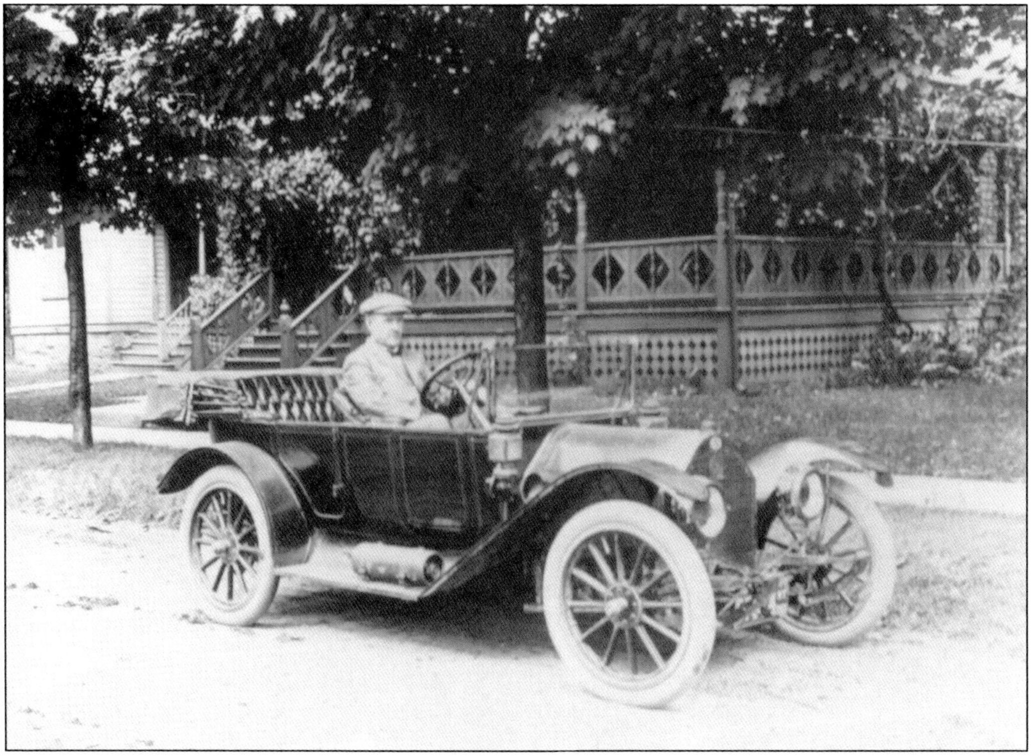

All of the construction no doubt would have been staggering to former mayor A.D. Stevens. Having gone to the trouble of having a photograph made, he was presumably proud of his Regal Buick. However, one would never guess it from his facial expression.

Herbert Johnson was "jailed" and had to be ransomed for the 1950 Colonial Days celebration. William Cumminsky is running the cash register while Niel Calter stands guard. The boys are, from left to right, Jerry Rarmes Jr., Al Hemley, and John Durkin.

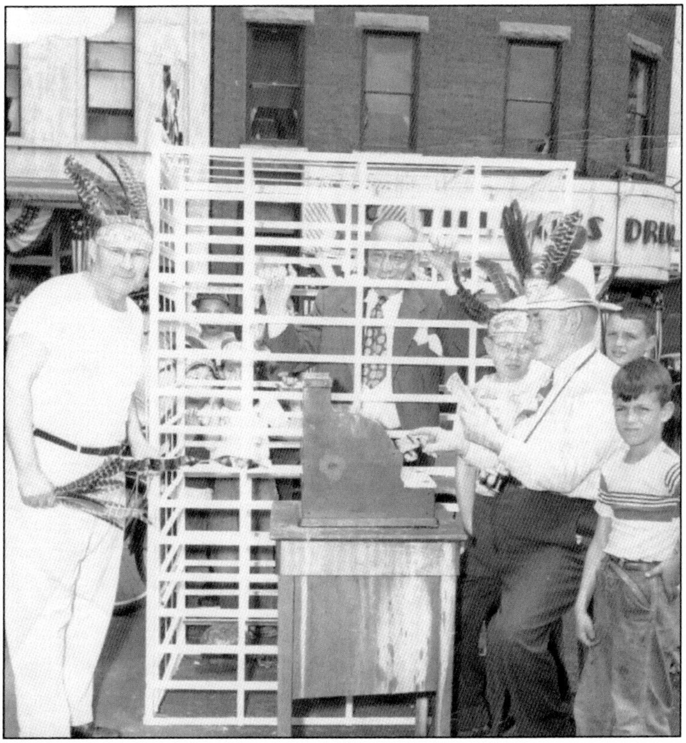

Colonial Days in Hodgman Park has always been a huge event. Visible in this aerial photograph are the Baptist Church (upper right) and the Ingersoll-Rand facilities just beyond it. Hodgman Park is located on Water Street.

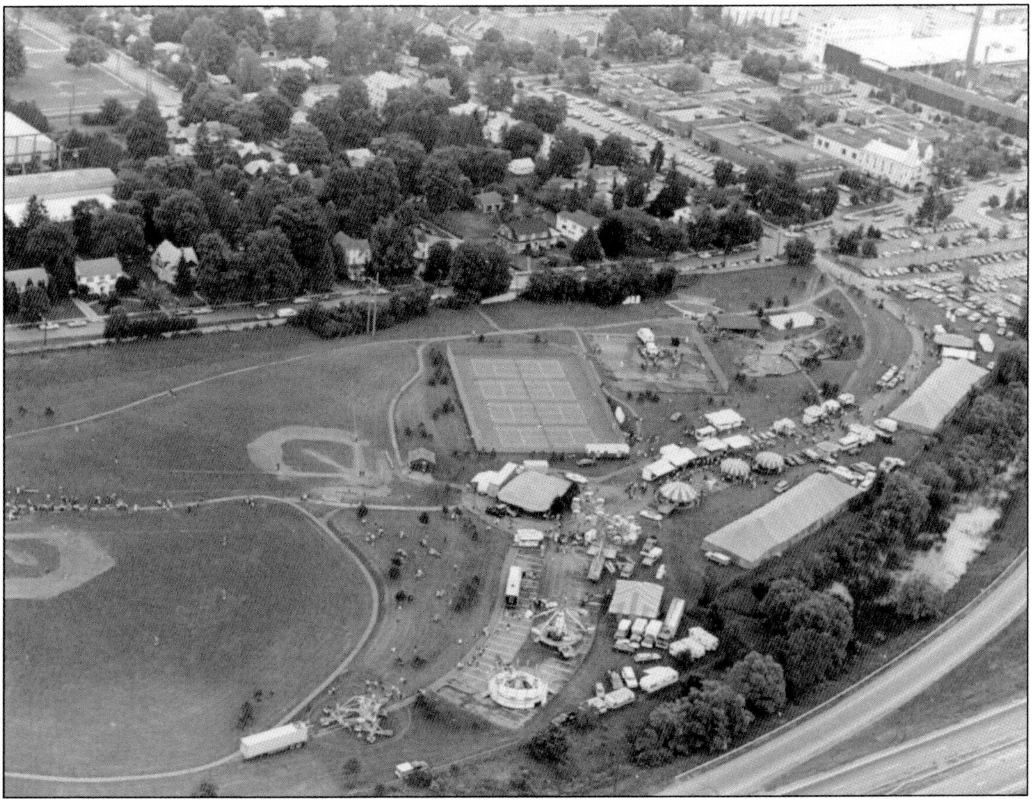

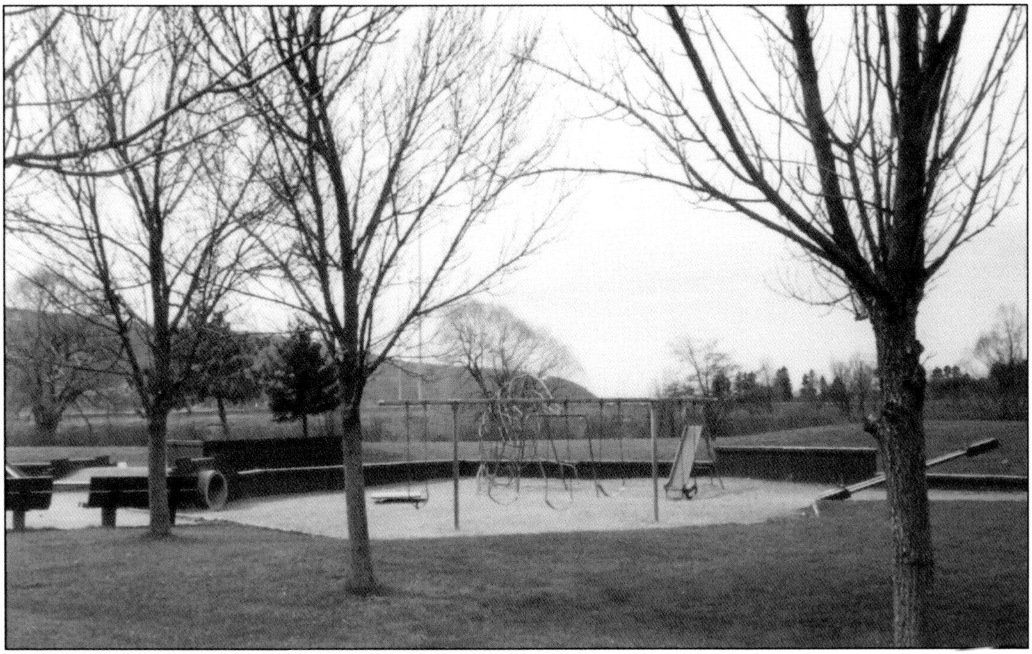

Even without Colonial Days, Hodgman Park is a popular spot for families. (Photograph by Stanley Weisenfeld; SCH.)

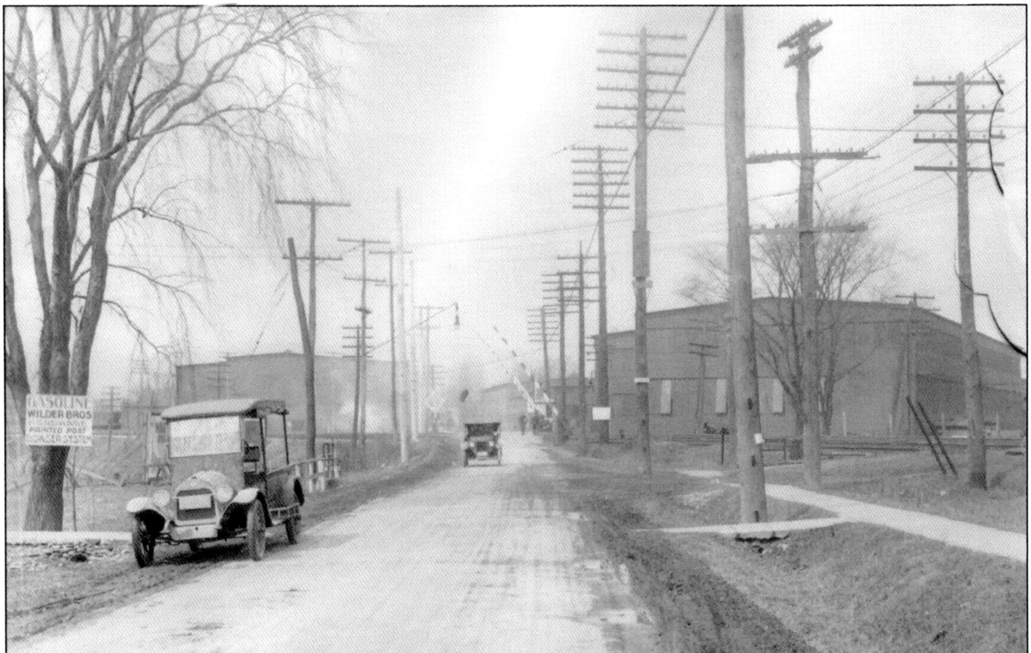

"The Rand" and the railroad tracks are in the background of this photograph. A short walkway leads from the sidewalk to the unpaved street just in front of the utility pole on the right, then resumes over the little culvert on the left. Included in this photograph are two automobiles, two pedestrians, and a cyclist. The sign on the left announces that Wilder Brothers Hardware in Painted Post carries gasoline. The infrastructure of service stations did not yet exist.

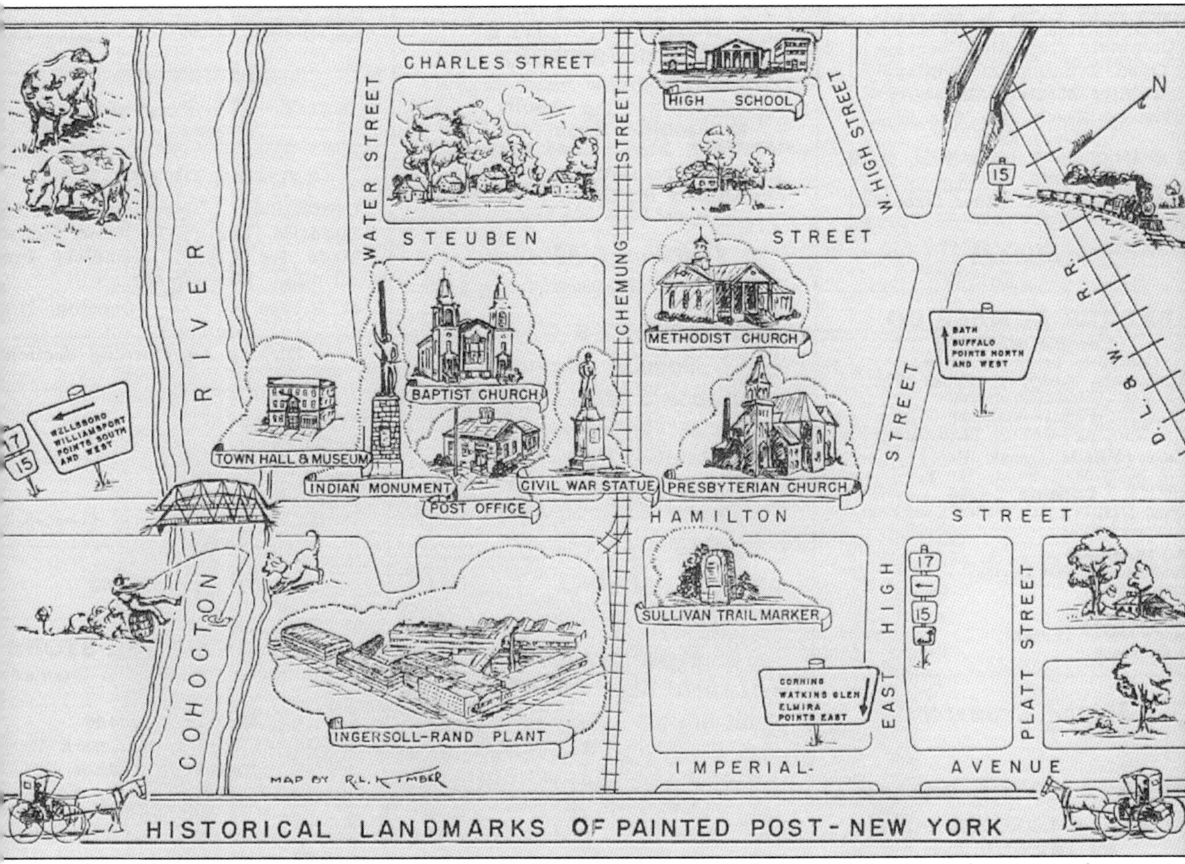

This 1950s tourism map does not show today's interstate routes, I-86 running between the river and Water Street, and I-99 running south across the river. The Methodist and Presbyterian Churches combined their facilities after the 1972 flood. The DL&W is no more, but tracks and trains still run down Chemung Street. Painted Post High School closed a few years after the 1956 merger of 62 systems into the Corning–Painted Post School District. The building now houses district offices. The map's buggies were merely quaint historical illustrations. Since the time of this map, however, conservative Anabaptists have indeed returned buggies to the region. (SCHS.)

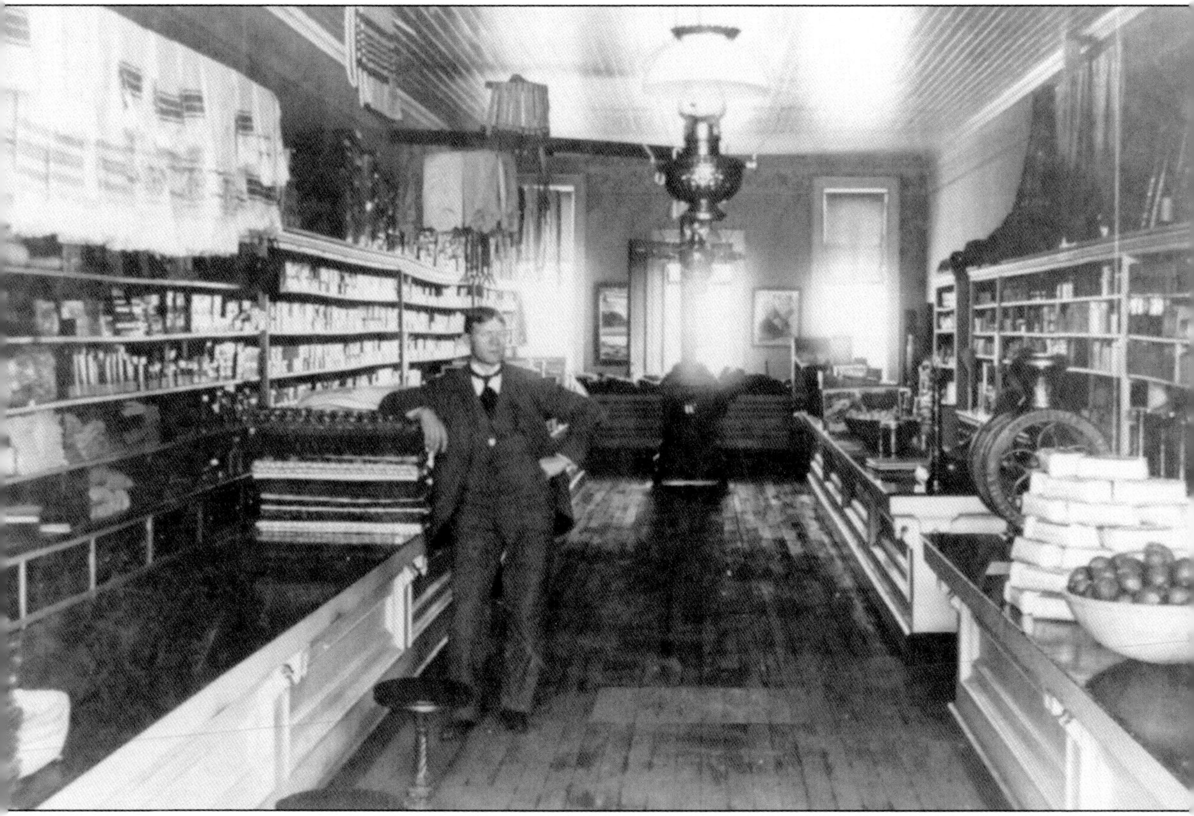

Asah Peck, seen here in 1901, took pride in his Painted Post grocery store. Note the elaborate chandelier, and the heating stove in front of the window. The counter stools at left have decorative uprights. Peck is leaning on dry goods, which fill much of the space on the left. At the right, note the coffee grinder and the large bowl of apples, as well as a bowl of what may be walnuts farther back. This space was Langworthy's Department Store in 1919, Benjamin Brown's Department Store from 1922 to 1962, and then Tallman's from 1962 until Hurricane Agnes struck 10 years later.

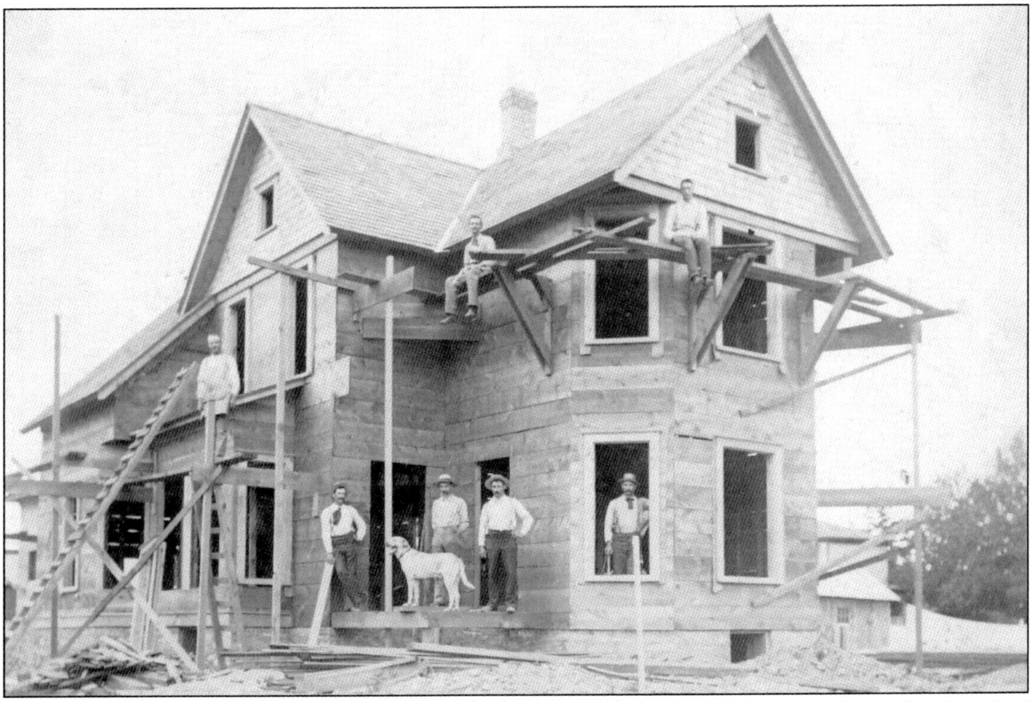

Richard Henry Packer built this fine house, the location of which is uncertain. The only identified persons are a Mr. Putnam, standing in the window, and Hulah C. Wilson, one of the men on the scaffolding. Note that several of the men are wearing hats, while some wear neckties while on the job. The dog must be a foreman.

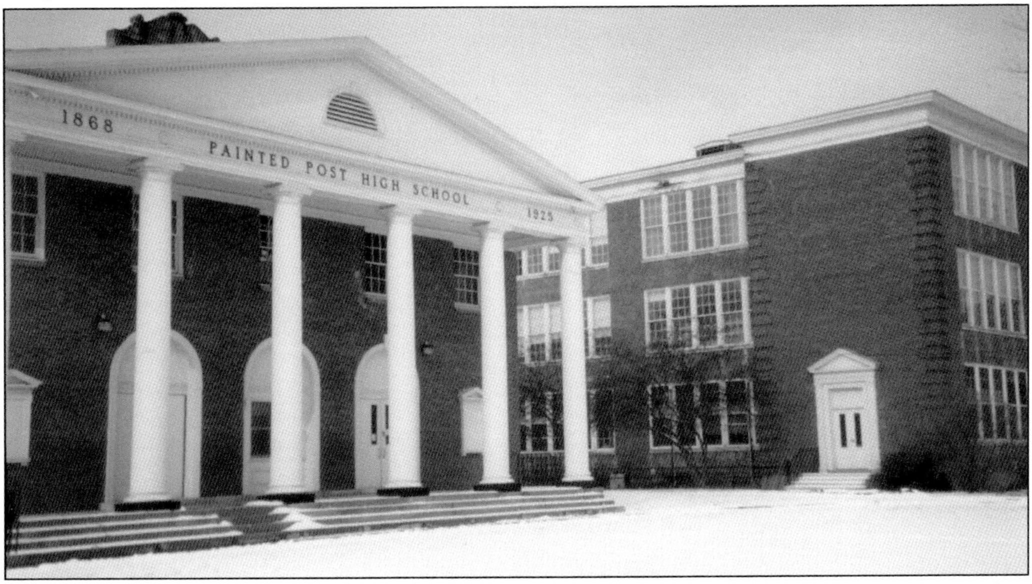

In 1957, the Corning–Painted Post School District was formed, a result of the merging of 62 districts, most with a single one-room school. Painted Post High School (shown here) was one of three in the new entity, the others being Corning Northside and Corning Free Academy. As two high schools rather than three were planned for the new district, PPHS became the district's administrative headquarters. (SCH.)

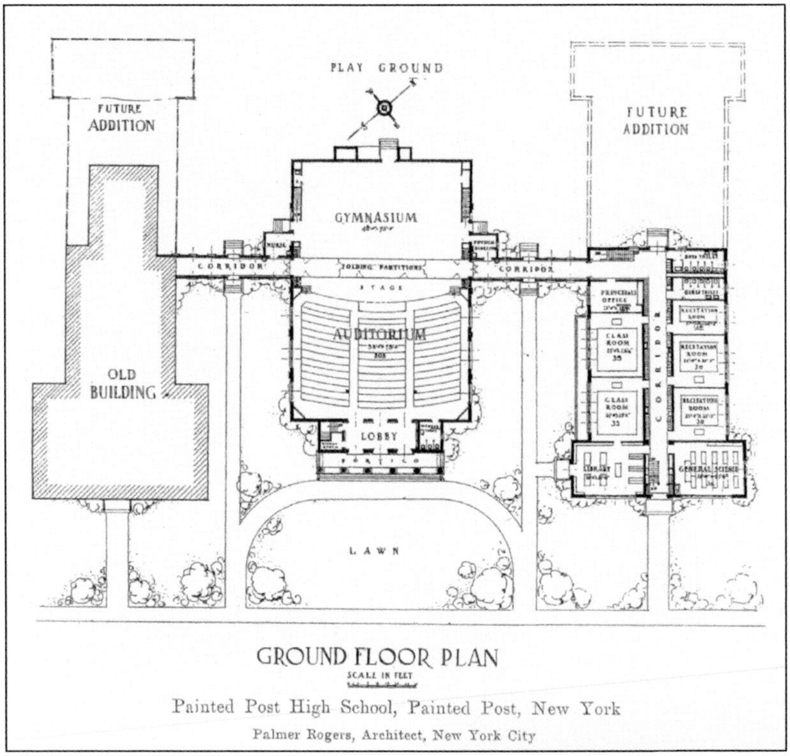

Painted Post High School was so advanced at the time of its construction that it was written up in the professional magazine *The Architect* in January 1929. (SCHS.)

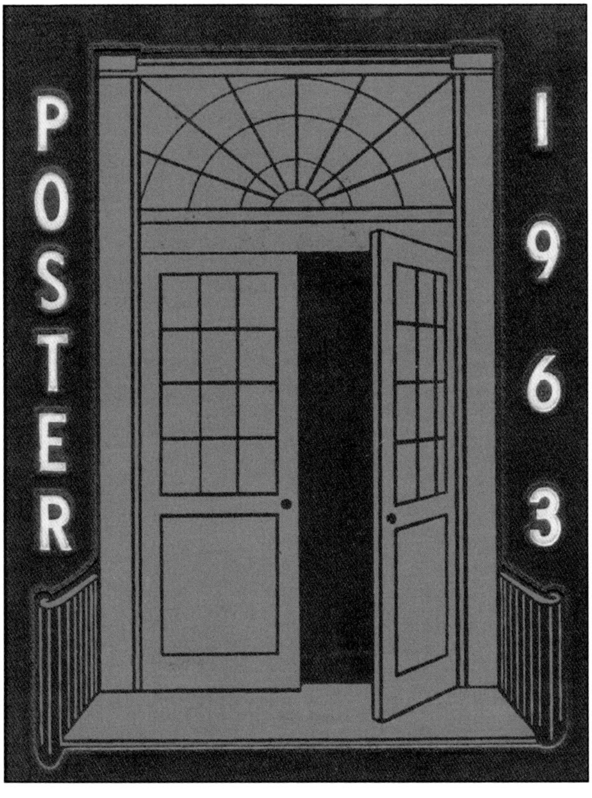

The 1963 *Poster* yearbook was a hail and farewell for Painted Post High School. (SCHS.)

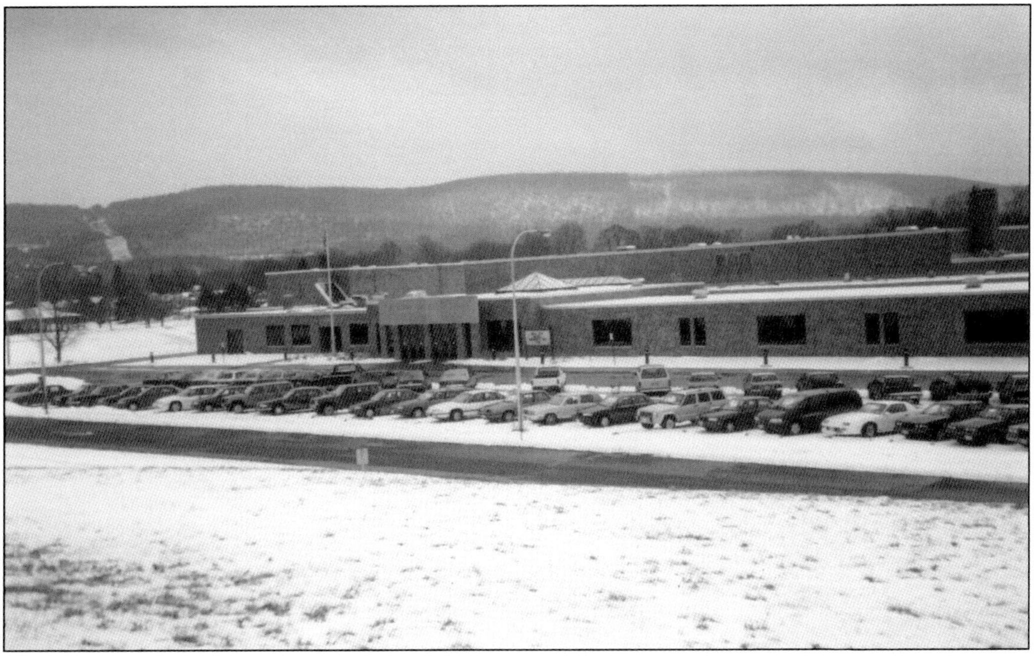

Corning–Painted Post West, one of two high schools created for the new district, lies within the village limits of Painted Post. The new district also created modern elementary facilities in Gang Mills (Erwin Valley School) and Coopers Plains (Frank Pierce School). In 2014, "West" (shown here) is scheduled to become a middle school. (SCH.)

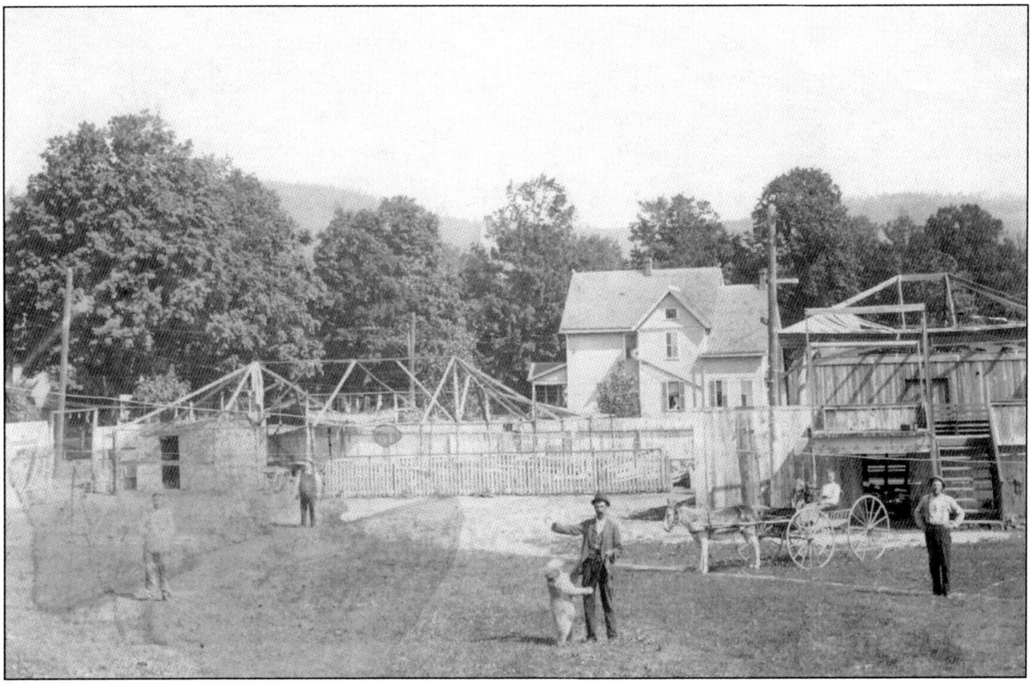

The J.W. Boret Hotel is shown here going up near Bronson Park in 1900. It looks as though the children have their wagon hitched to a mule or donkey. The fellow in the center appears to be training a bear cub!

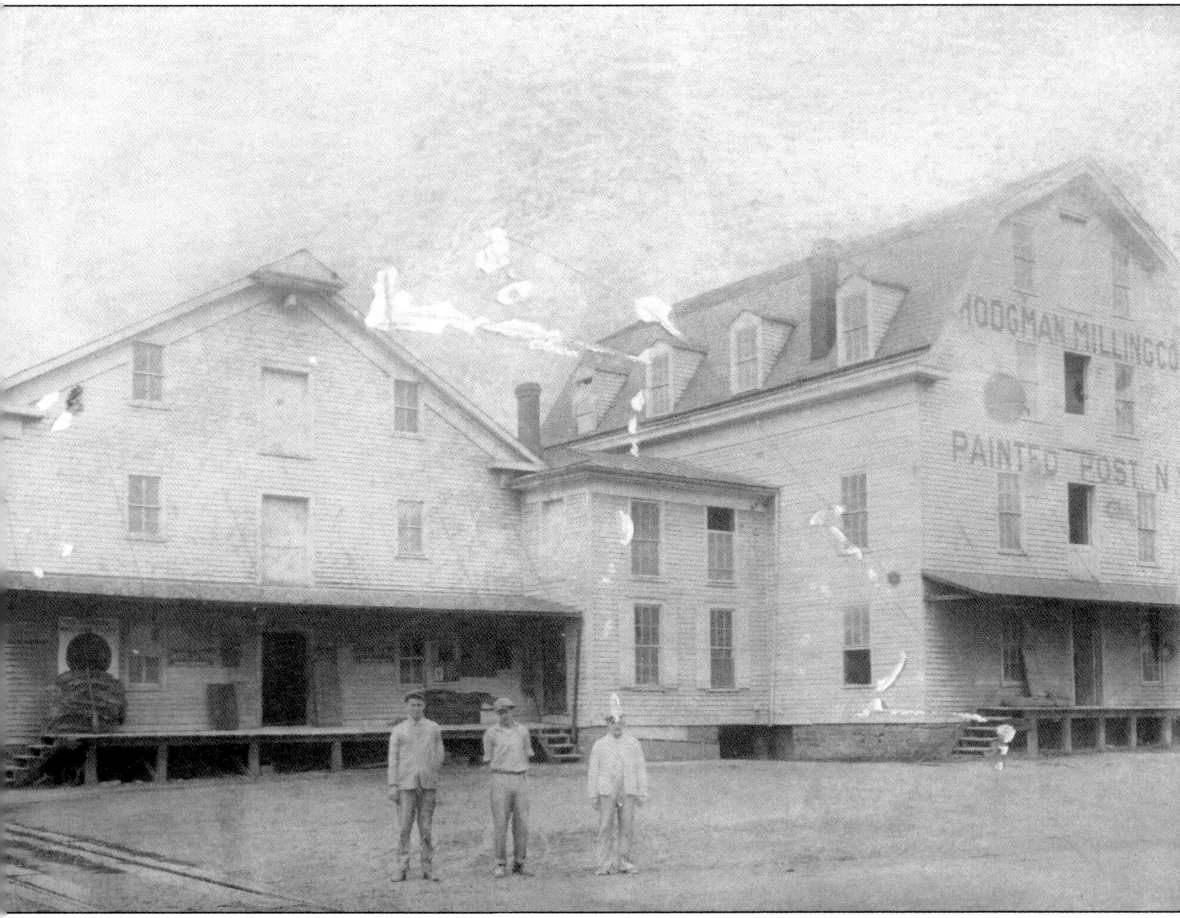

Posing in front of Hodgman Milling are Fred Morse (left), Ray Margeson (center), and millwright Charlie Hubard. The poster at left, partly obscured by a broom and a pile of empty bags, advertises The Standard American Brand.

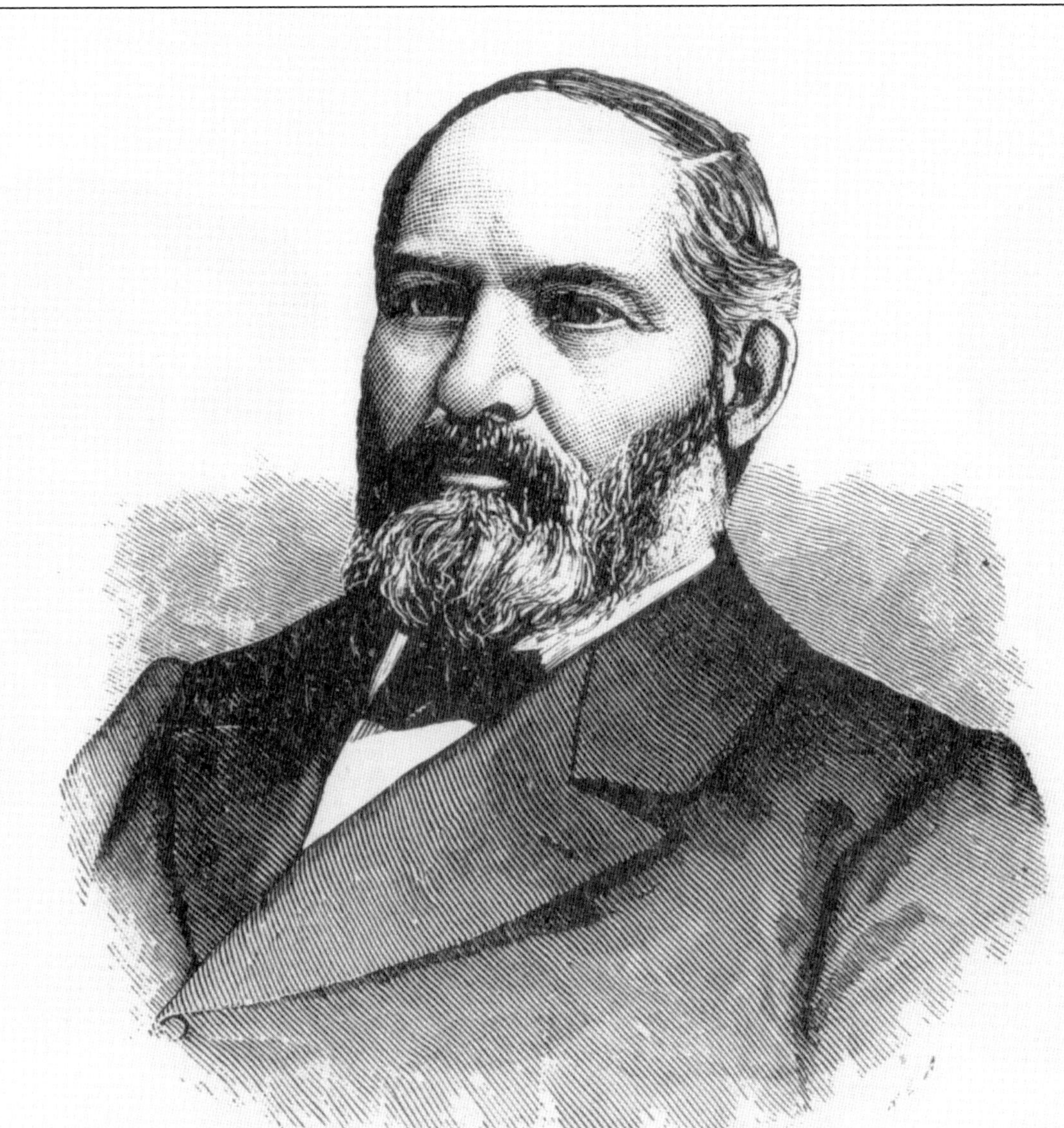

Warren S. Hodgman was already a successful businessman when he moved to Painted Post in 1850. Besides operating the grist and sawmills, he was a prominent Presbyterian, a leader in the Republican Party, tax assessor, town supervisor, and president of the board of education. He married the daughter of Judge Lyman Balcom. (SCH.)

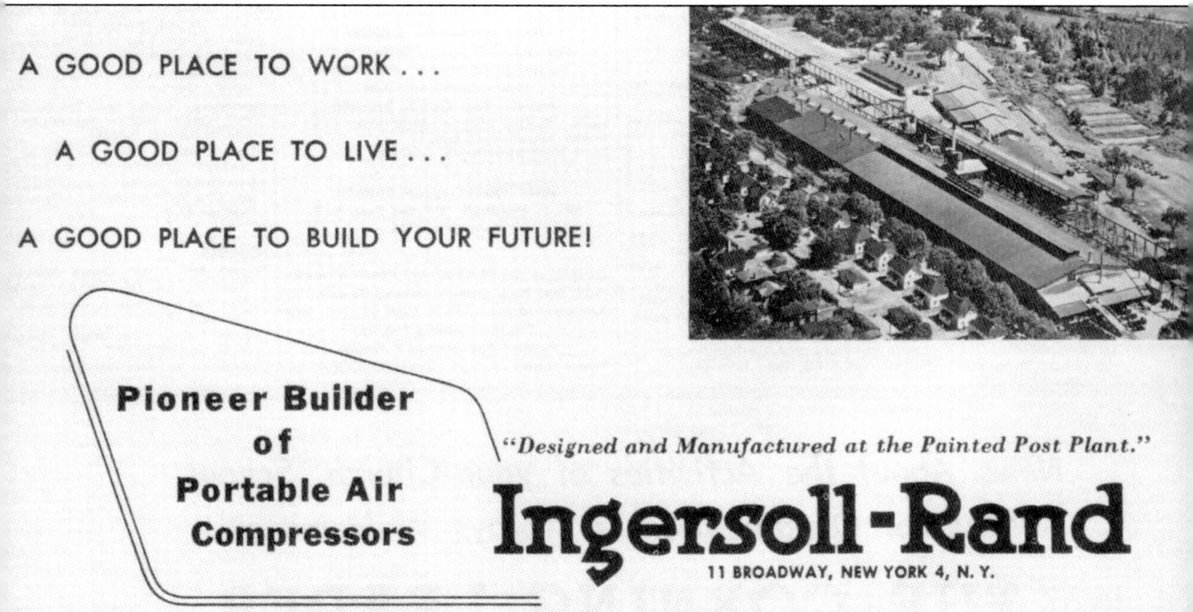

According to this Ingersoll-Rand advertisement, Painted Post was a good place to work, a good place to live, and a good place to build your future. (SCHS.)

Two

The Hamlets

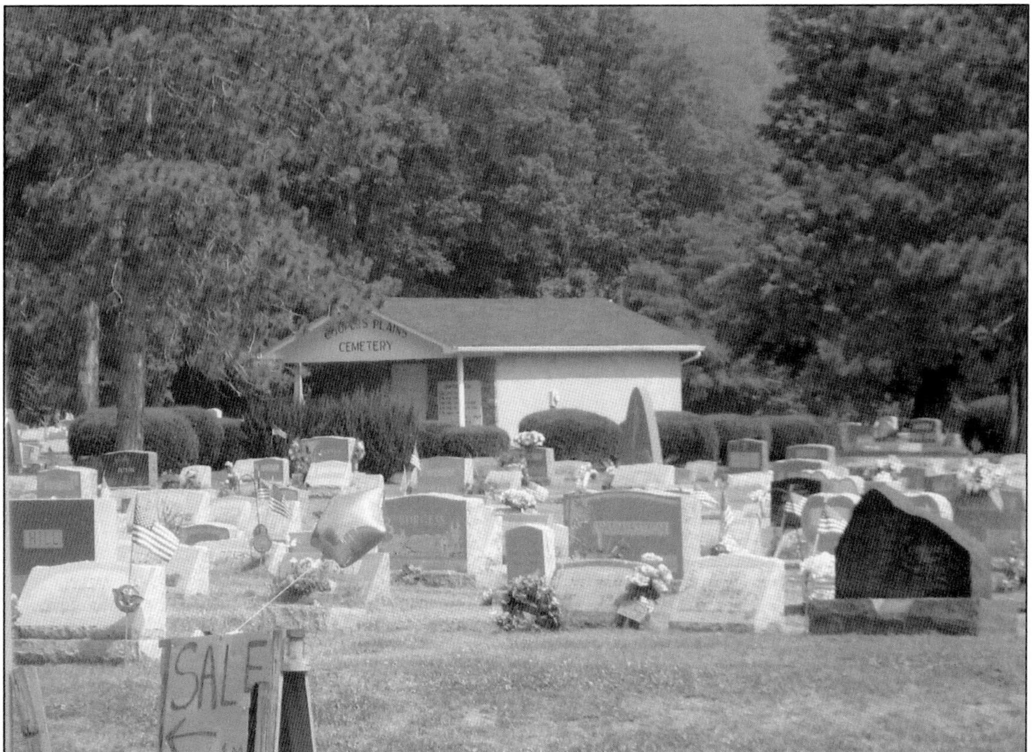

Outside Painted Post, Erwin has nonofficial settlements as well. Gang Mills in many ways seems an extension of Painted Post and Corning. Coopers Plains (with its lovely cemetery) and Erwins maintain individual identities. Long-ago hamlets include Erwin, Erwinna, Erwindale, Erwin Centre, Erwin Junction, Erwin Station, and Townsend's Grove. Beartown was never much more than a one-room school. But Beartown Road, and businesses bearing the old name, keep its memory alive. (KWH.)

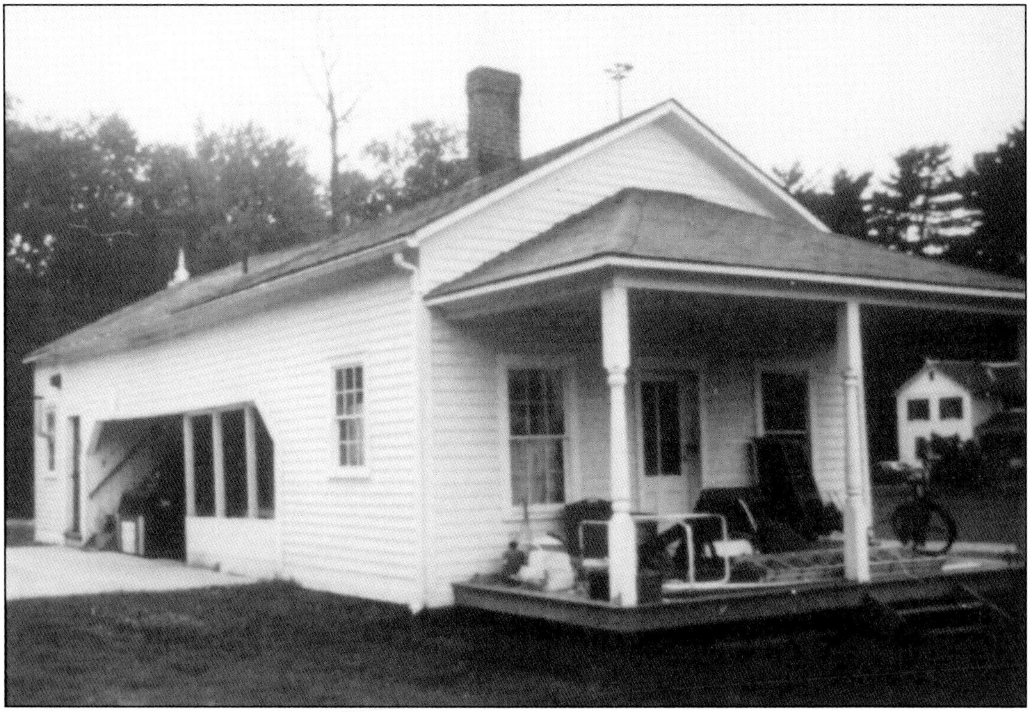

An early post office in Erwin was at the hamlet of Townsend's Grove, near Townsend-Erwin Cemetery on Route 417. Edward C. Townsend was postmaster in 1873. (SCH.)

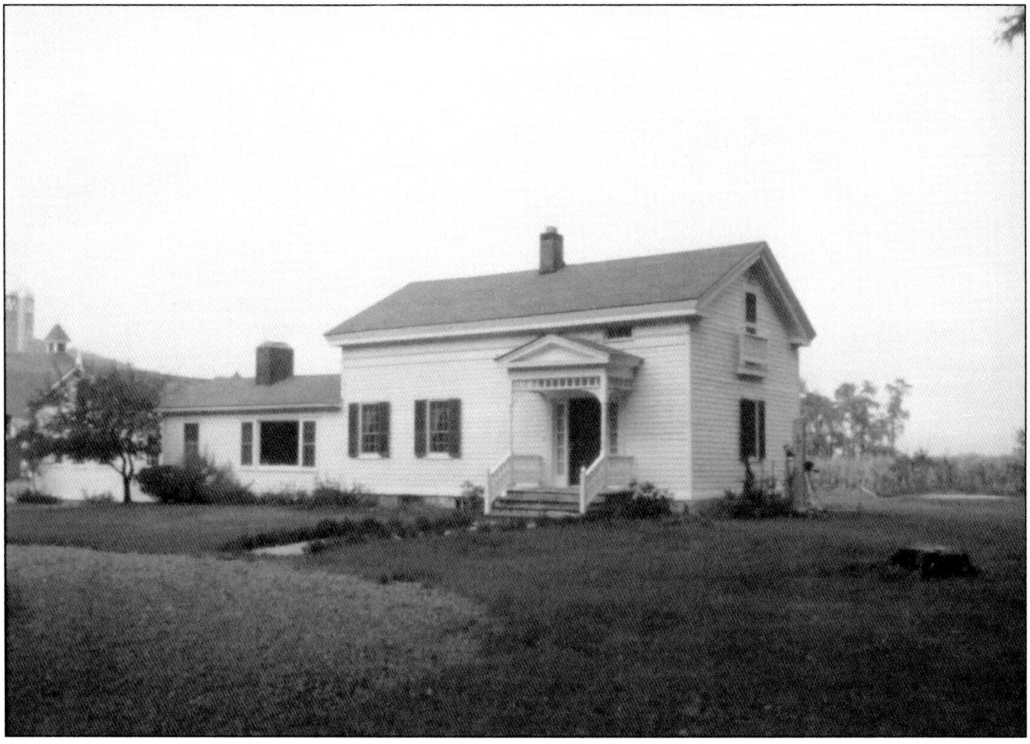

The Townsend family built this home in 1848. Note the barn in the background at left.

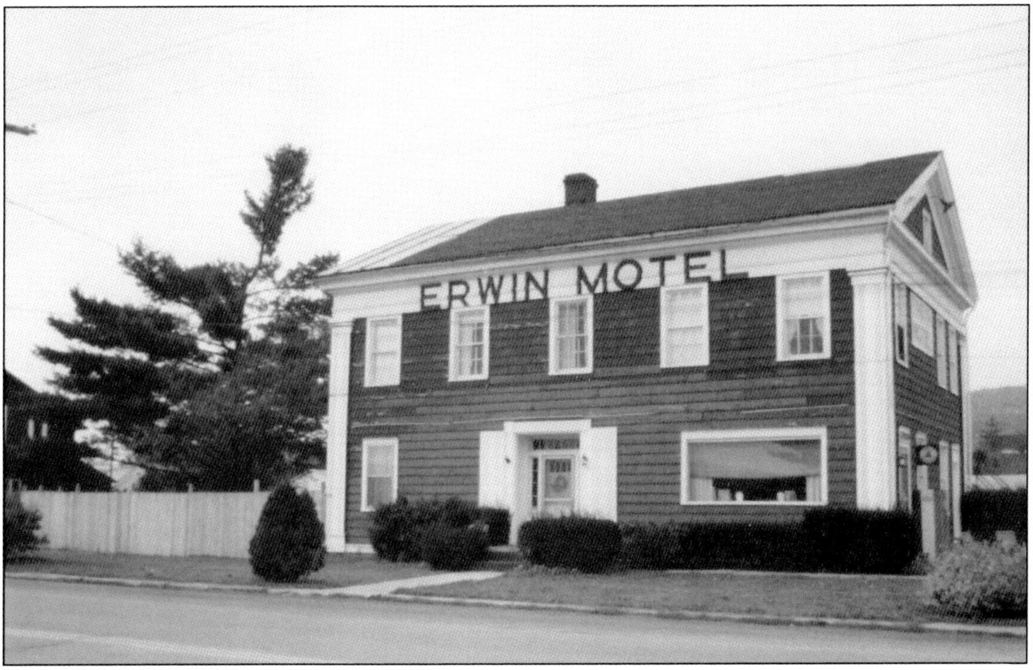

This large house, now the heart of the Erwin Motel in the hamlet of Erwins, has been a stopping and gathering place since the 1800s. Long ago, grateful travelers climbed down from their stagecoaches here. Today, it lies conveniently close to an exit on the new I-99.

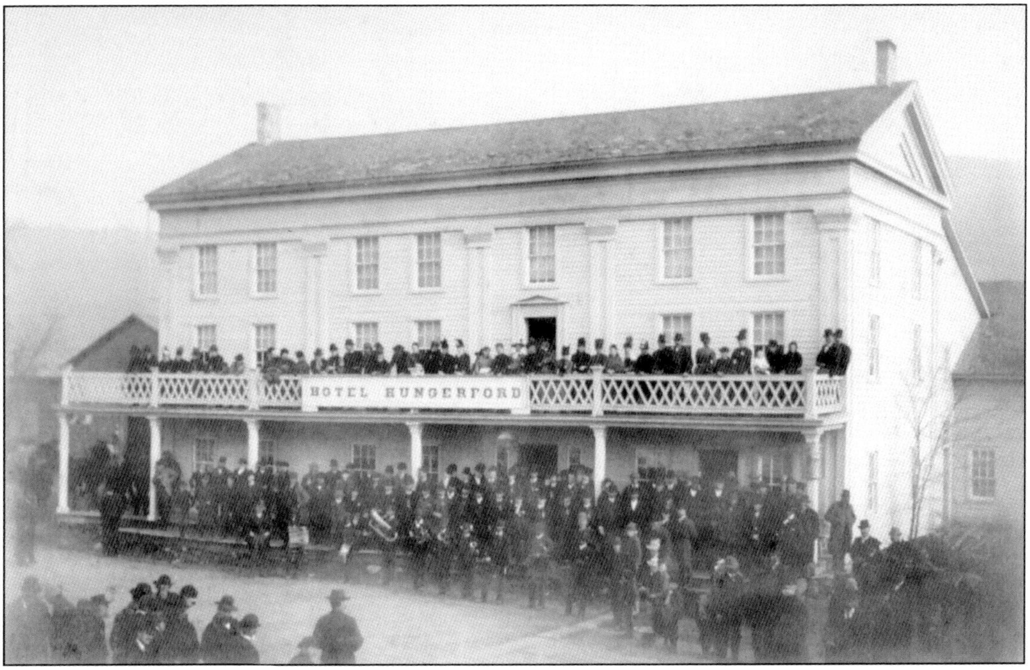

Hotel Hungerford, in the hamlet of Coopers Plains at Race and North Main Streets, hosted this large gathering sometime in the 19th century. And no gathering back then was complete without a community band. The quiet Greek Revival architectural elements work perfectly with the hotel's large size. Fire destroyed the structure on May 4, 1914.

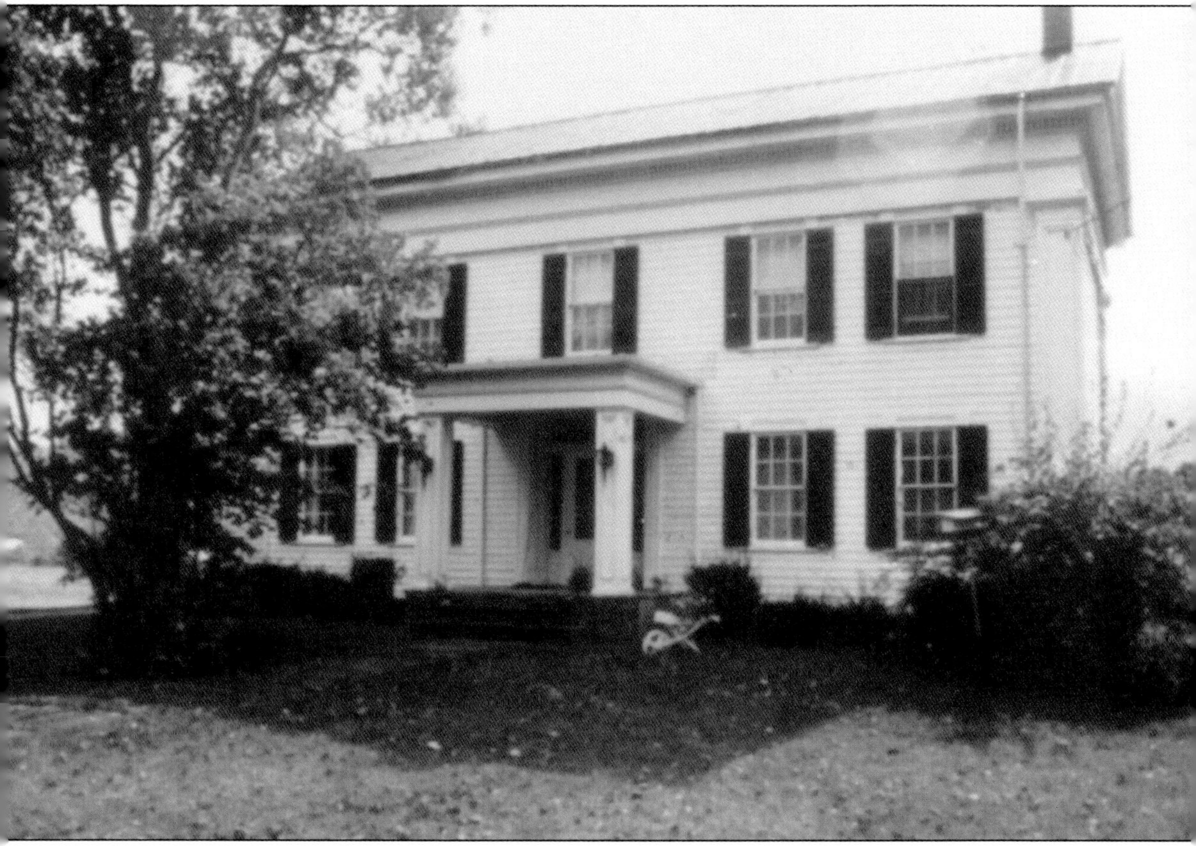

Dr. John Cooper and his wife, Mary Erwin Cooper, built this home in Coopers Plains at what is now Main Street and State Route 415 in 1839. He started selling lots in 1841. (SCH.)

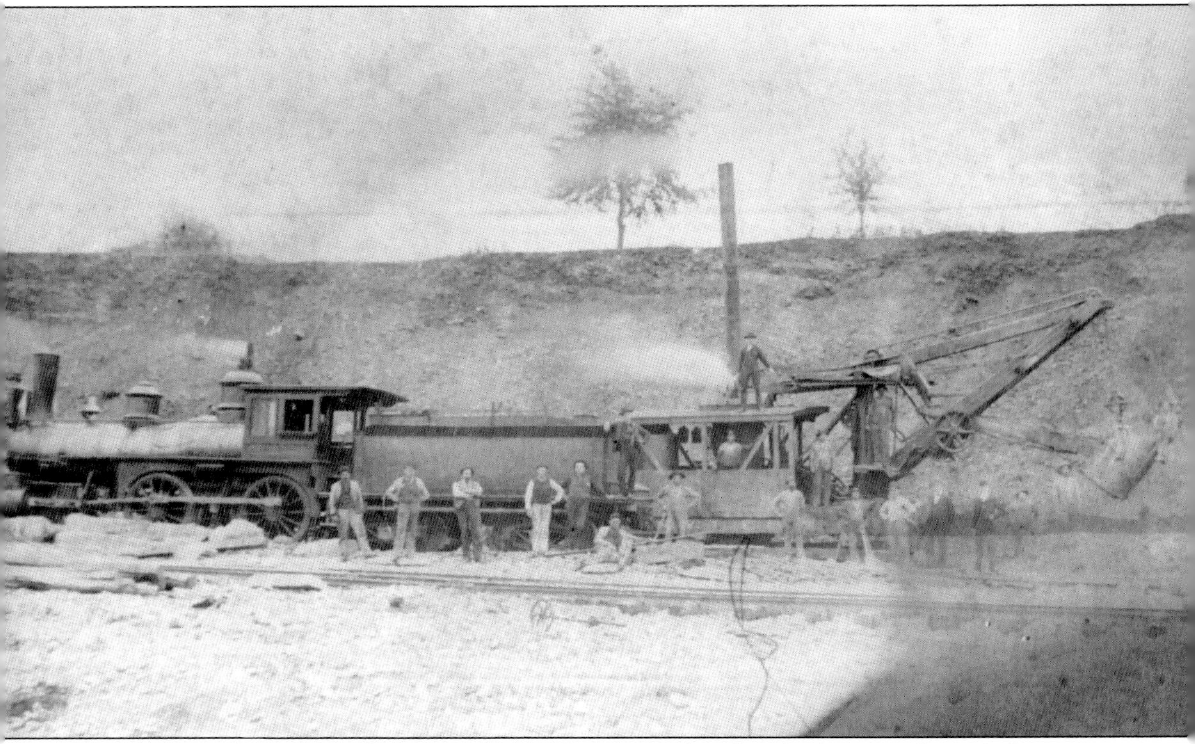

Not long after the Coopers built their home, the Erie Railroad pushed its way through Coopers Plains, installing its main line from New York City to Lake Erie.

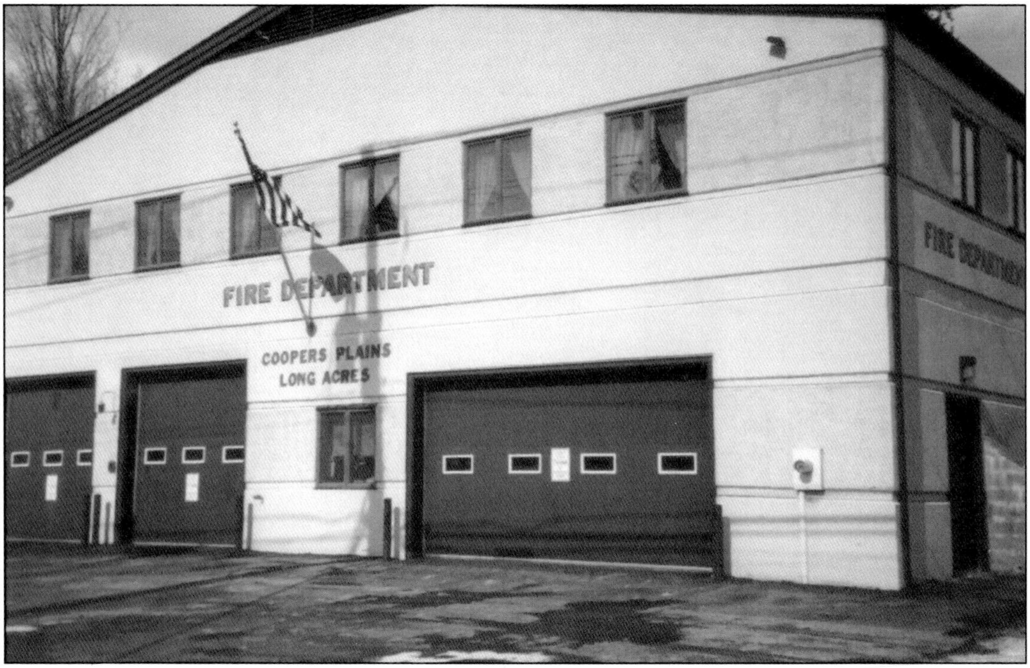

Coopers Plains has its own fire company, organized in 1953. This building went up in 1989, and it is seen here in 1996. (SCH.)

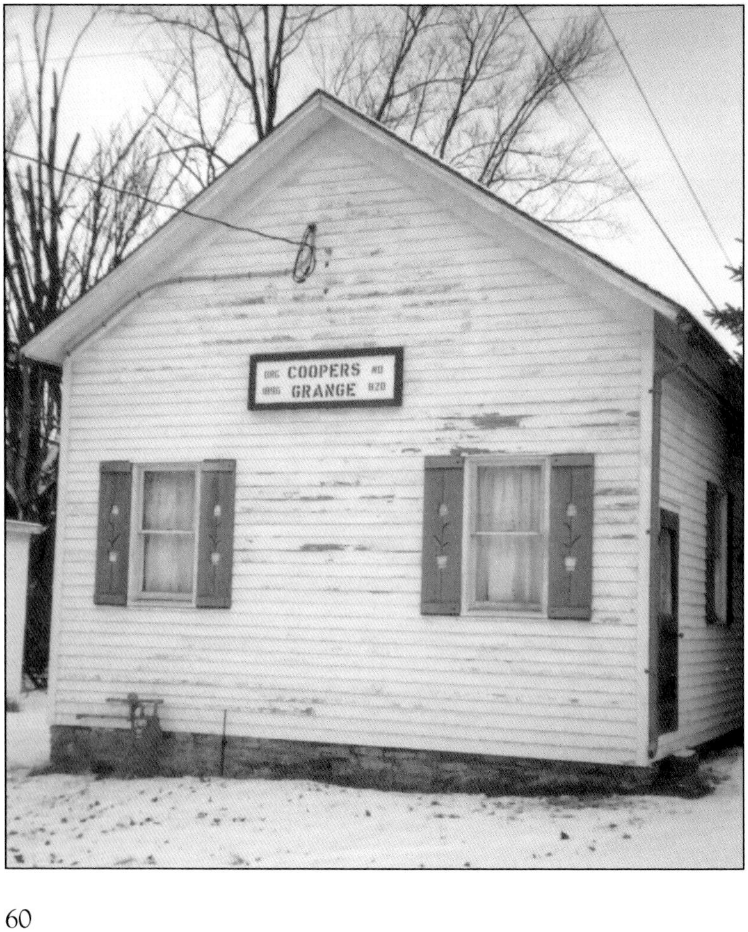

Unfortunately, the Coopers Grange, which celebrated its centennial in 1996, is no more. Like many granges, its membership melted away as farm life dwindled. (SCH.)

J.J. Baker may well have belonged to the Coopers Grange. As if the Great Depression weren't bad enough, his farm and his stock were clobbered by the 1935 flood.

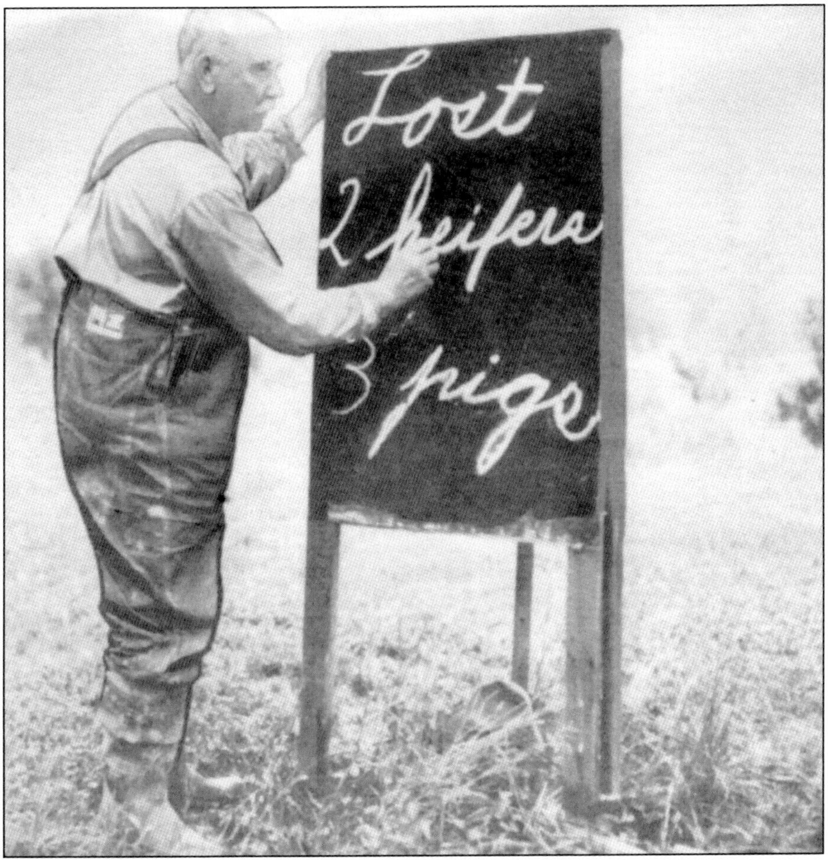

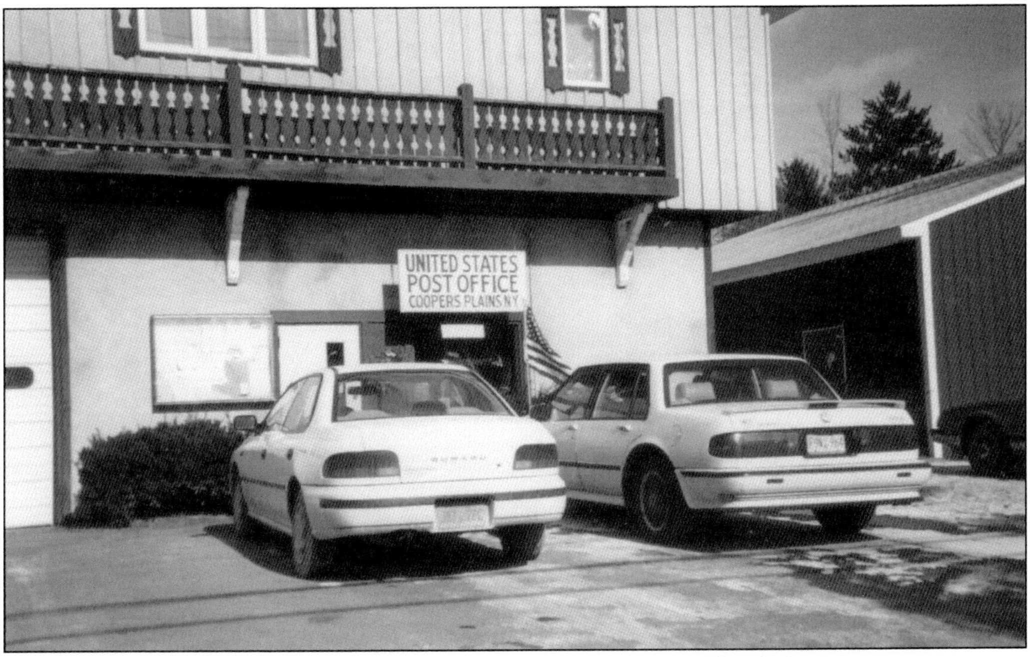

The Coopers Plains post office on Main Street still serves the public. (SCH.)

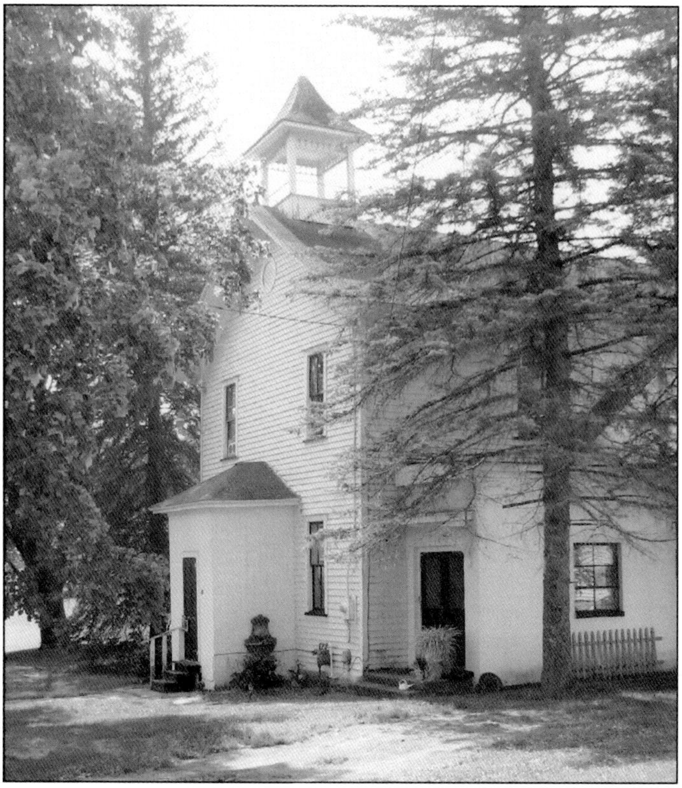

In the days of one-room schools, Coopers Plains rejoiced in an unusual and interesting two-story school, complete with bell tower. The building is now a private home. (KWH.)

Hard by the old school, clinging to the hillside, is Campbell-Erwin Baptist Church. The congregation dates to 1820, but the current 1896 edifice was remodeled in the 1950s with help from IBM president Thomas Watson, who was born and brought up just over the town line in Campbell. (KWH.)

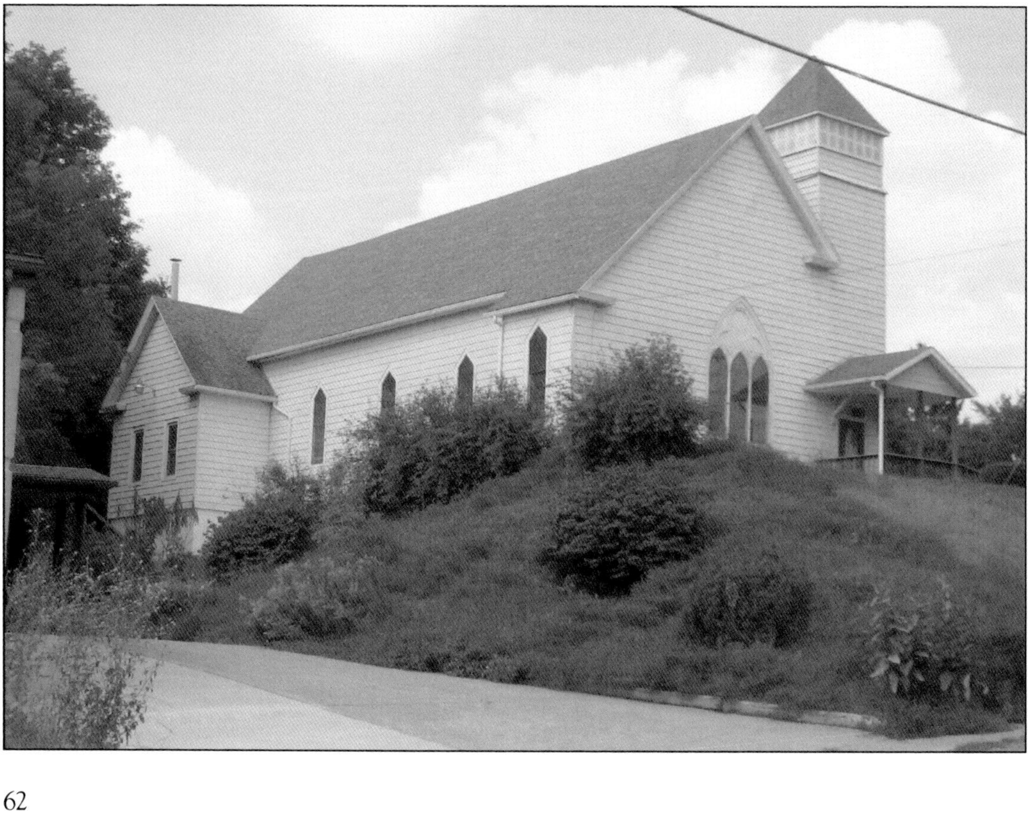

The attractive and understated Coopers Plains United Methodist Church bespeaks the New England roots from which many of the area's first white settlers sprang. The Baptist and Methodist Churches, now pastored by a single minister, serve the community via the Coopers Plains United Church. (KWH.)

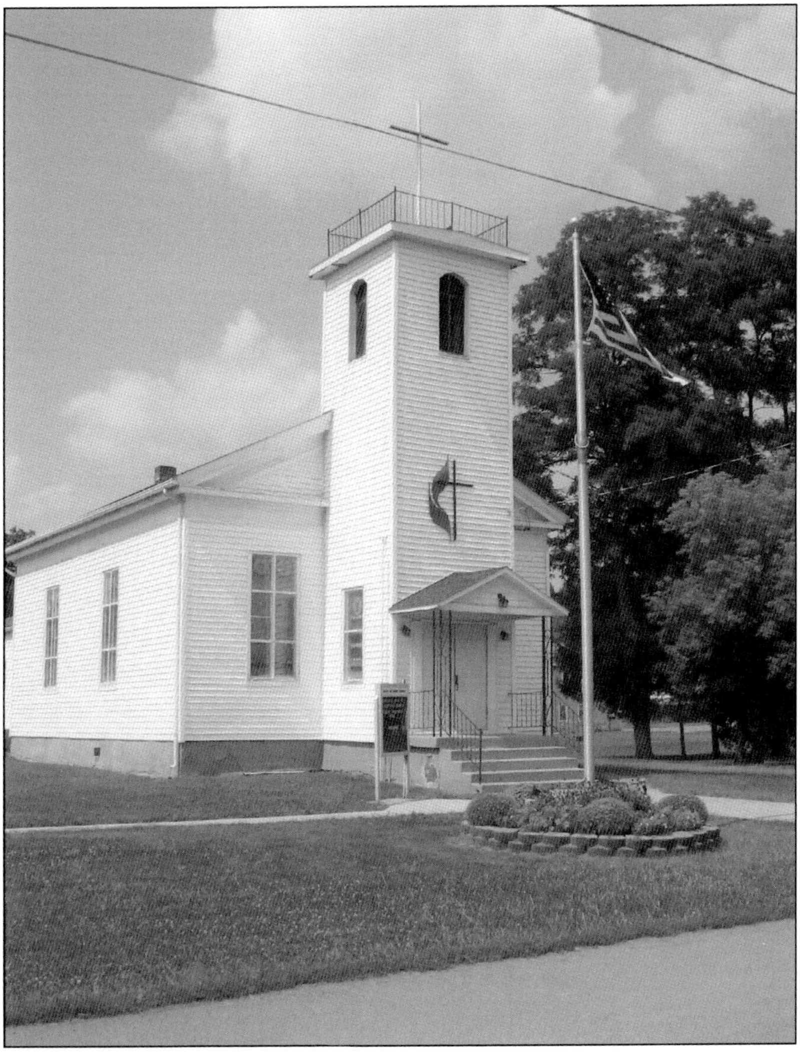

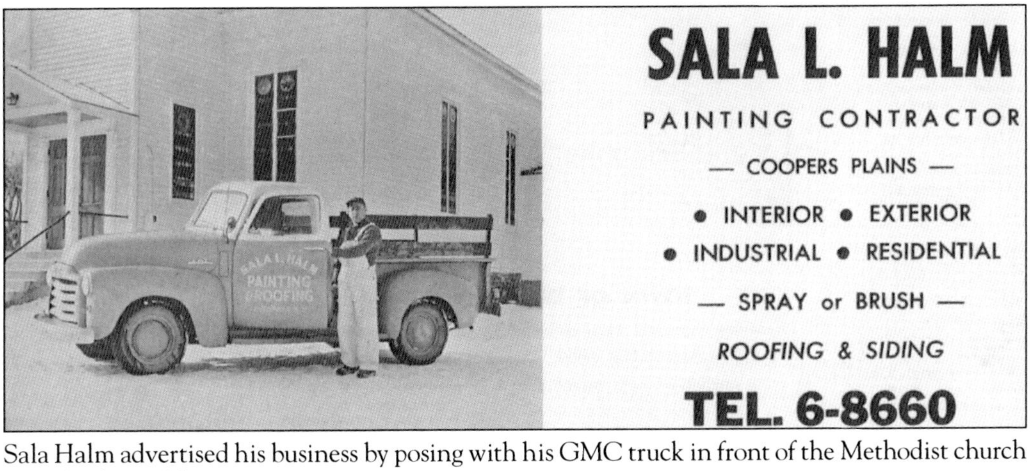

Sala Halm advertised his business by posing with his GMC truck in front of the Methodist church in 1956. (SCHS.)

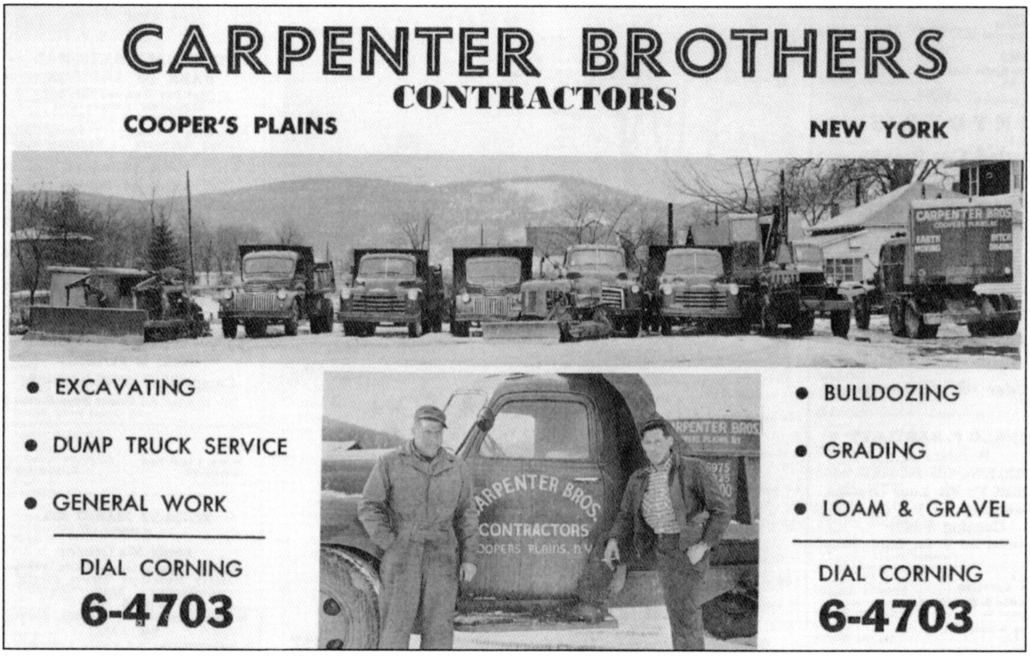

The Carpenter Brothers were contractors who undertook ditch digging and earth moving, among other tasks. Judging from this photograph, they operated quite a fleet in Coopers Plains. The brothers, posing in snow in this advertisement, apparently ran their business from the front, rather than the office. (SCHS.)

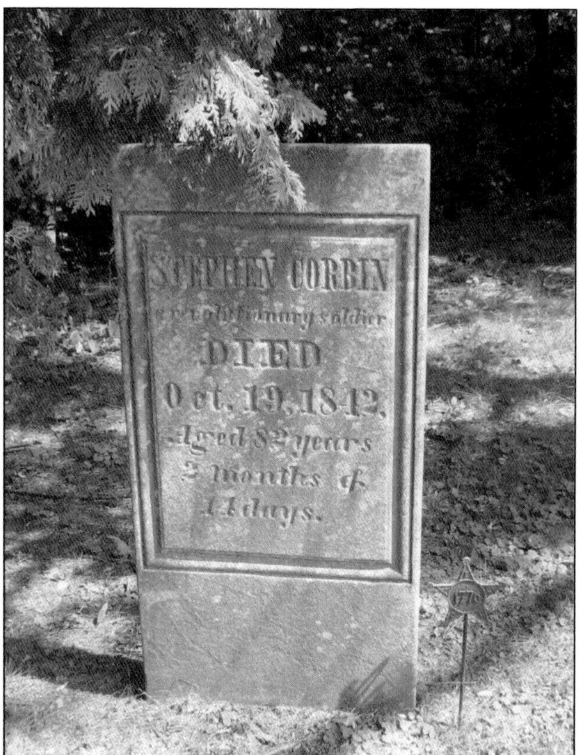

Coopers Plains Cemetery is still active. Its first interment was John Williams in 1817, a Hessian soldier who served with British general Burgoyne during the Revolutionary War and may have deserted. His stone describes him as "a pioneer settler and first builder in this community." Also buried here is Stephen Corbin, an American veteran of the Revolution. One wonders what they would make of I-86, with its exit just a few yards away. (KWH.)

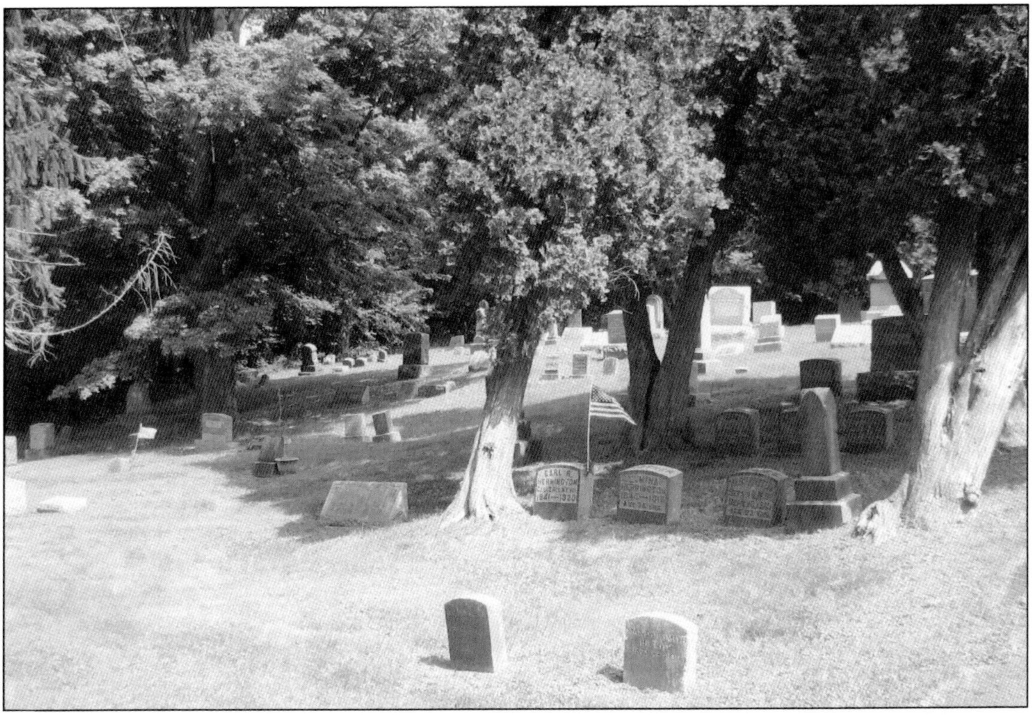

Styles in Coopers Plains Cemetery slide gently from old to new, making it a lovely study of changing times. Campbell-Erwin Baptist Church operates the cemetery. (KWH.)

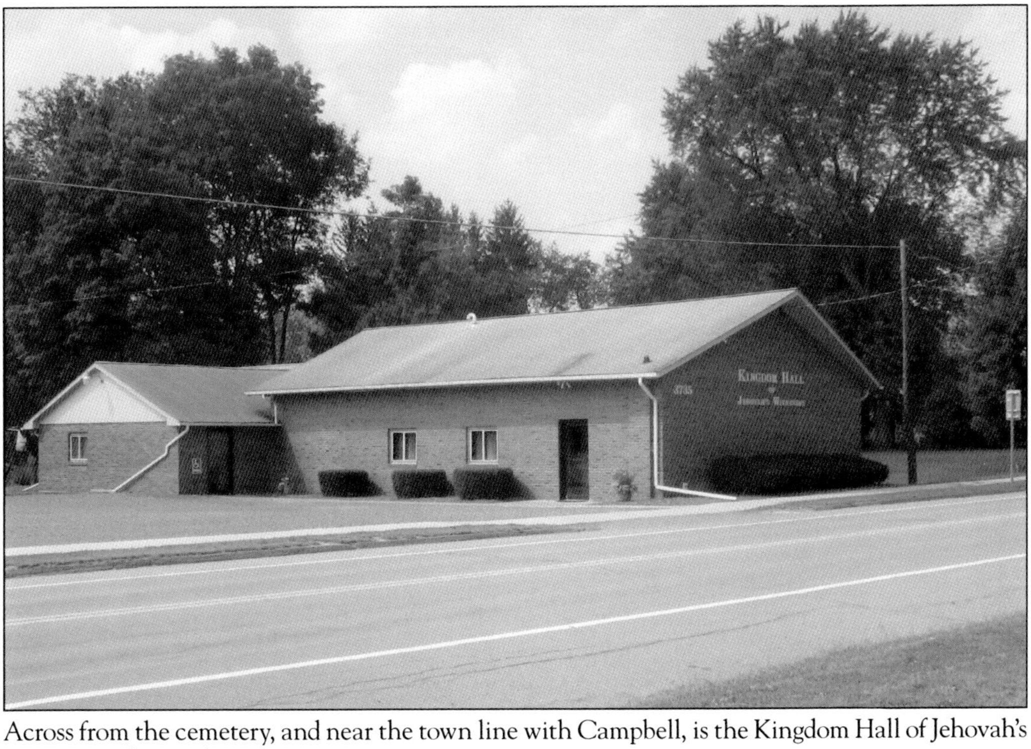

Across from the cemetery, and near the town line with Campbell, is the Kingdom Hall of Jehovah's Witnesses. (KWH.)

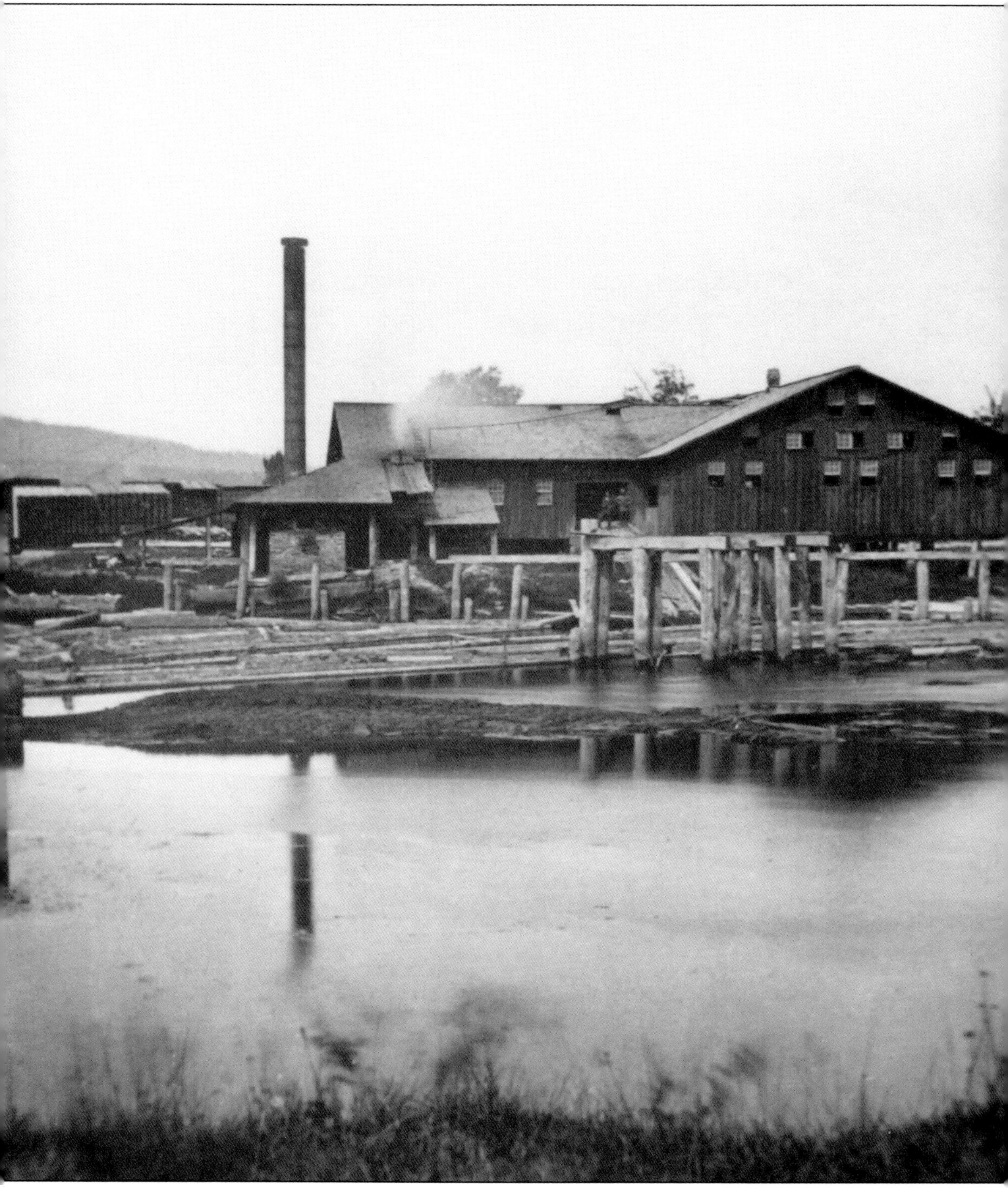

Isaac Gray and partners bought 4,000 acres of timber and set up a water-powered sawmill in 1832, converting to steam 14 years later. Lumber mills such as this one gave the hamlet of Gang Mills the name it still bears today. One such operation eventually became today's Dresser-Rand. Erwin was a lumbering town as early as the 1790s. Logs were still rafted downstream well into the 20th century.

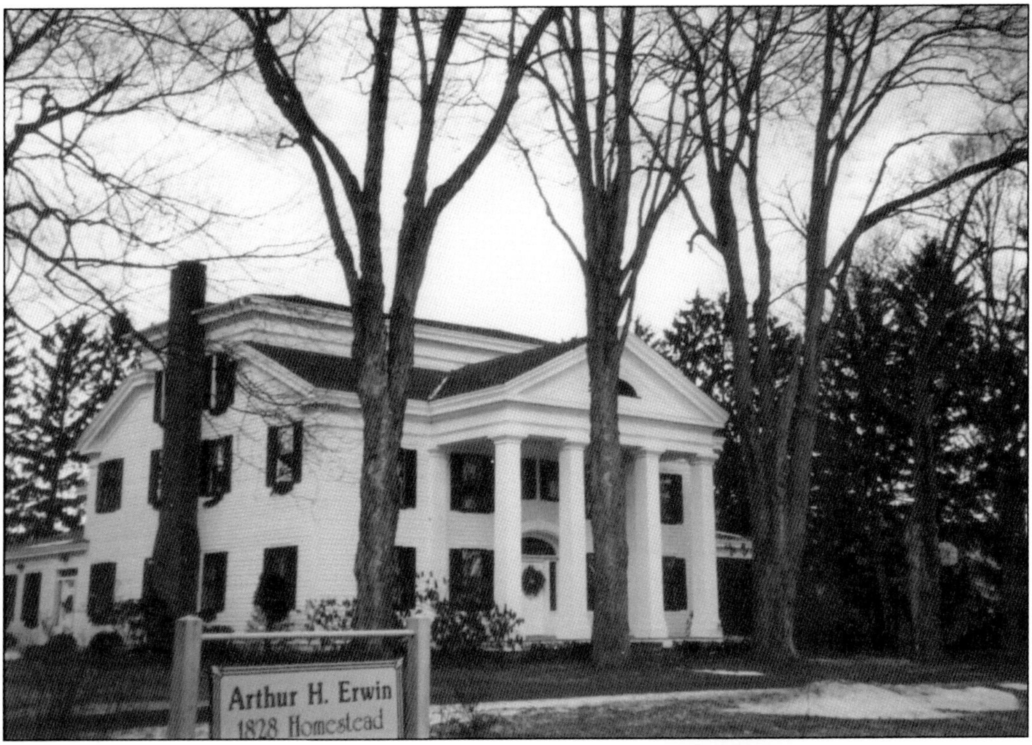

Arthur H. Erwin started this Gang Mills home on Canada Road in 1828, but died before finishing the job. His son Samuel E. Erwin completed the project in 1850. (SCH.)

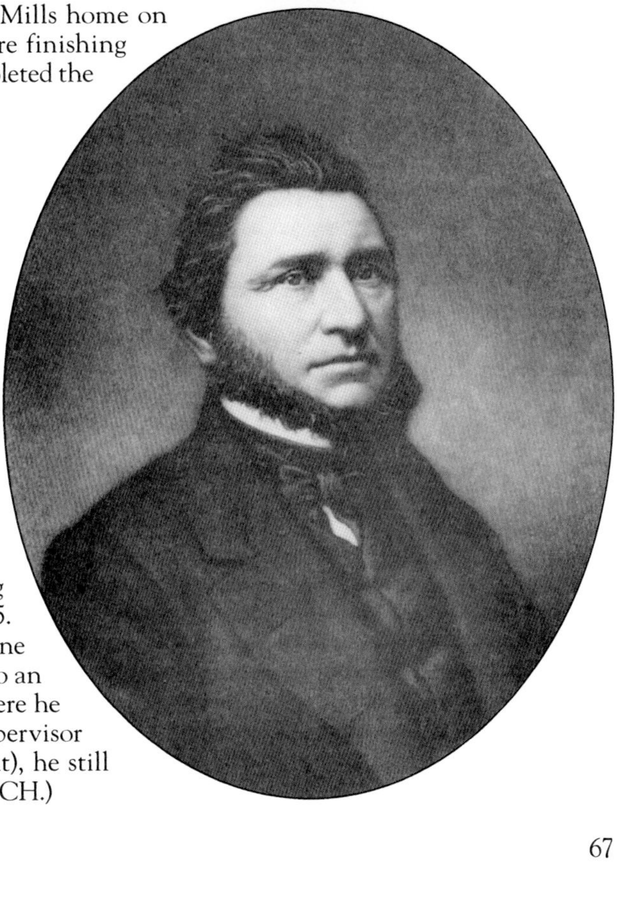

Arthur, grandson of his town-founding namesake, was born in Erwin in 1805. He was educated as best as could be done there in those raw days, before going to an academy in Easton, Pennsylvania, where he met his future wife. Elected town supervisor eight times (as a Whig or a Democrat), he still held office at the time of his death. (SCH.)

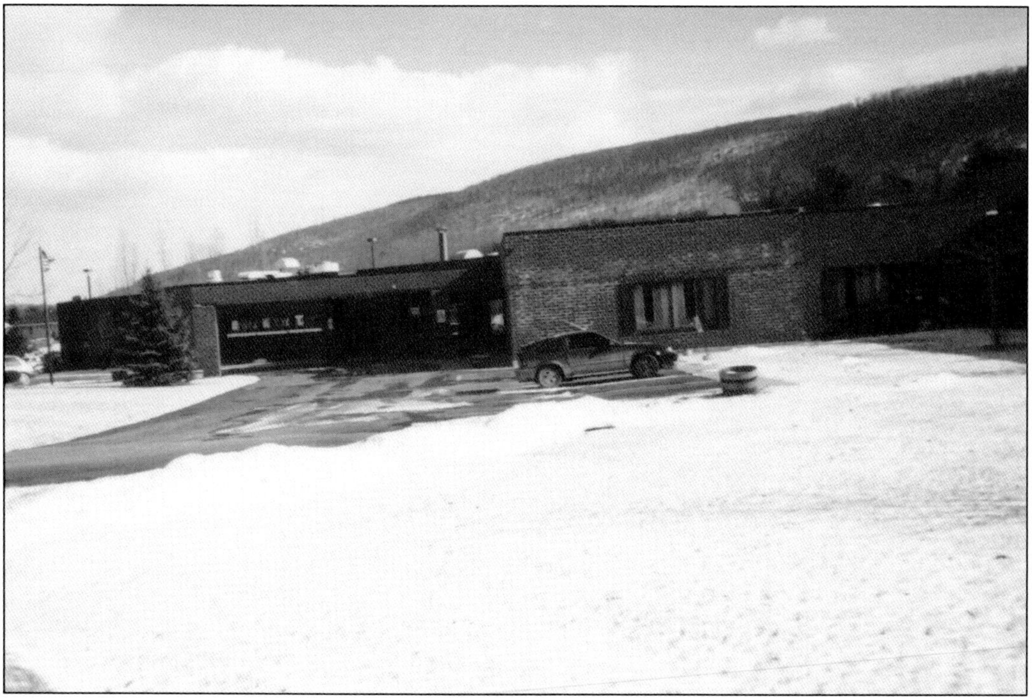

This Gang Mills building originally housed Three Rivers Health Care, a nursing home. It is now a 120-bed facility specializing in short-term rehabilitation and long-term skilled nursing care, operated by Absolut Care. (SCH.)

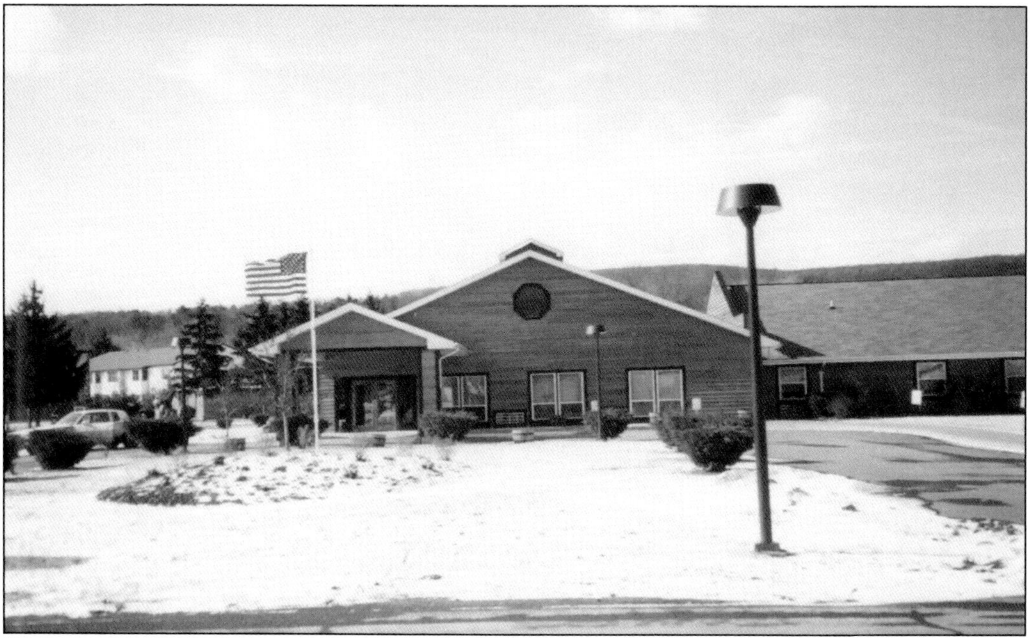

Green Meadows Adult Care facility in Gang Mills was created as a single-level semi-retirement home. As of 2013, the facility is Emeritus at Painted Post, "cradled between the gently sloping residential hills of Erwin and . . . only a short drive from the bustling business districts," according to the company's website. (SCH.)

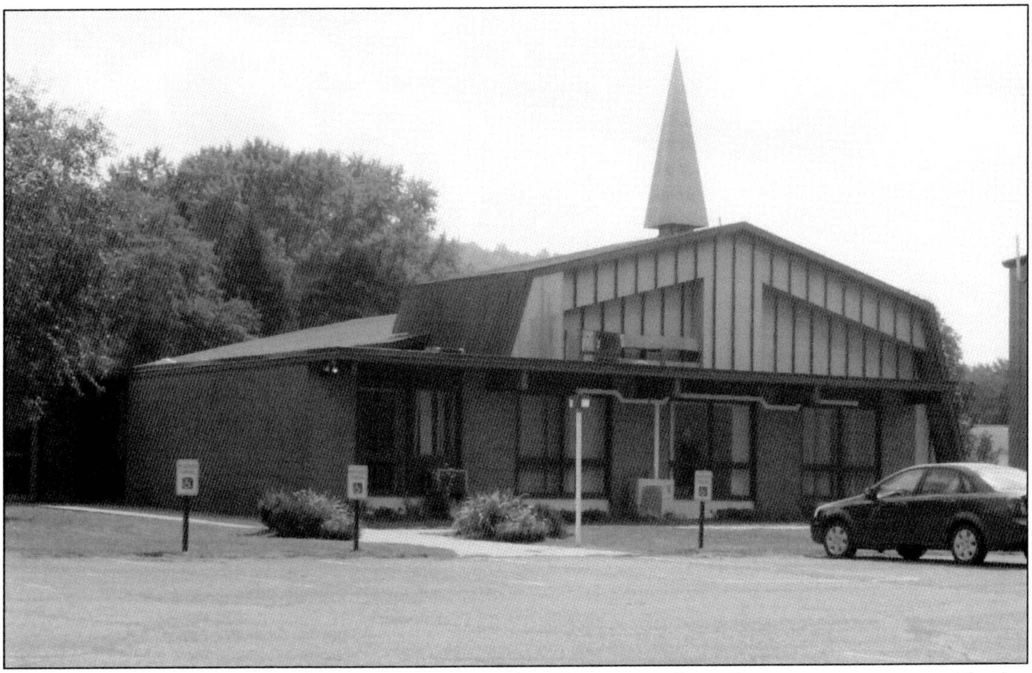

Beartown Road Alliance Church in Gang Mills affects a modern design, in contrast with the Baptist and Methodist churches in Coopers Plains. The congregation traces its roots to a Corning woman's encounter with Rev. A.B. Simpson in the late 1800s. The current building was erected in 1967. (KWH.)

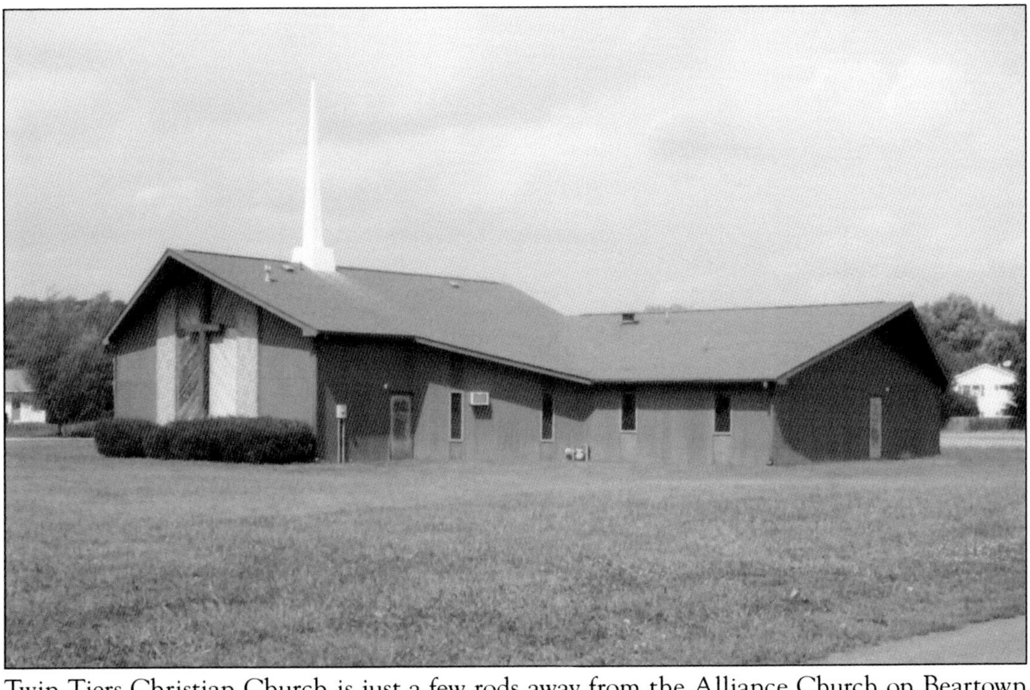

Twin Tiers Christian Church is just a few rods away from the Alliance Church on Beartown Road. The name "Twin Tiers" represents the Southern Tier of counties in New York, and the adjoining Northern Tier of counties in Pennsylvania. (KWH.)

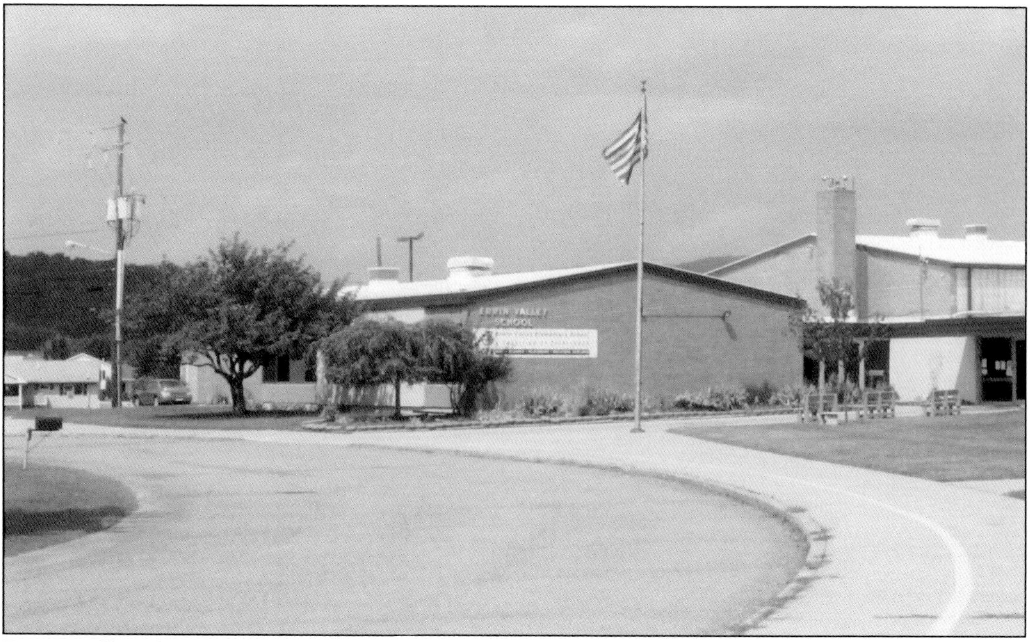

Erwin Valley Elementary School opened in 1957 as part of the new Corning–Painted Post district. In June of that year, the last of the district's one-room schools closed its doors. Erwin Valley, just minutes by foot from the town's high-water mark, became a center for relief following the 1972 flood. (KWH.)

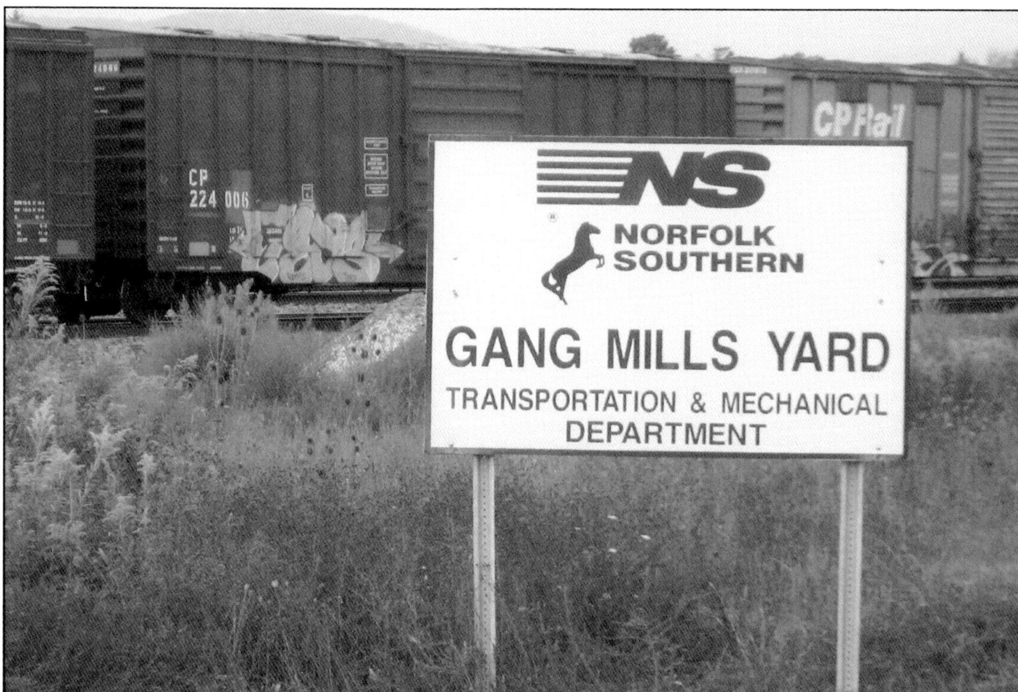

Major rail yards formerly north of Corning were moved to Gang Mills in the 1950s. Half a century later, hundreds of cars are usually on site at any given time. (KWH.)

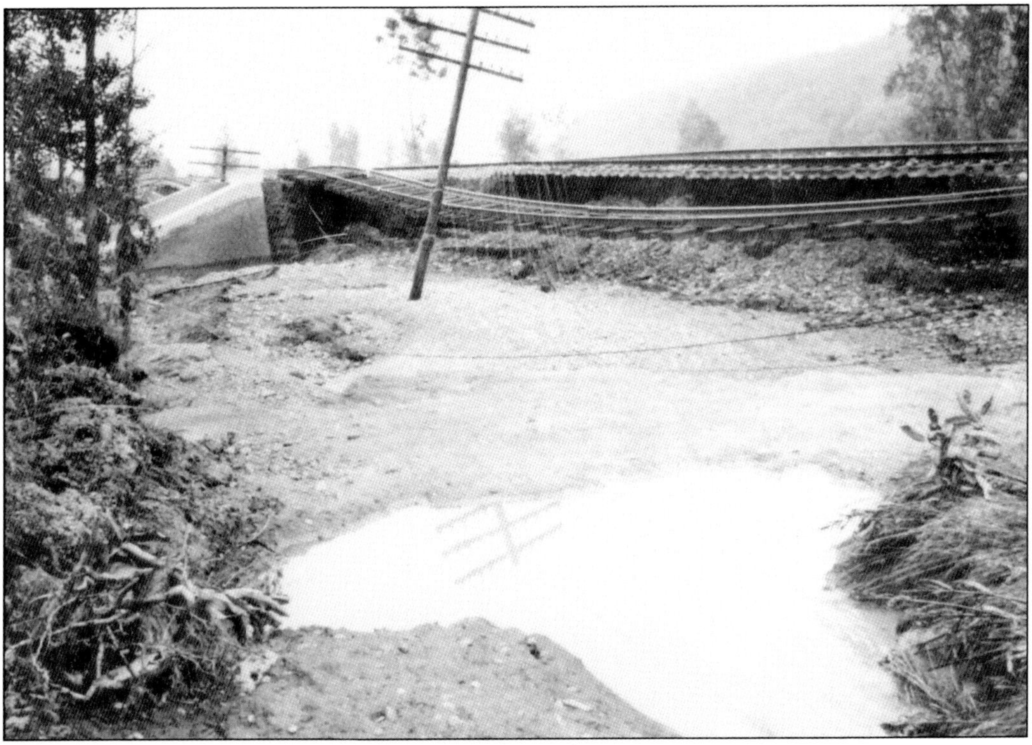

The yards were devastated in the 1972 flood. (ELHS.)

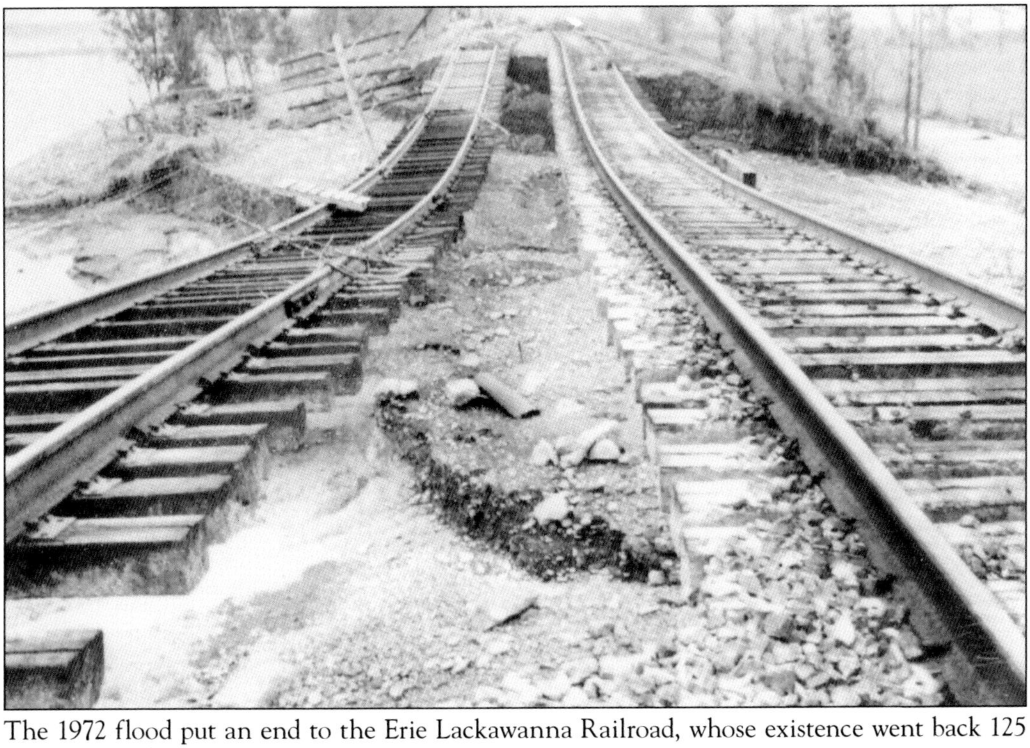

The 1972 flood put an end to the Erie Lackawanna Railroad, whose existence went back 125 years. (ELHS.)

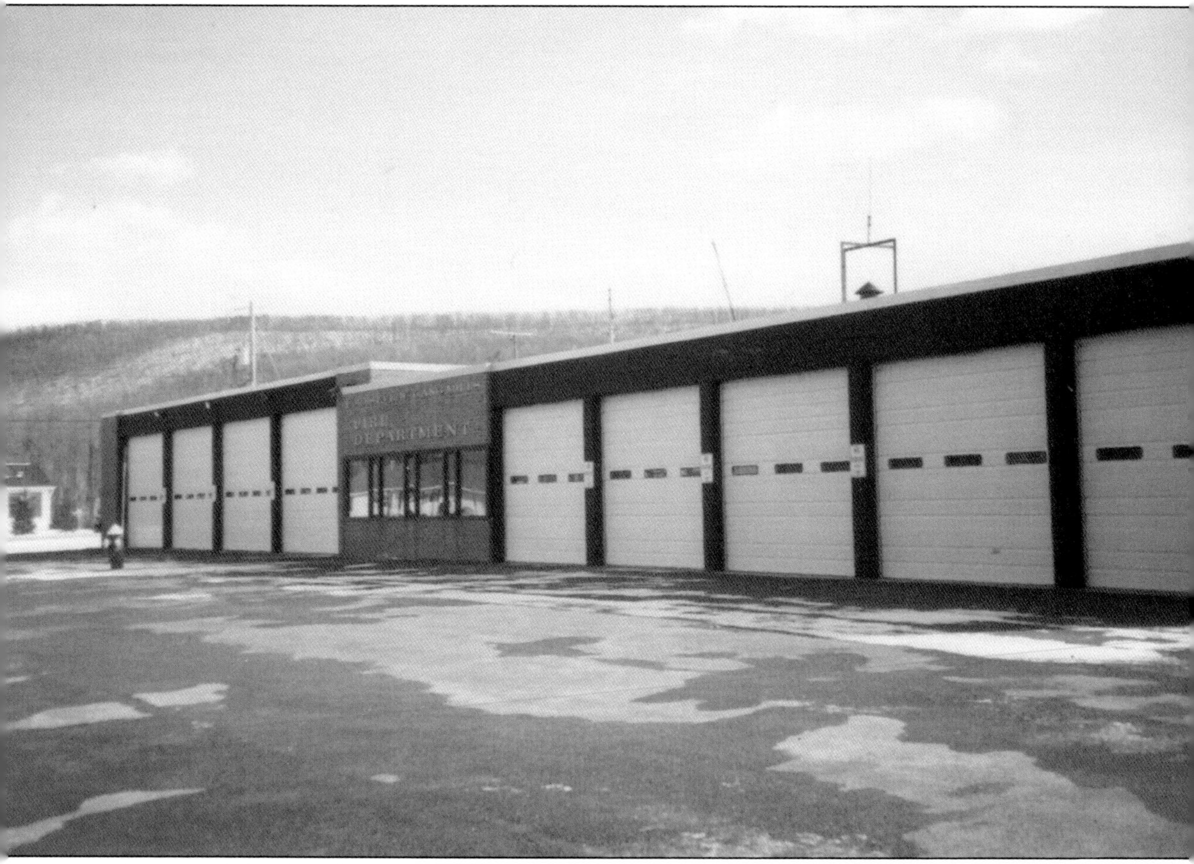

The Gang Mills Fire Department was organized in 1942; this structure dates to 1980. Assistant Chief Hobart Abbey was the first of 18 victims from the Erwin-Corning area in the 1972 Hurricane Agnes flood. That number represented three-fourths of the total victims in New York State. Abbey was lost while searching for the body of a man swept downstream from Bath. (SCH.)

Three

The Countryside

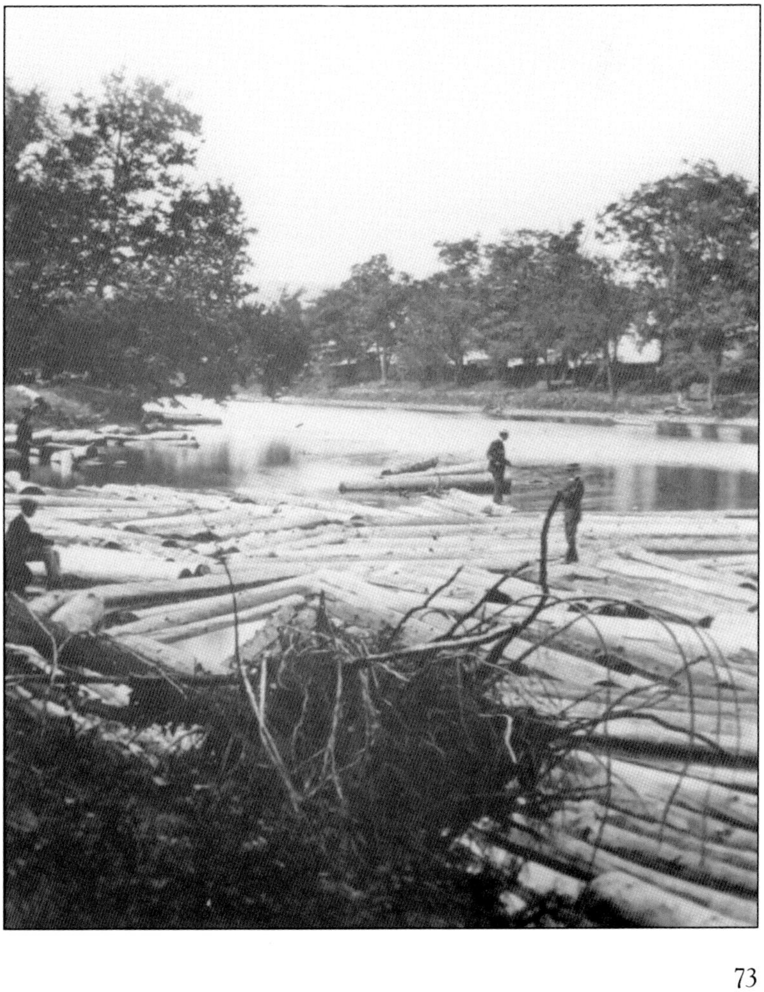

Despite the semi-urban village of Painted Post and the booming hamlet of Gang Mills—both of which blend into the neighboring "metropolis" of Corning—most of Erwin is forest and field, home to deer and turkey and even bear. Hunting is big business and important work. The Great Eastern Trail runs through on its way to Alabama. Tiny cemeteries and one-room school sites reveal a lifestyle now gone, but which flourished not so long ago.

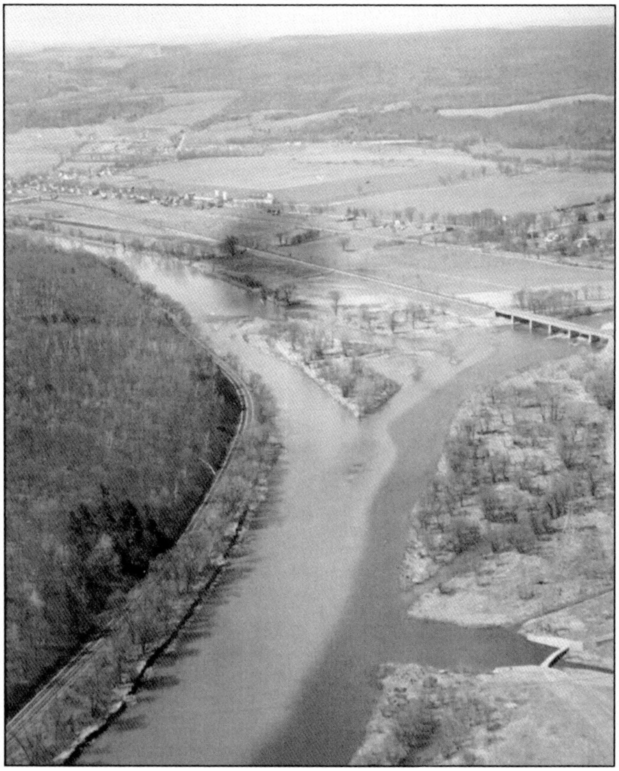

The Tioga (upper left) and Conhocton Rivers come together in Erwin just above Painted Post, forming the Chemung River. Dann's Dairy is visible in the midground, just to the left of the confluence. Much of that farmland is now retail and hotel complexes in the hamlet of Gang Mills. Rail lines at the left lead to a large rail yard, just beyond the bridge in the distance at left. The bridge at right carried old Route 15 on its way from Rochester to Virginia.

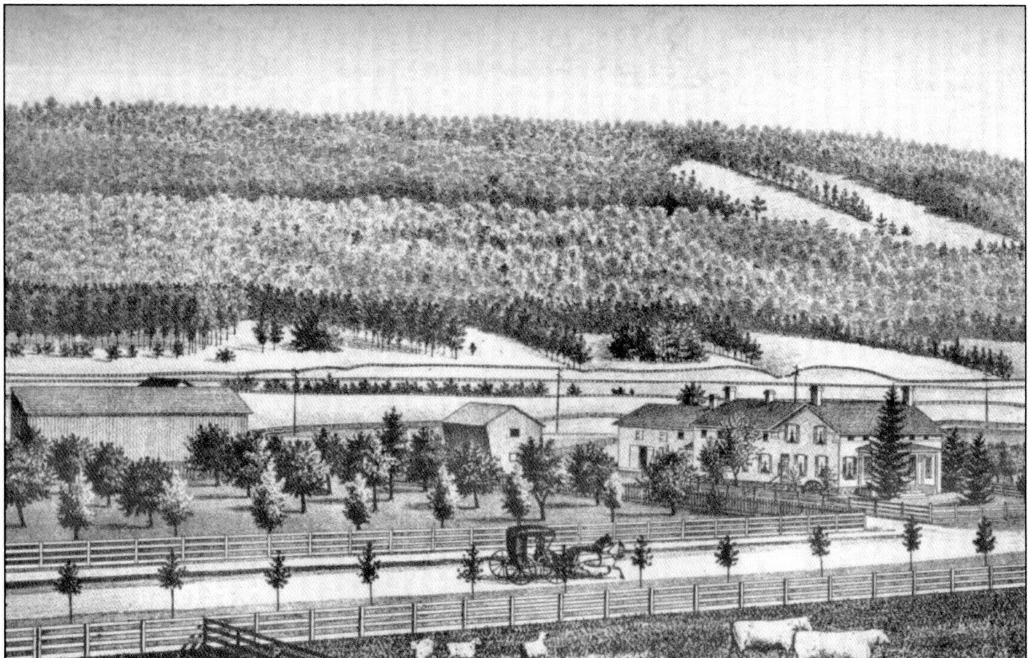

Judge Lyman Balcom settled in Erwin in 1852, buying this home two years later. Situated on very level ground on the northwest side of the Tioga River, half a mile above its confluence with the Conhocton, the farm was reputed to be one of the most productive in the state. (SCH.)

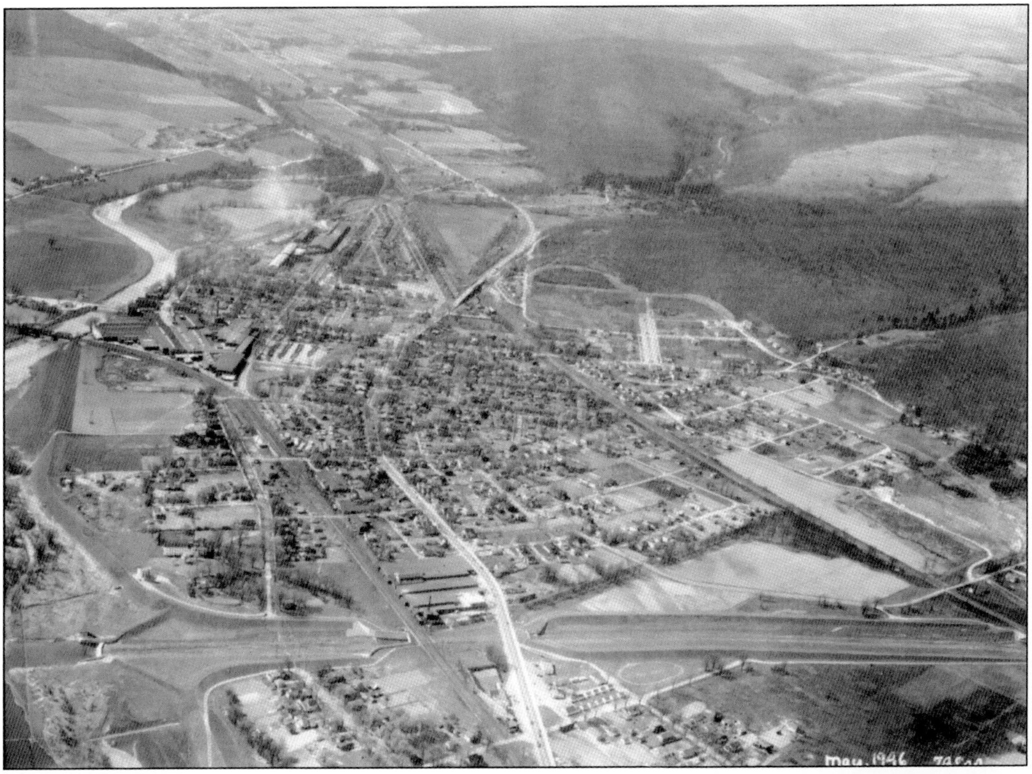

Dairying was once a major part of Erwin's economy. Far fewer farms dot the landscape now than in this 1946 aerial photograph. Some areas, such as those in the upper left, have been taken over for housing, retail, industrial, and office use. But other land once devoted to farming has reverted to forest, such as those hilltop spaces on the right. Extensive state lands now cover much of the town, including Erwin State Wildlife Management Area, Erwin Mountain State Forest, Erwin Hollow State Forest, and McCarthy Hill State Forest.

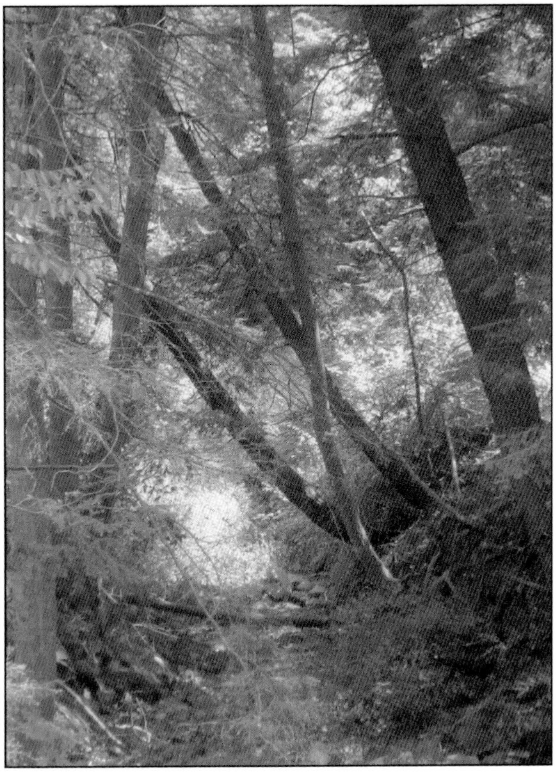

The 44-mile Crystal Hills Trail (CHT) wends its way through Erwin. The CHT is a branch of the Finger Lakes Trail and is the northern terminus of the Great Eastern Trail. On this trail, a recent hiker has encountered deer, owls, turkeys, pileated woodpeckers, a peregrine falcon, and a copperhead snake.

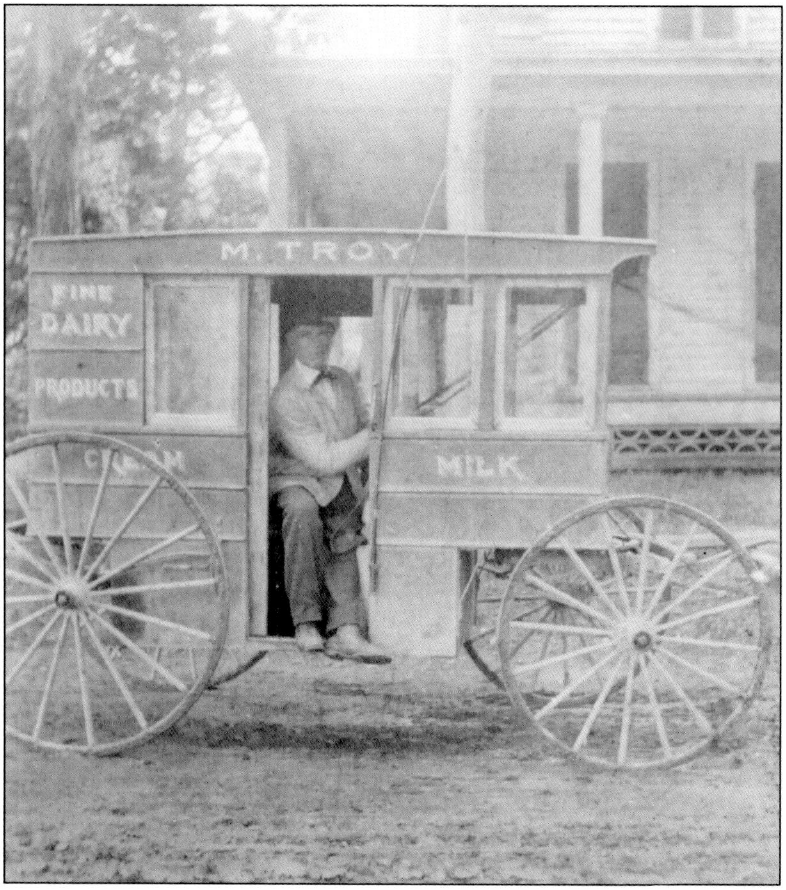

Michael Troy was an Erwin dairy farmer around 1898. The chassis of his carriage rides high, a concession to contemporary road conditions. His whip is mounted just outside the door. Troy's reins rise up above the windshield, then drop down to the horses, allowing him to control the horses while staying warm and dry inside. One thing it looks as though Troy could not do, curiously, is carry much by way of cream, milk, and "fine dairy products," as there is scarcely any cargo space.

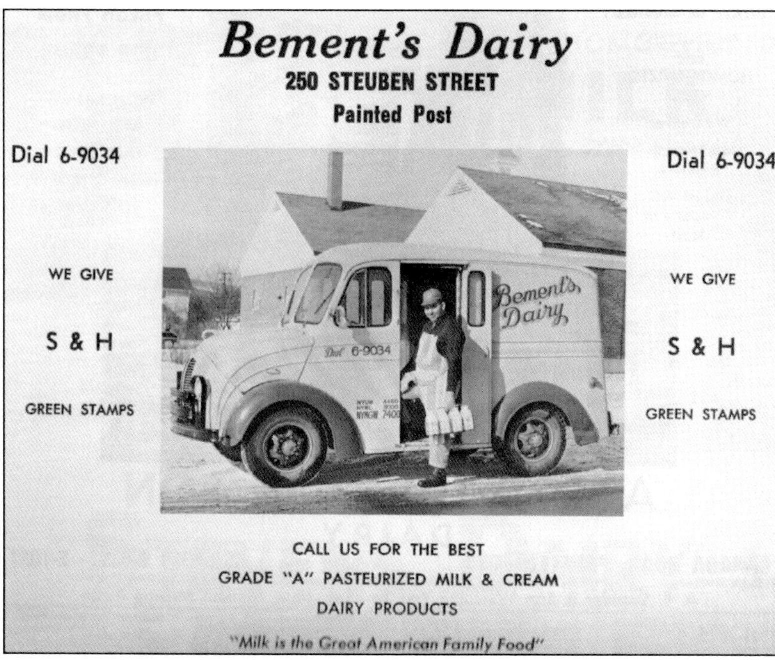

Bement's Dairy not only delivered; it also gave S&H Green Stamps, which could be redeemed in nearby Corning. (SCHS.)

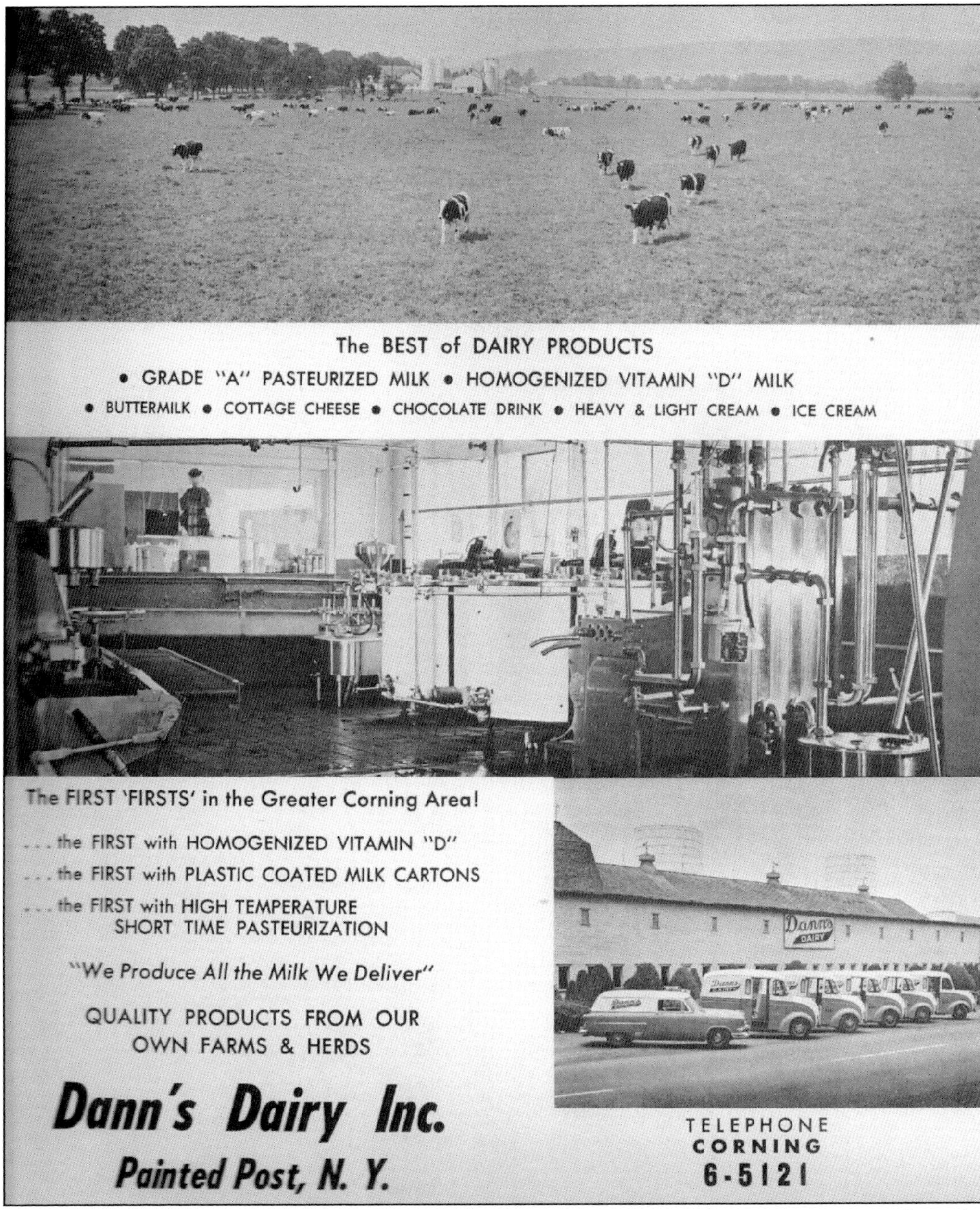

Robert Dann's 1956 delivery fleet was just a little bit speedier, and more capacious, than the carriages of old. In addition, the trucks had refrigeration. Much of the large Dann farm is now retail and hotel space in Gang Mills. (SCHS.)

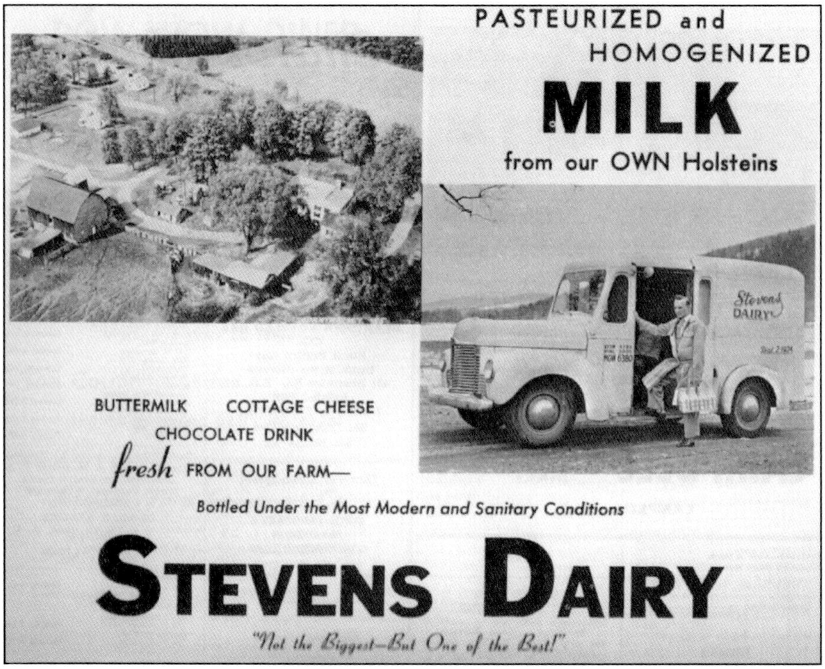

Stevens Dairy in Coopers Plains advertised that its milk came from the dairy's own Holstein herd. (SCHS.)

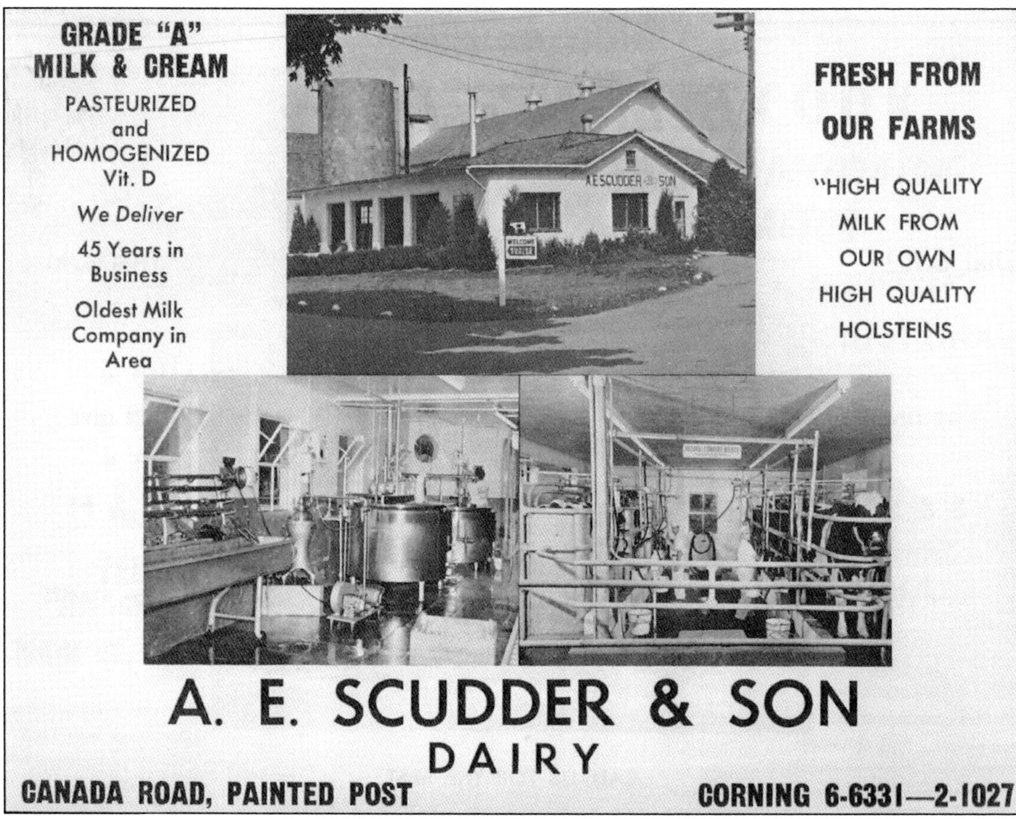

A.E. Scudder & Son operated its dairy on Canada Road. The Scudders, unsurprisingly, had extensive milking and processing facilities. (SCHS.)

In 1948, Erwin town historian Ellsworth C. Cowles supervised an archeological dig on the Dann farm. (SCH.)

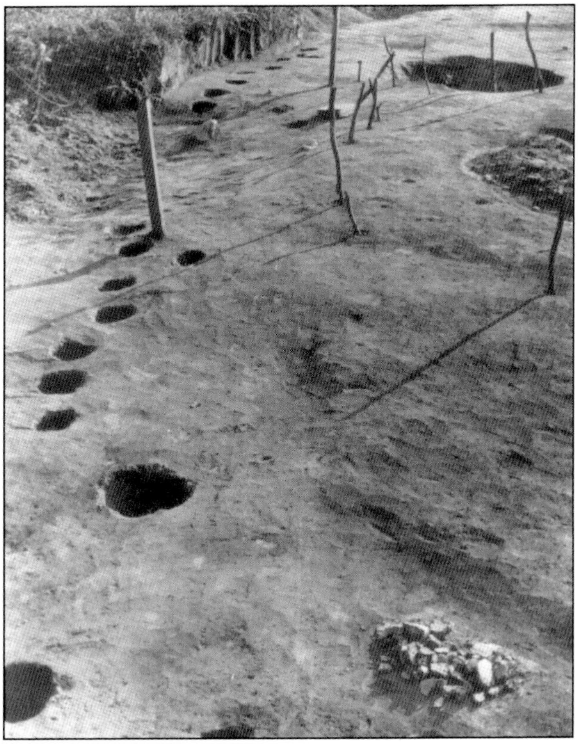

Among the findings from Ellsworth Cowles's excavation were two Native American graves. Many scholars were quite cavalier about Indian remains in those days, but Cowles left them in place and covered them up again. (SCH.)

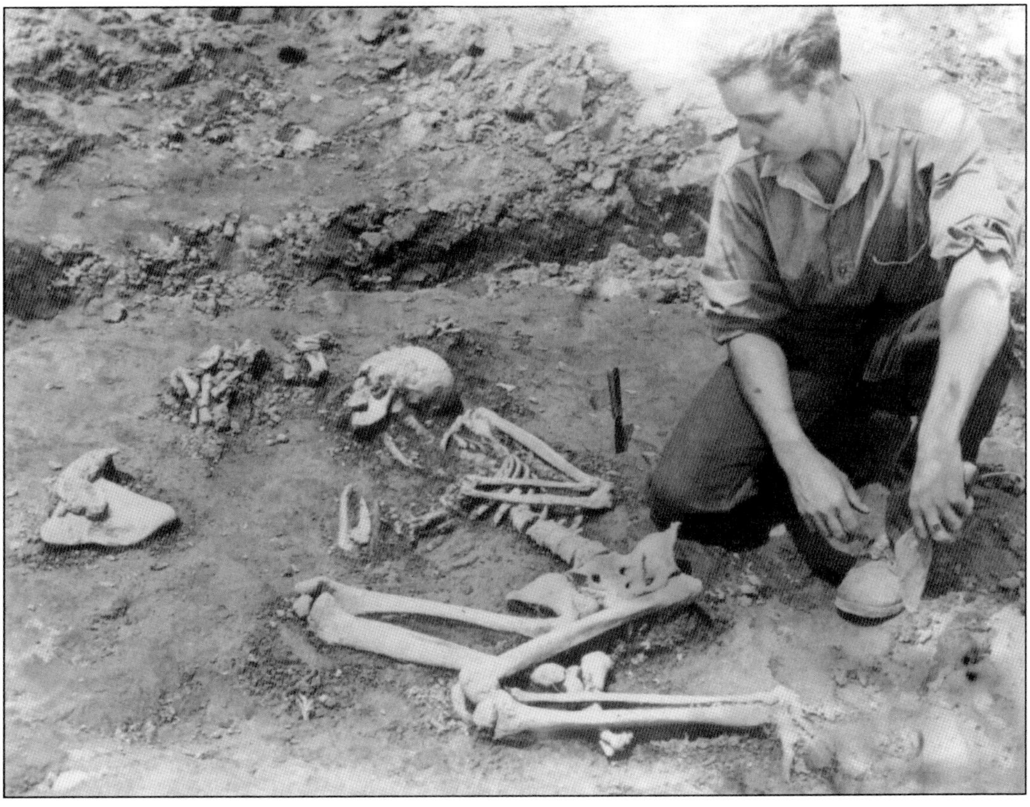

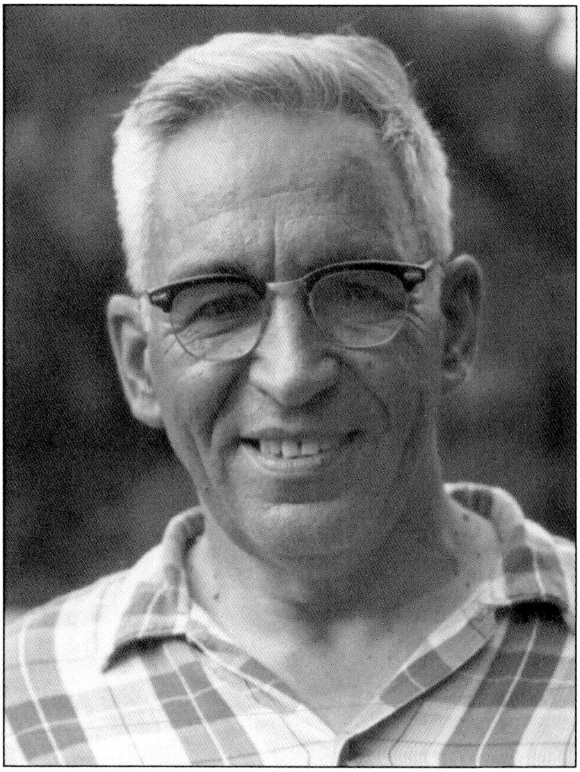

Joseph A. Costa, seen here in later years, attempted a single-engine solo round-the-world flight in 1937. Born on Madeira in 1909, Joe Costa passed away in the far-different time of 1998. (SCH)

Joe Costa's Lockheed Vega, the *Crystal City*, honored Erwin's next-door metropolis of Corning. He force-landed in Brazil, ending the journey. At least Costa, with his Portuguese heritage, was able to speak the language. (GHCM.)

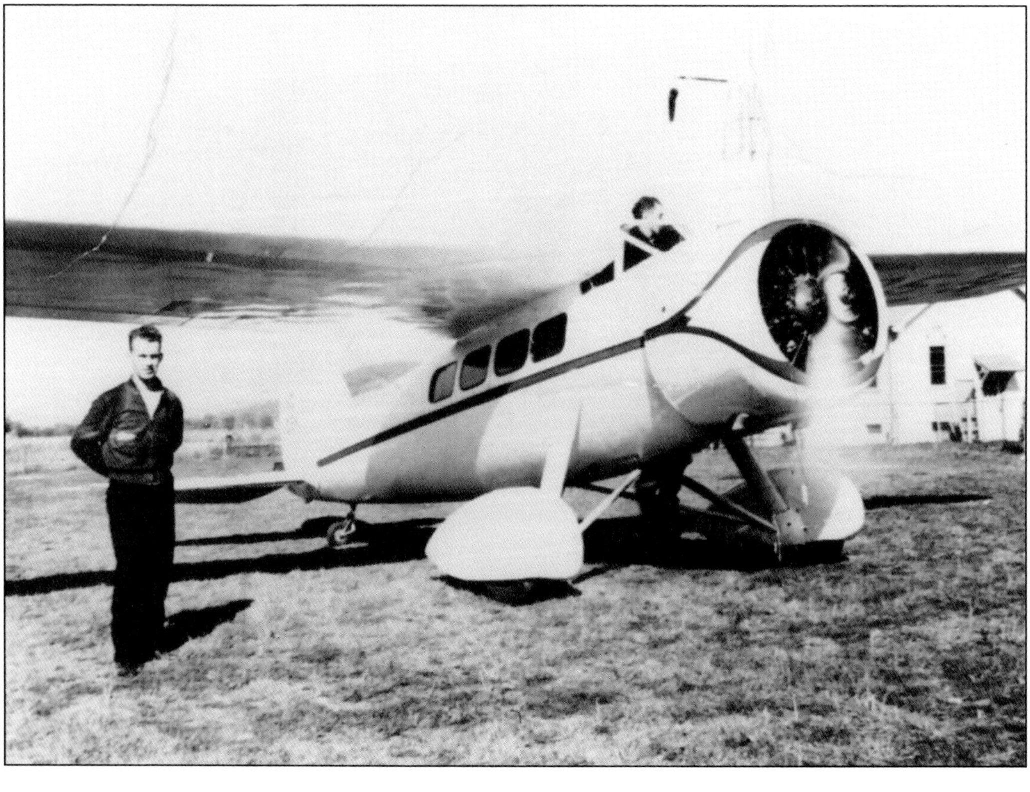

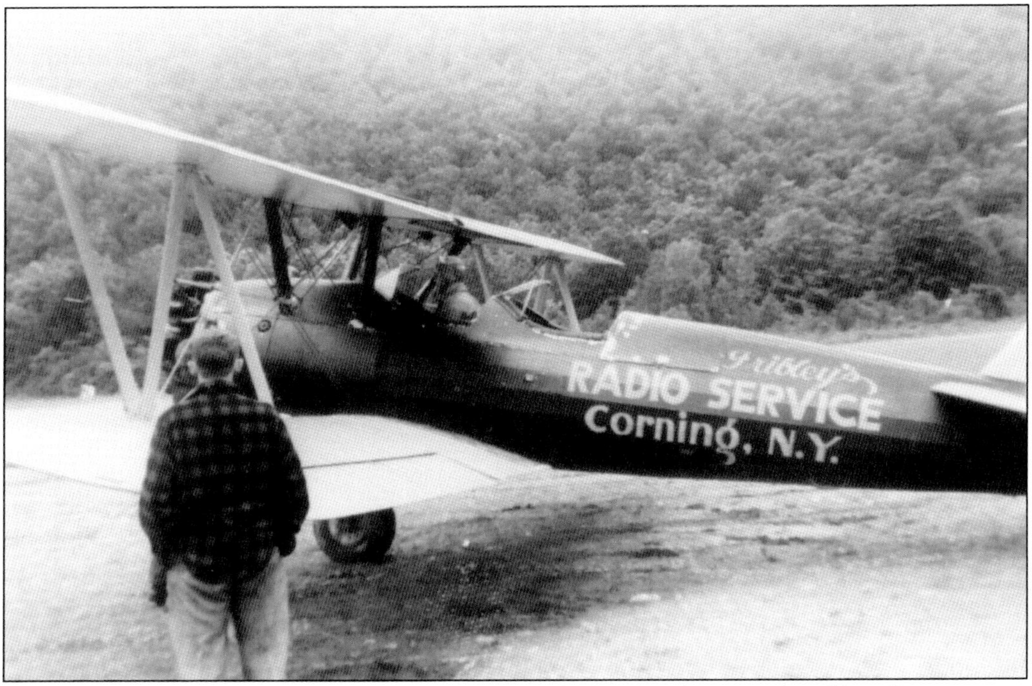

From 1930 to the end of his life, Joe Costa operated what has became the oldest flying service in New York, on his privately owned airfield just off Victory Highway in rural Erwin. The family still has both businesses. Some of the soaring scenes from the 1999 movie *The Thomas Crown Affair* were filmed here. This aircraft, advertising Fribley's Radio Service, is taking off in 1947. Fribley's was on Bridge Street in Corning. (GHCM.)

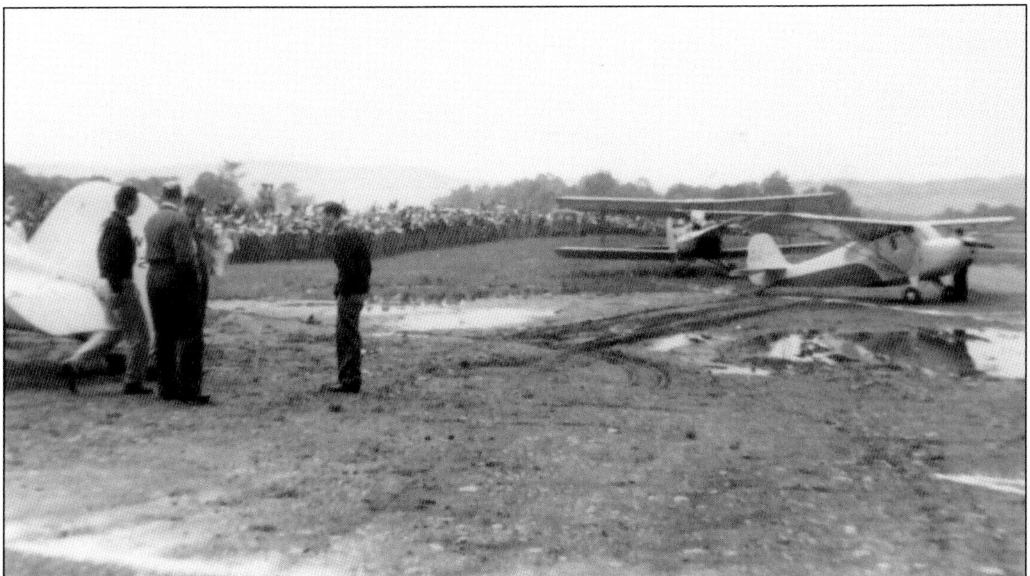

Costa's Field hosted this air show in 1947 or 1948. Grass airfields are romantic, but this image clearly shows their limitations. The 3,270-foot runway was finally paved at the dawn of the 21st century. Running alongside I-86, the airstrip gets plenty of attention from passing drivers and passengers. (GHCM.)

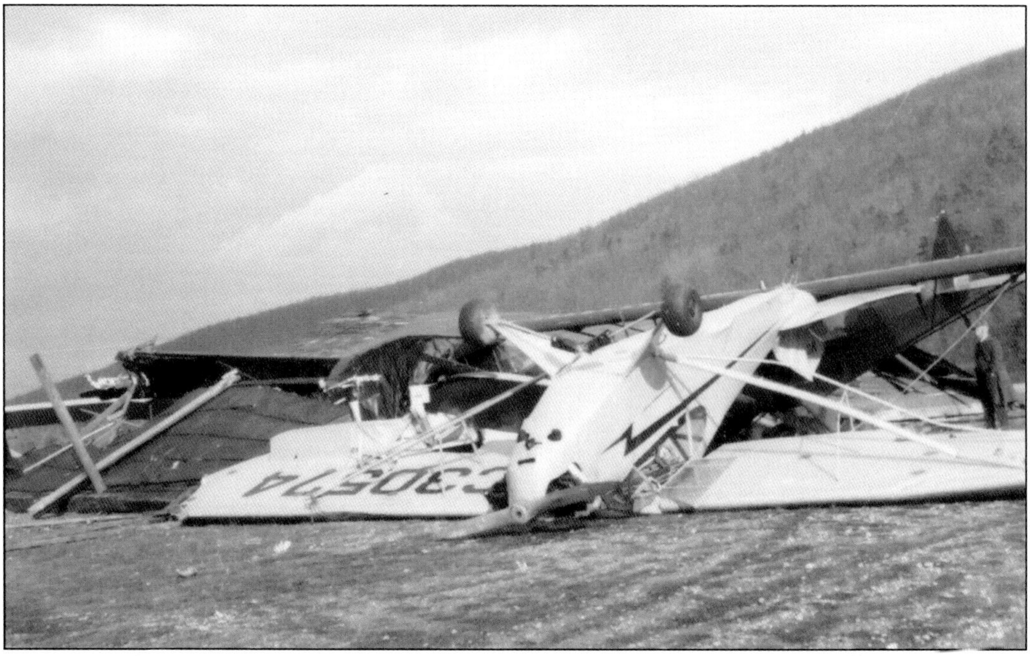

A 1948 windstorm wrecked airplanes and buildings alike at Costa's Field. Officially the Corning–Painted Post Airport (though whimsically known locally as Corning International), the general aviation facility handled over 9,000 aircraft operations in a recent 12-month period. Today, 28 aircraft are based here. (GHCM.)

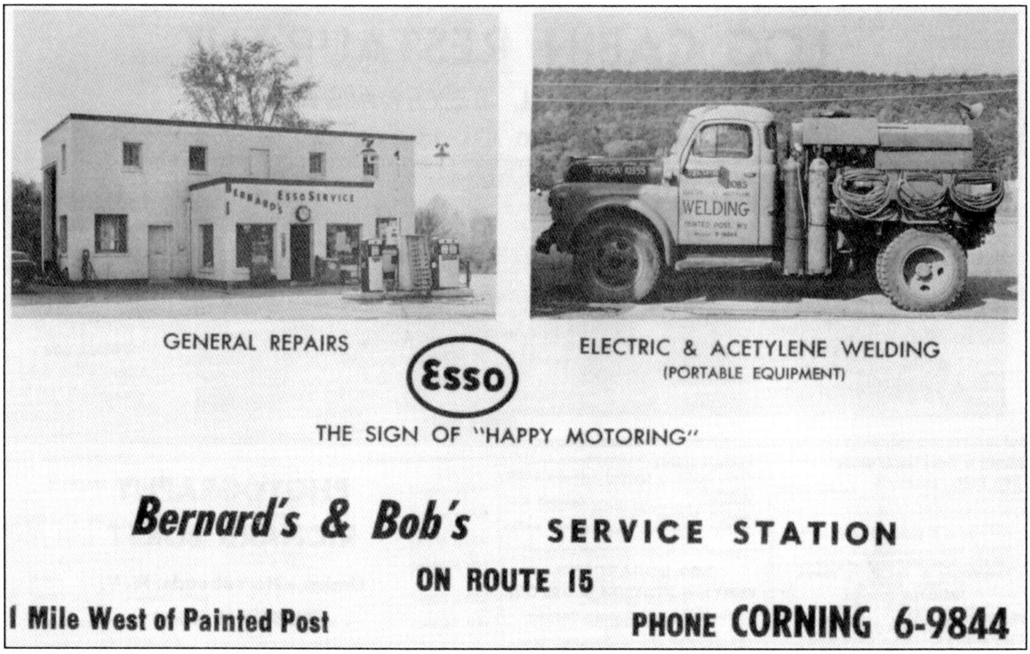

Bernard and Bob were clearly ready to take on welding jobs just about anywhere. (SCHS.)

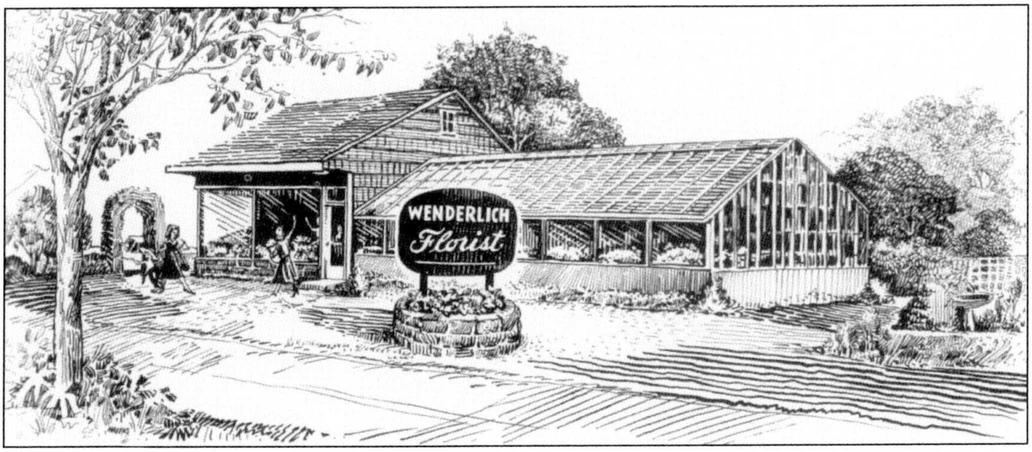

Wenderlich Florist operated on Victory Highway in the 1950s. (SCHS.)

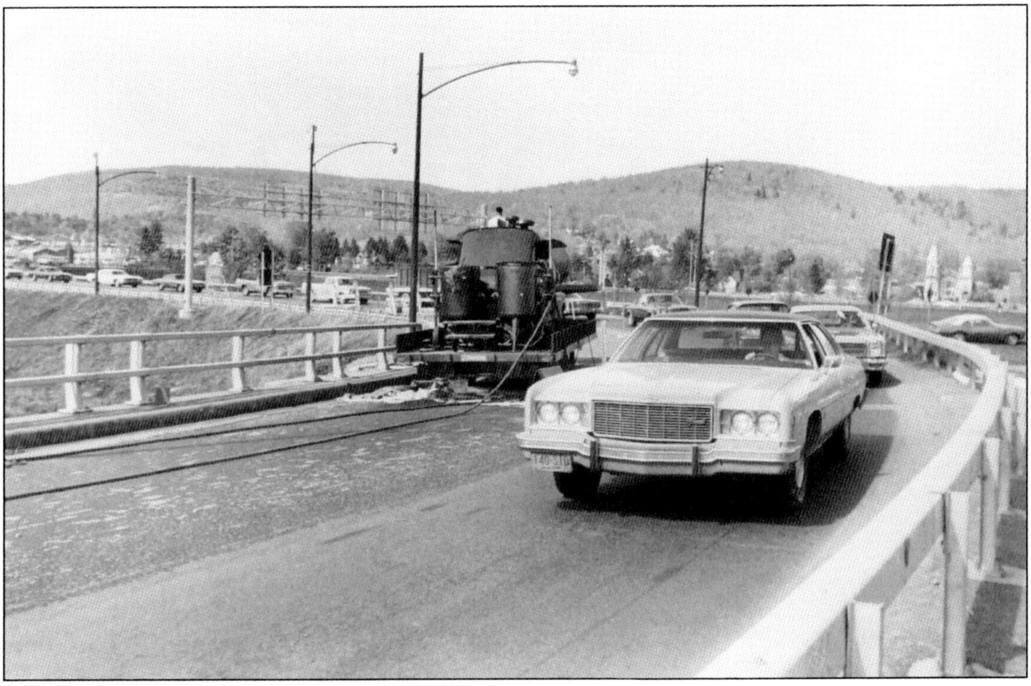

Interstates 99 and 86 meet in Erwin, making the town a southern gateway to Corning and the Finger Lakes. In the right background of this photograph are the twin spires of the Baptist church in Painted Post. The 1922 Erwin municipal building is just visible in the far right background.

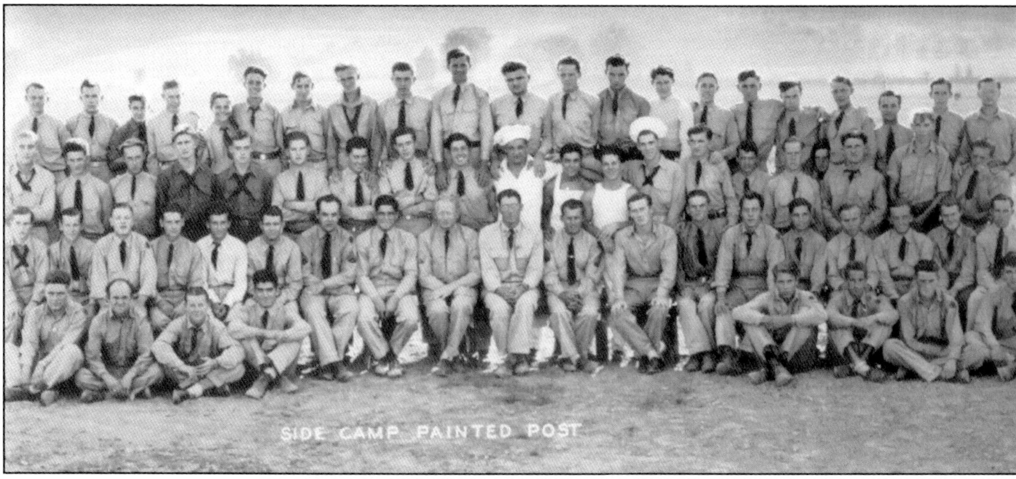

In the 1930s, Erwin played host to the Civilian Conservation Corps (CCC). This New Deal program gave meaningful work to young men and World War I veterans, along with training, bed, board, uniforms, and pay. In addition, the CCC provided a stipend to their families, who were also relieved of the expense of their support. The CCC was a vital part of combating the Great Depression. (SCHS.)

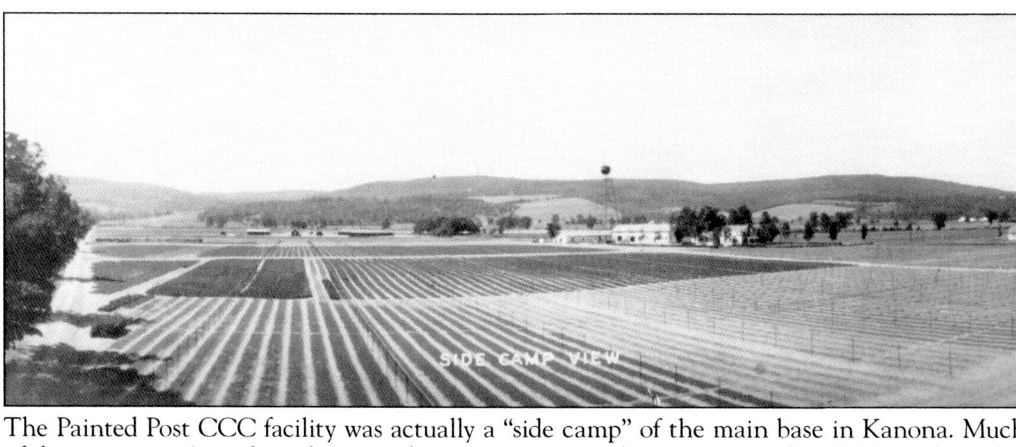

The Painted Post CCC facility was actually a "side camp" of the main base in Kanona. Much of the young men's work in the immediate area was in soil conservation, but CCC workers also developed much of the infrastructure still in use at Stony Brook State Park and Watkins Glen State Park. This photograph probably dates to 1938. (SCHS.)

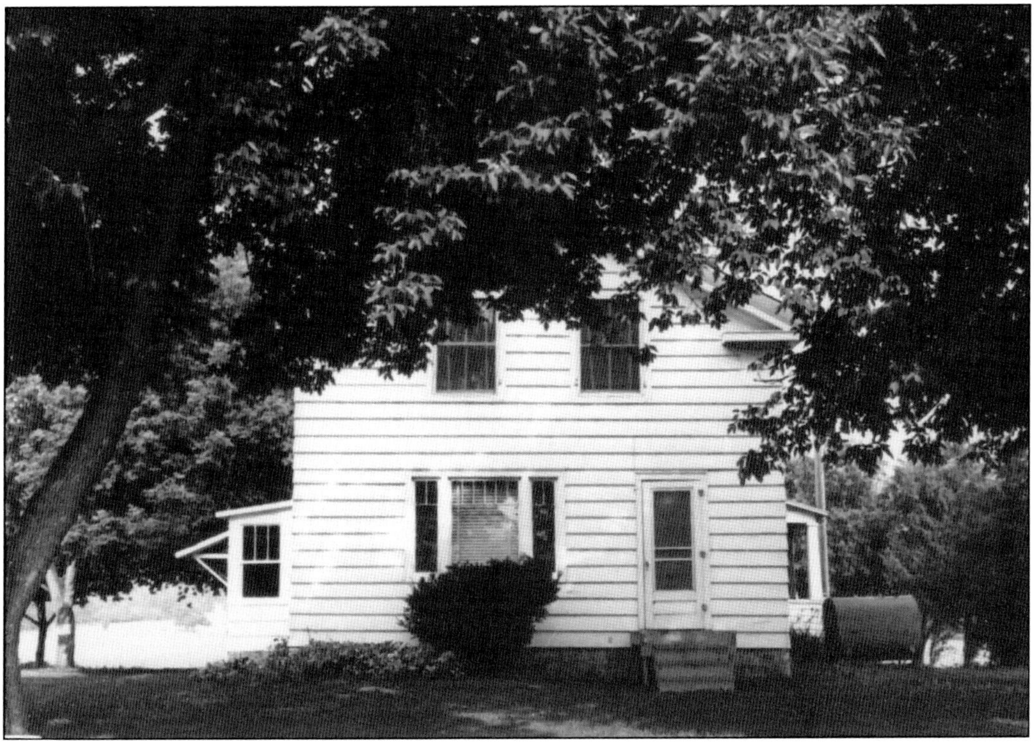

Indian Hills Golf Club, seen here in September 1964, its first year of operation, lies south of the hamlet of Erwins. New York State acquired the 18-hole course, which features 2,400 feet of Tioga River frontage and panoramic views of the Southern Tier hill country, in 2007. (SCH.)

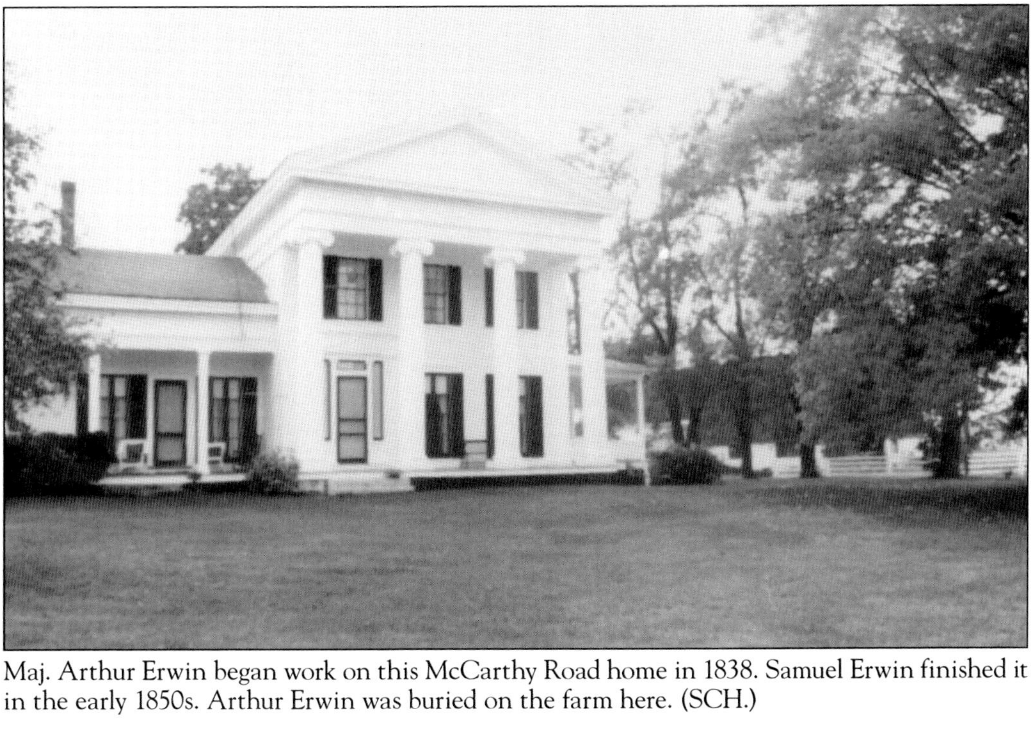

Maj. Arthur Erwin began work on this McCarthy Road home in 1838. Samuel Erwin finished it in the early 1850s. Arthur Erwin was buried on the farm here. (SCH.)

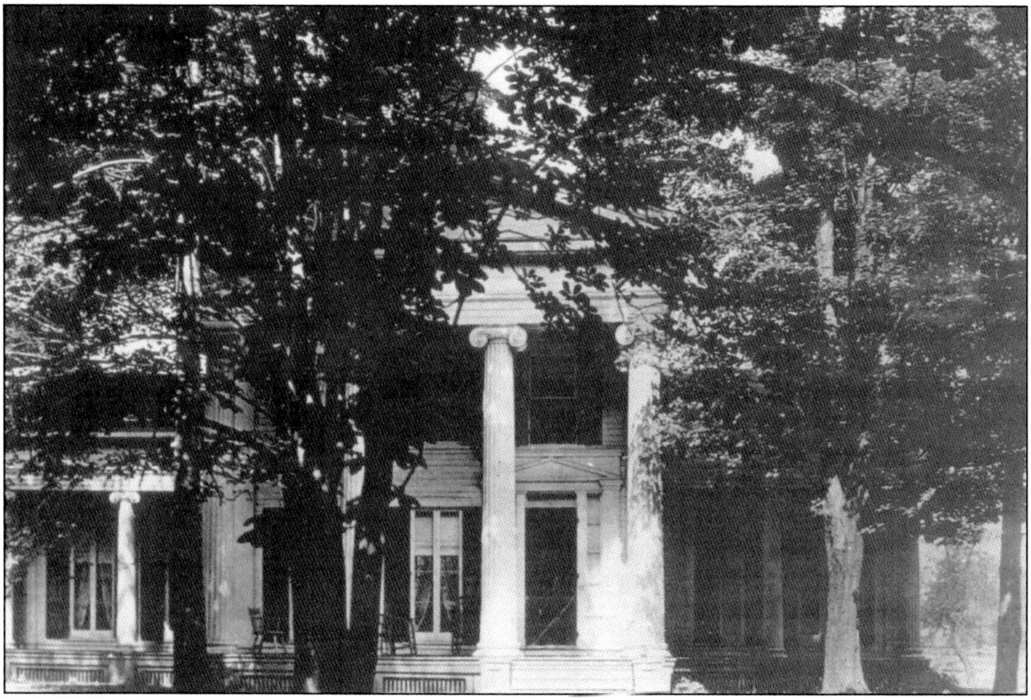

Cephas Platt and his wife, Mary Elizabeth Erwin Platt, built a fine mansion near Painted Post in 1852. Their grandson Gerald E. Platt was operating it as a tourist home when it was destroyed by fire in 1931. The porch and the shade trees must have made for lovely sitting on summer days. (RP.)

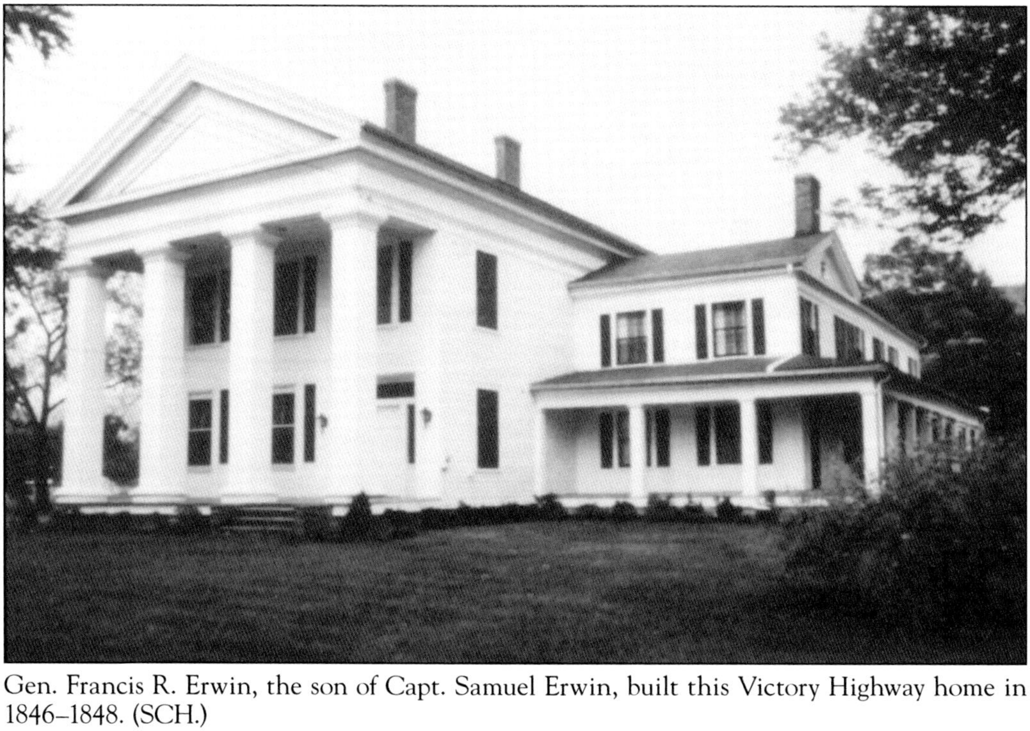

Gen. Francis R. Erwin, the son of Capt. Samuel Erwin, built this Victory Highway home in 1846–1848. (SCH.)

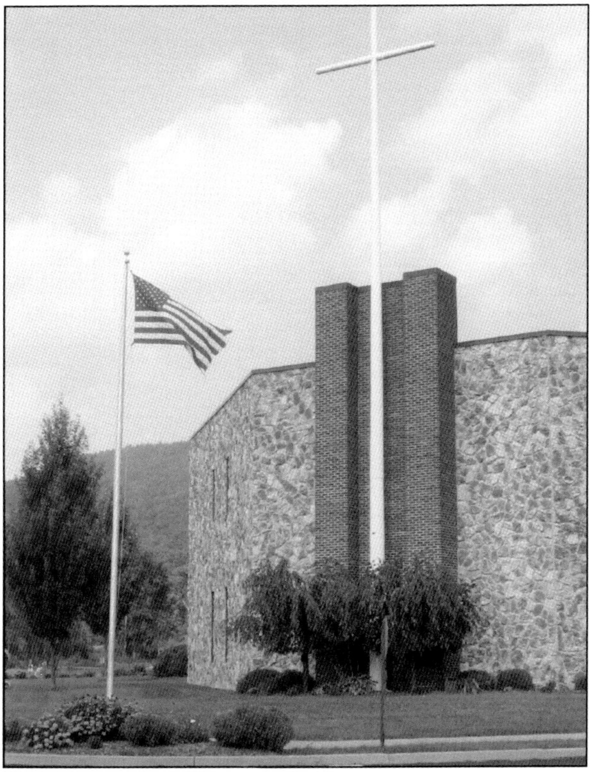

General Erwin's home later became the parsonage for Victory Highway Wesleyan Church (shown here), just to the east. (KWH.)

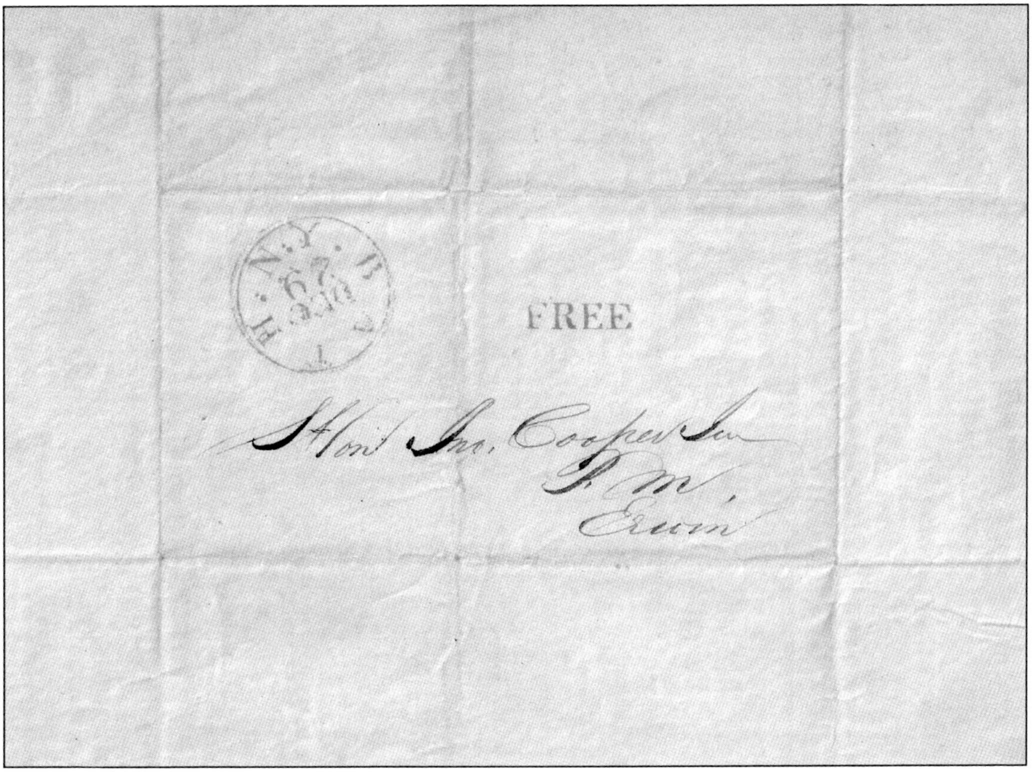

General Erwin received an 1837 invitation to the Civic and Military Ball in Bath. The invitation, folded over to make its own envelope, was postmarked in Bath. (SCHS.)

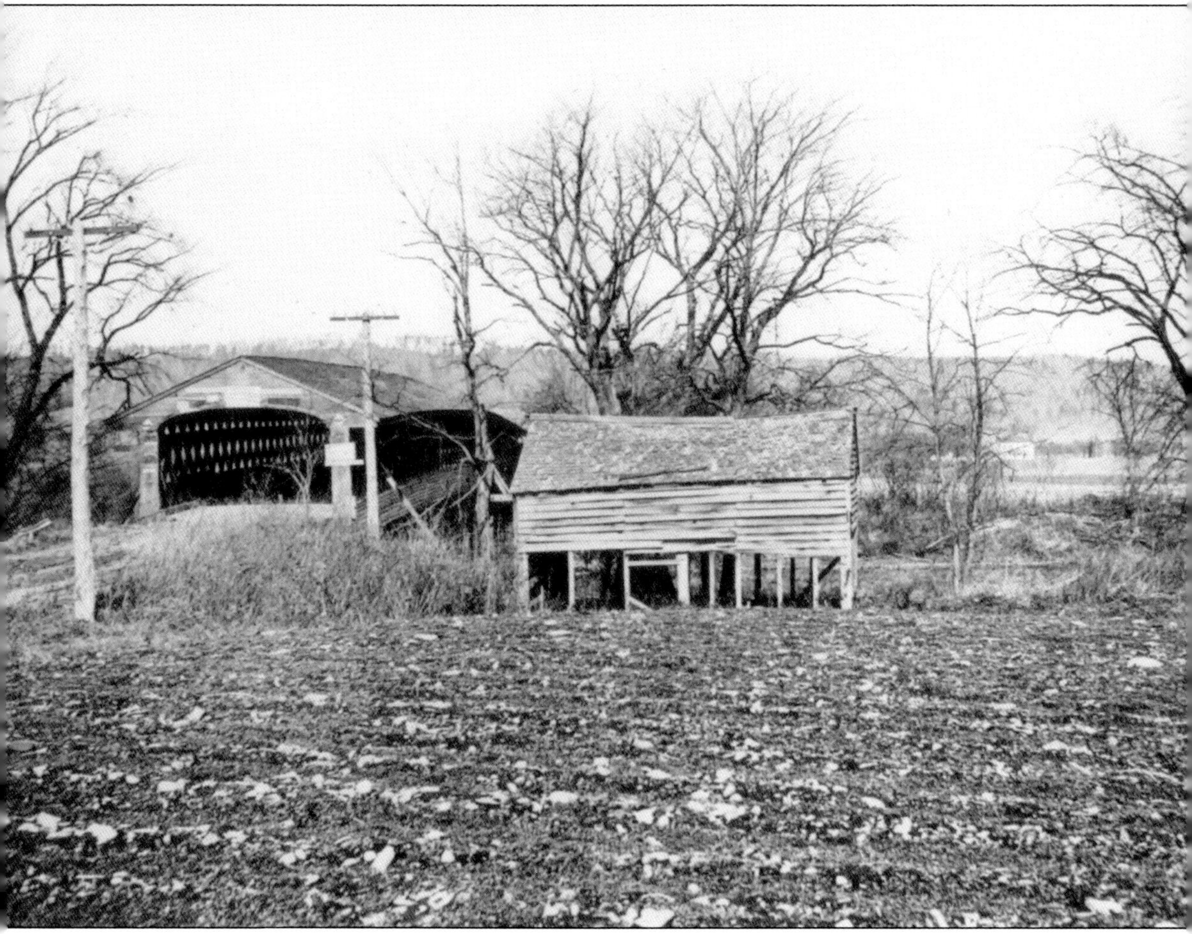

A covered bridge once carried the road to Presho. If the reported date of this photograph, 1880, is correct, the poles must be for telegraph wires. A set of such wires reached Painted Post in 1855, and another in 1857. The crude structure at center may be a tobacco shed.

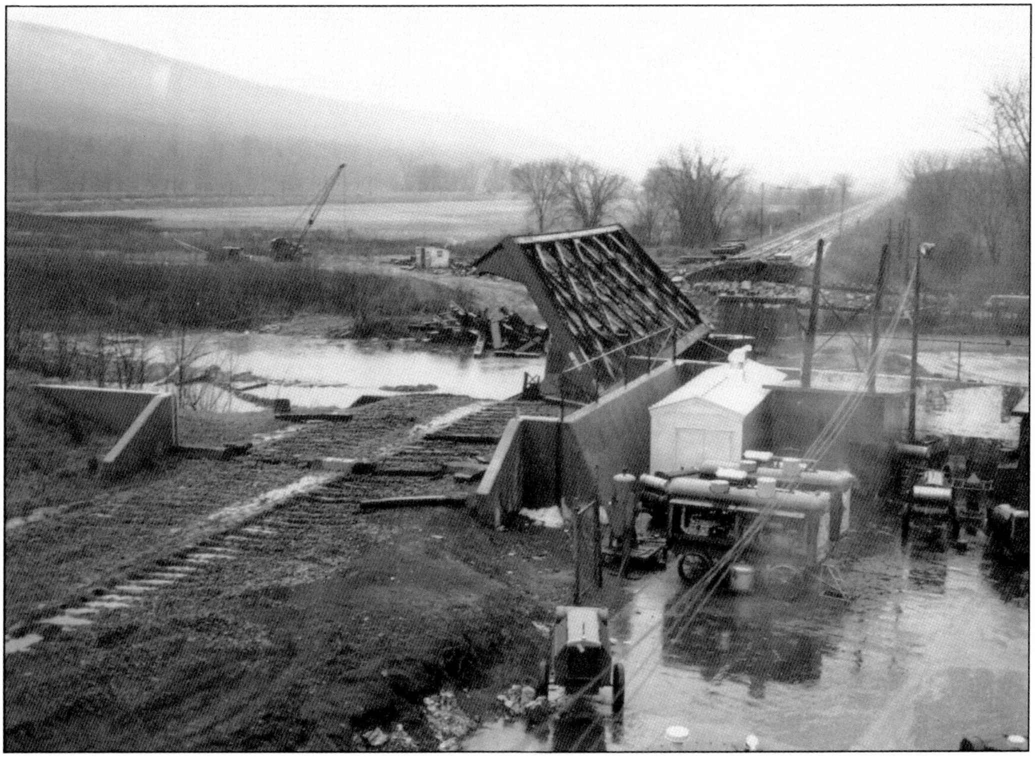

Another bridge, this one on the Erie Railroad, is being dismantled in December 1953. This is near the southeast corner of the Ingersoll-Rand test yard.

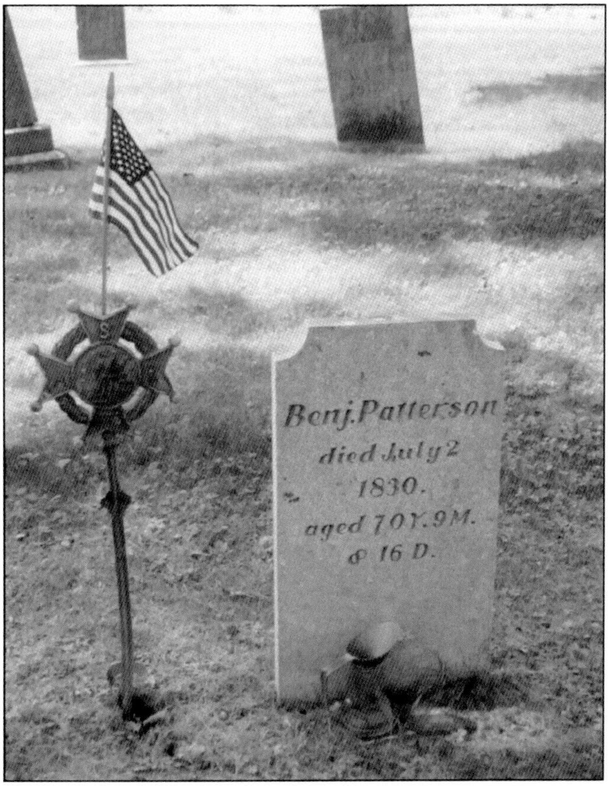

Townsend-Erwin Cemetery is the final resting place for Revolutionary War veteran Benjamin Patterson, who, when hunting, limited himself to taking 100 deer annually, in order to preserve the herd. The frontier entrepreneur promoted schools and operated a large inn, now home to the Corning–Painted Post Historical Society. Patterson arrived in the area in 1793. The cemetery was active from 1810 to 2000. Repeated flooding has displaced many stones. (KWH.)

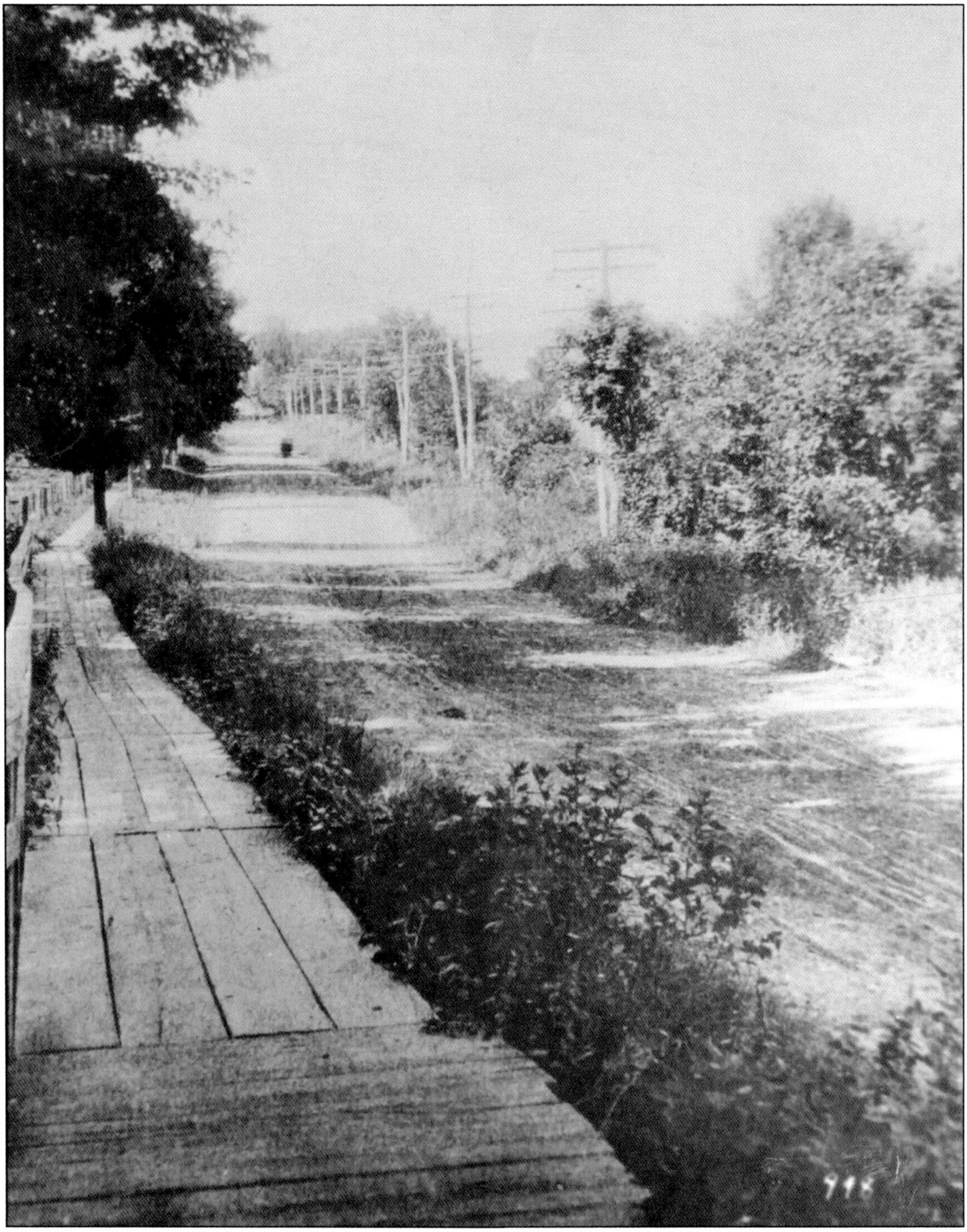

A fence and wooden sidewalk ran along South Hamilton Street (Addison Road) in 1890, but the road itself was still unpaved. Utility poles at the time of this photograph have multiple crossbars to carry the ever-increasing number of wires (telephone, telegraph, and electricity). This looks like a pleasant road to travel, assuming it is neither too wet and muddy, or too dry and dusty. This photograph was taken from the river bridge.

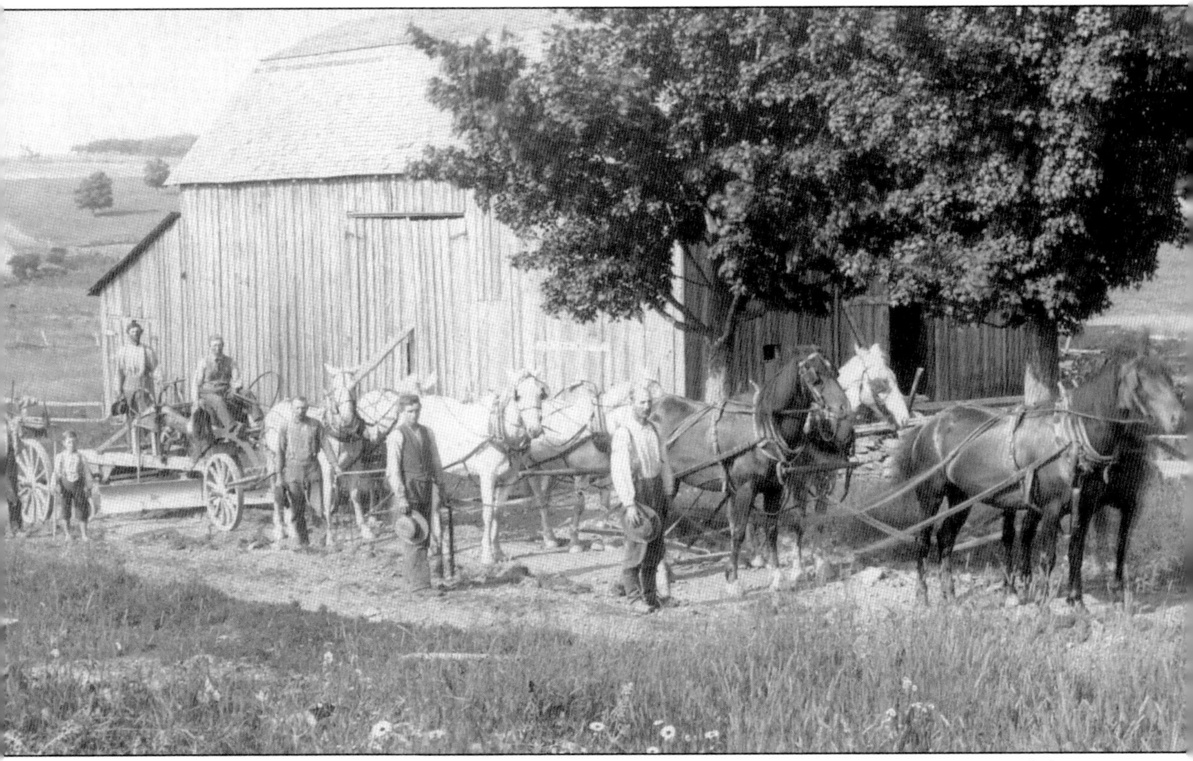

This eight-horse rig, apparently a grader, seems to require five or six men to operate, most of them just tending the teams. It may be that the young fellows at left—or at least the littlest guy—are just taking advantage of the chance to get their picture taken.

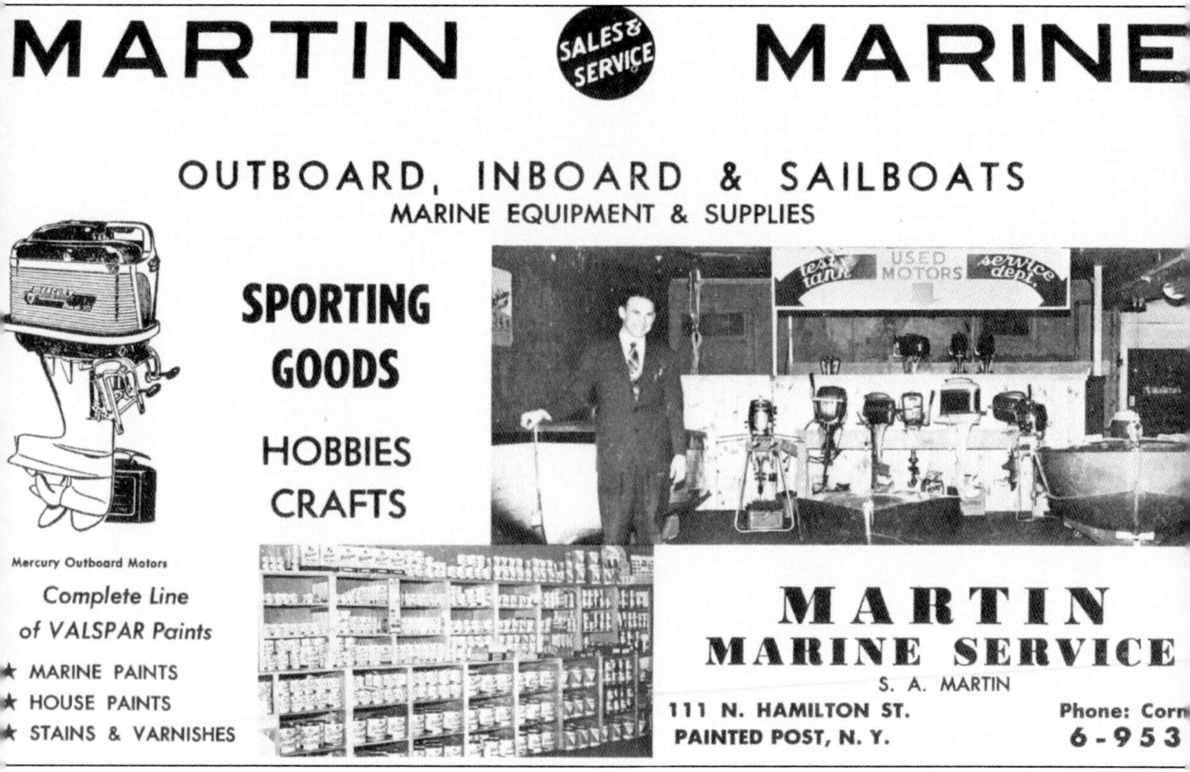

With Seneca Lake and Keuka Lake just a half hour away, not to mention Lamoka, Waneta, and Cayuta Lakes, demand for boating supplies was a constant. (SCHS.)

Four

The Industry

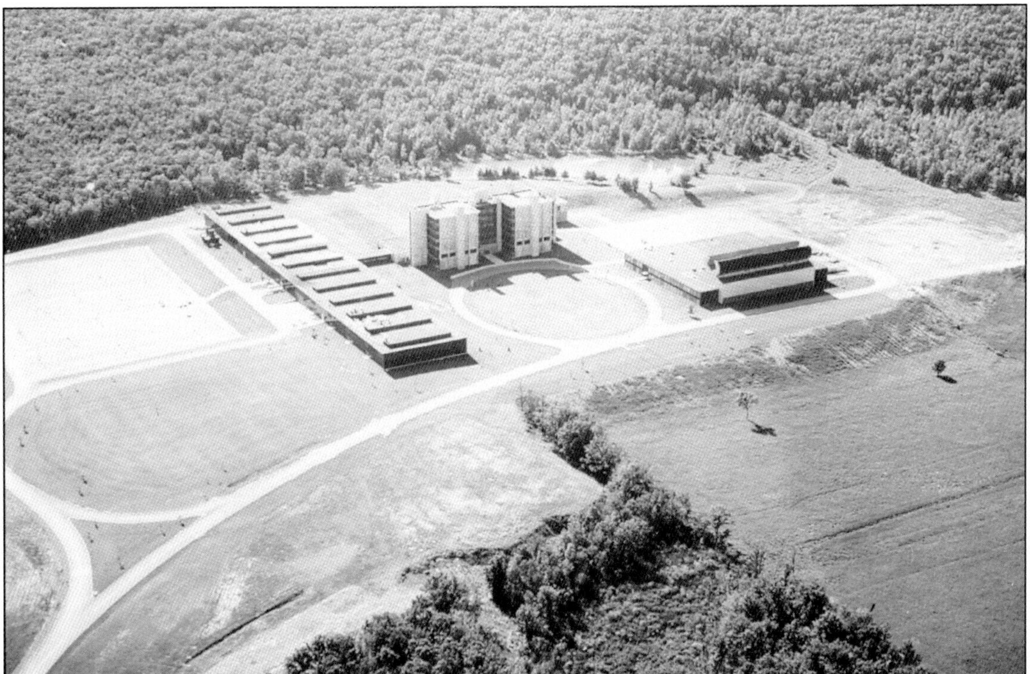

The rivers brought in raw materials, powered the mills, and carried out the product. Then, the railroads threaded their way up the rivers, making connections even easier. Industry attracted workers, and more workers fueled more industry, in a spiral of growth. With Dresser-Rand in the village and Corning Incorporated at Gang Mills and Erwin, this rural town is networked tightly into national and global business, industry, and innovation. Corning's Sullivan Park is shown above. (CI.)

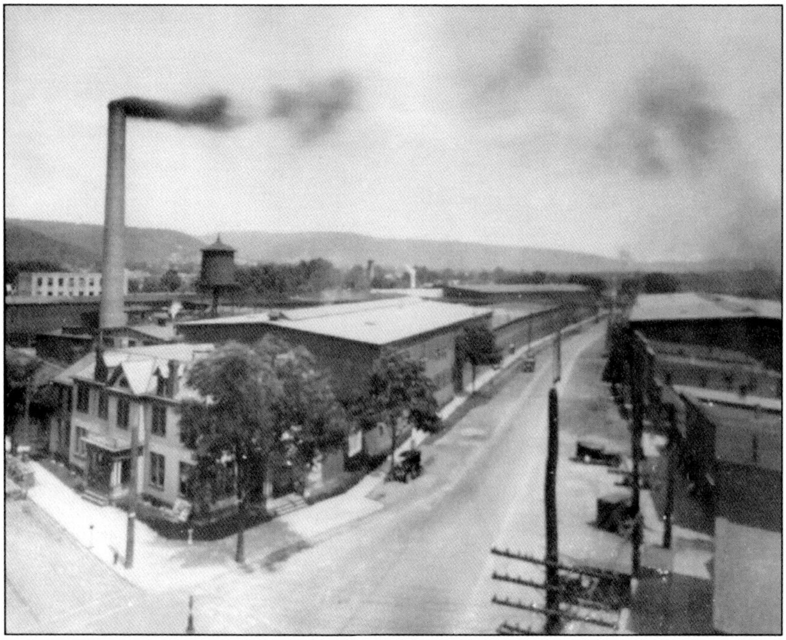

This 1921 photograph of Ingersoll-Rand is a reminder of the health hazards of a coal-fired economy. The hotel on the corner may also be clearly seen on page 14.

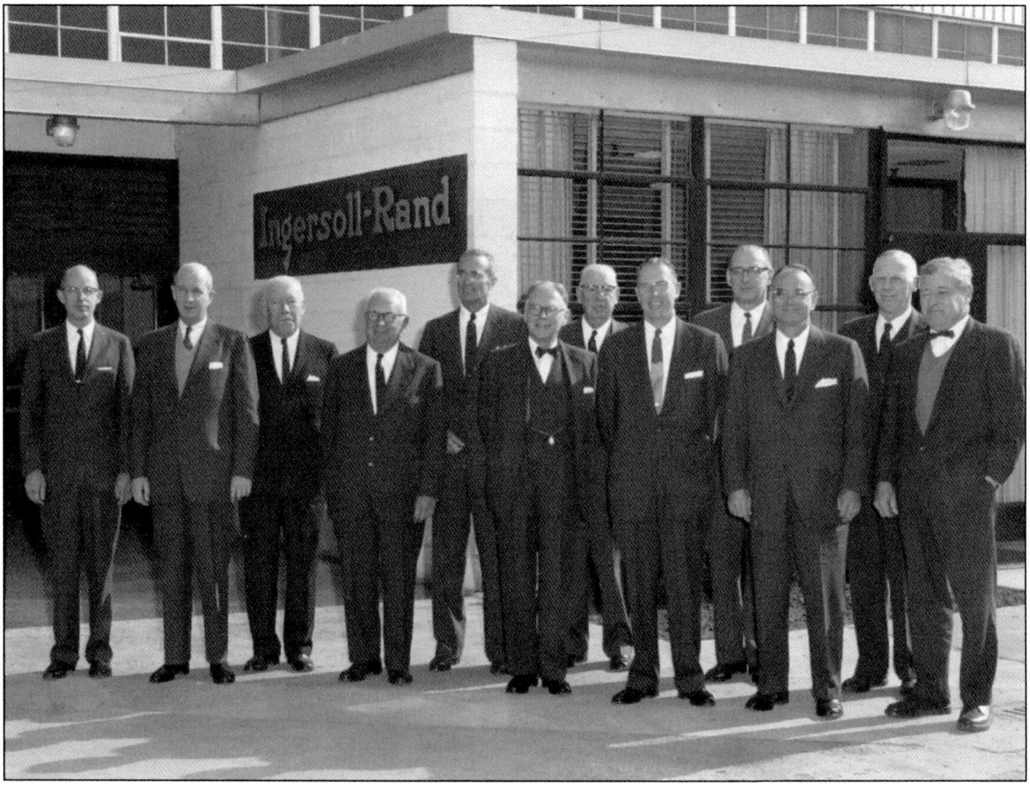

The Ingersoll-Rand corporate board gathered at the plant in September 1960. The board members are, from left to right, E.E. Teach, G.C. Doubleday, R. Carpenter, E. Raymond Sheerin, A.S. Blagden Jr., P.L. Loeb, E.J. Smith, L.C. Hopton, E.J. Parish, E.H. Johnston, M.C. Davison, and J.H. Phipps.

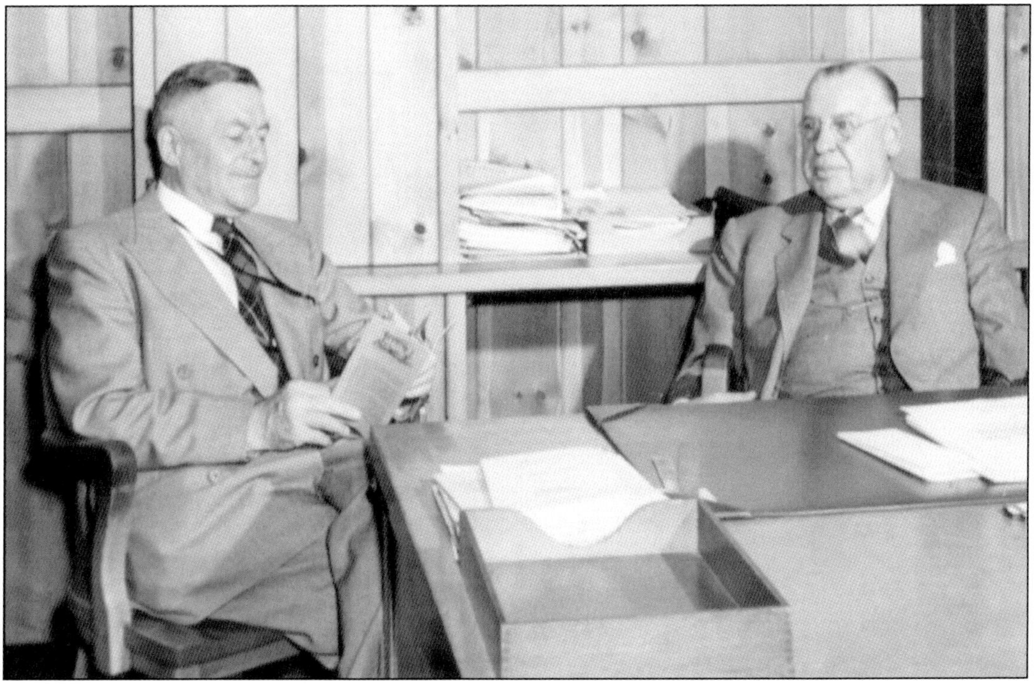

Rand general manager E.J. Smith (right) meets with Alexander Ruthvan from the University of Milwaukee. Ruthvan was doing an evaluation of company practices and procedures.

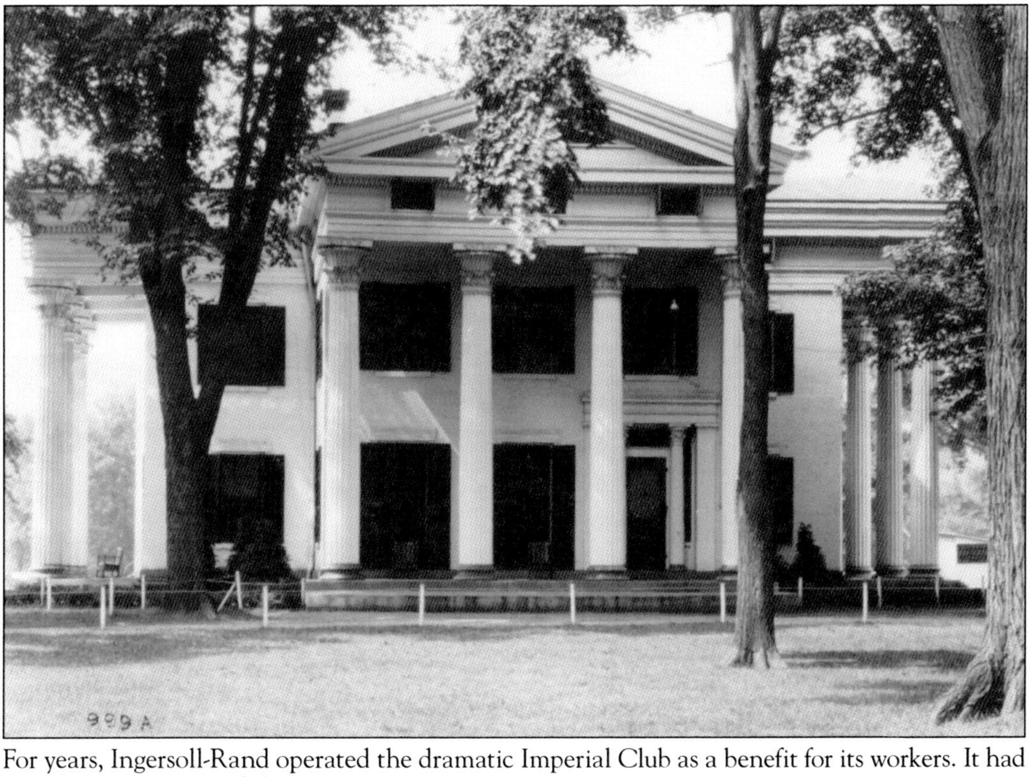

For years, Ingersoll-Rand operated the dramatic Imperial Club as a benefit for its workers. It had once been a country club.

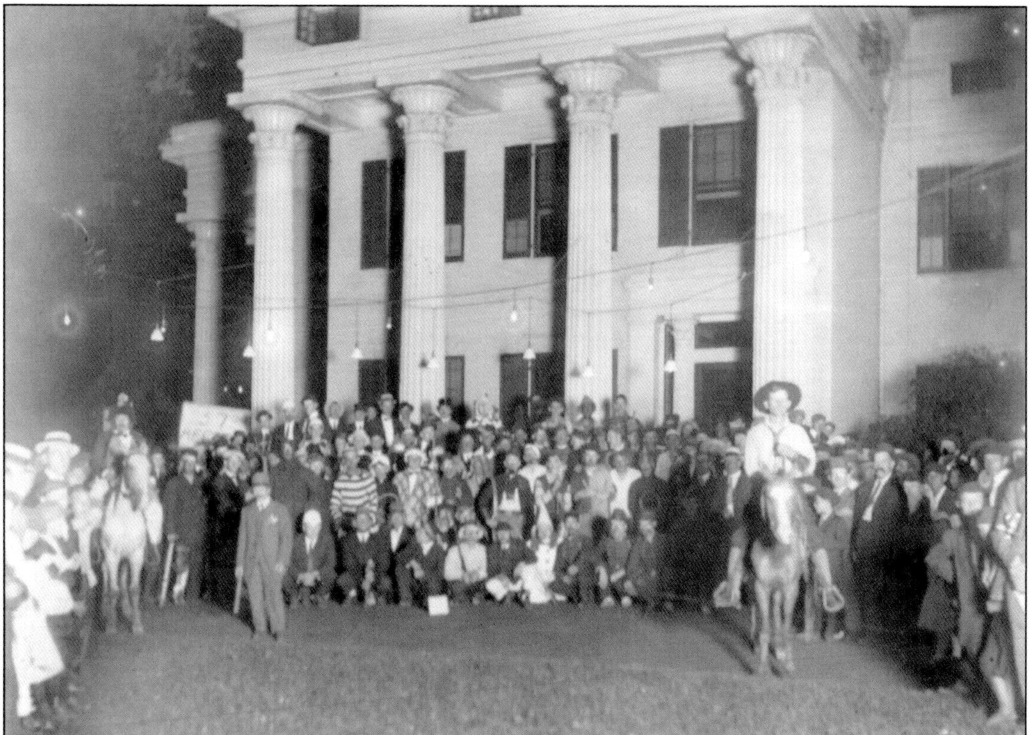

In this photograph, a large contingent gathers at the Imperial Club on September 1, 1914, for some sort of party and parade.

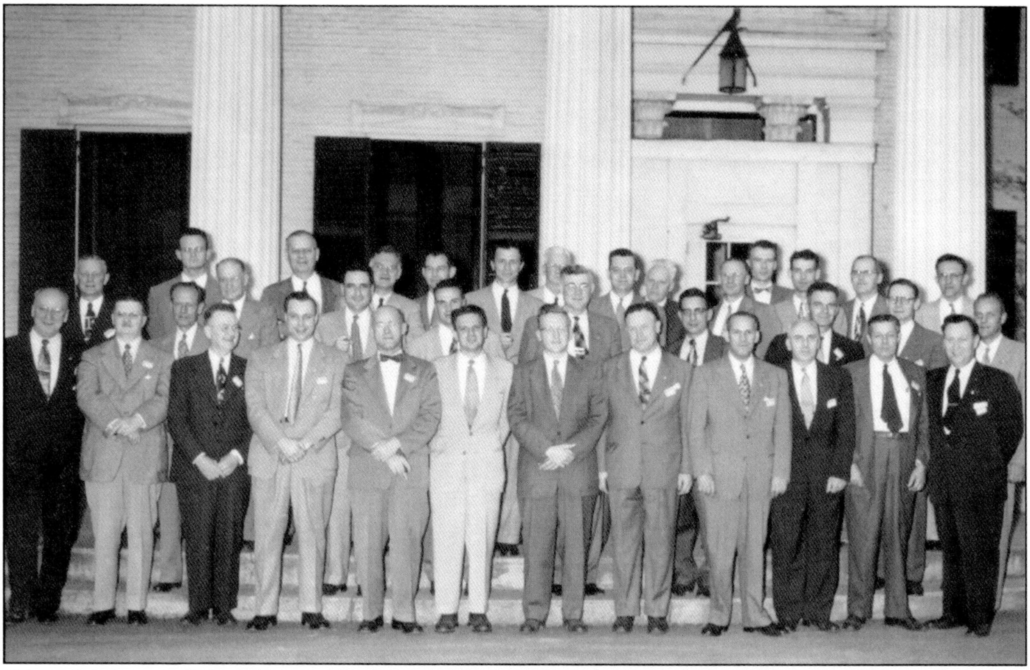

Cheerful Ingersoll-Rand general salesmen gathered at the Imperial for their conference on May 12, 1953.

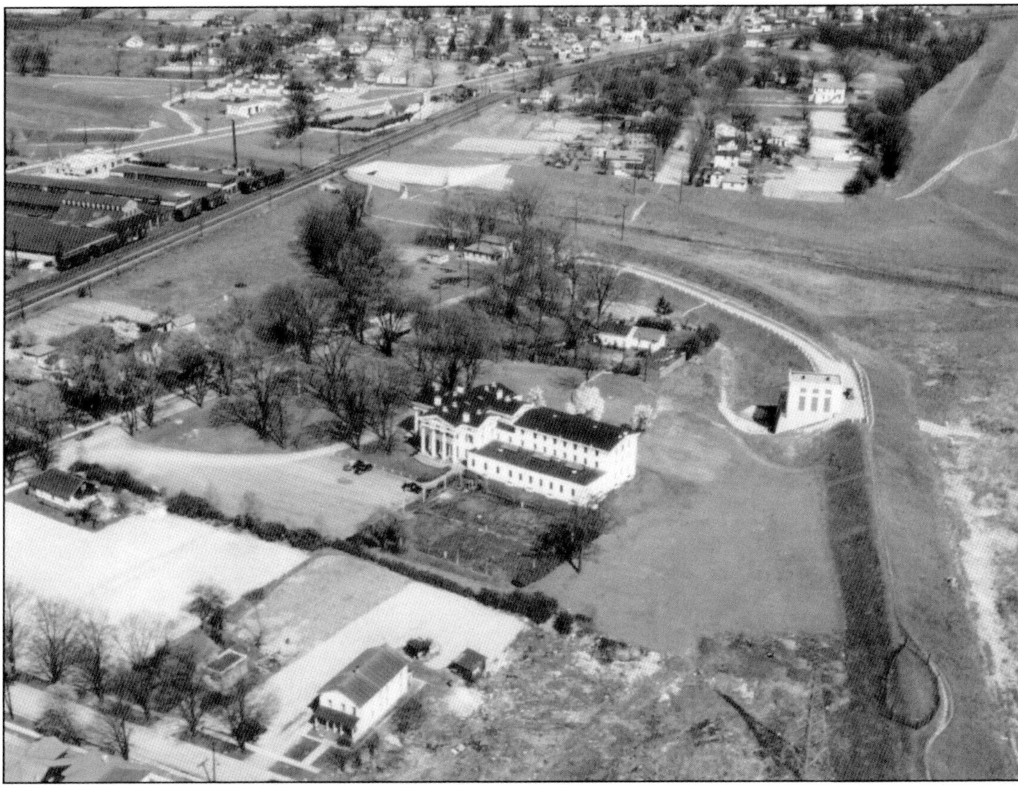

This aerial photograph of the clubhouse also shows the flood-control berms at right.

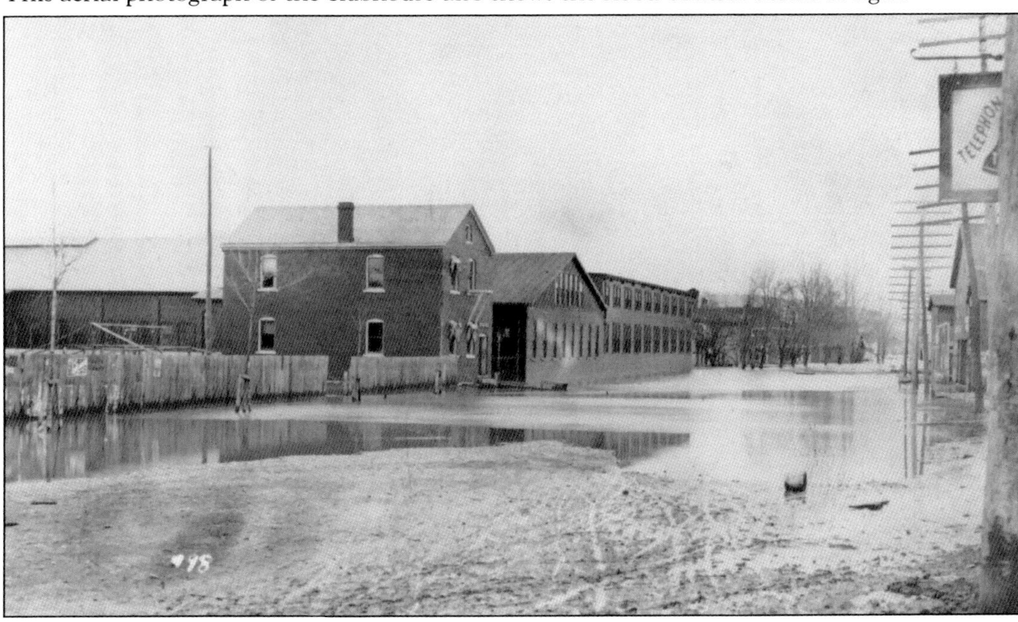

The name of the Imperial Club memorializes the Imperial Engineering Company (shown here), predecessor to Ingersoll-Rand. This Hamilton Street scene, near Water Street, shows the aftermath of a flood in 1901. The sign at right indicates that, even at that early time, there is a telephone booth available to the pubic.

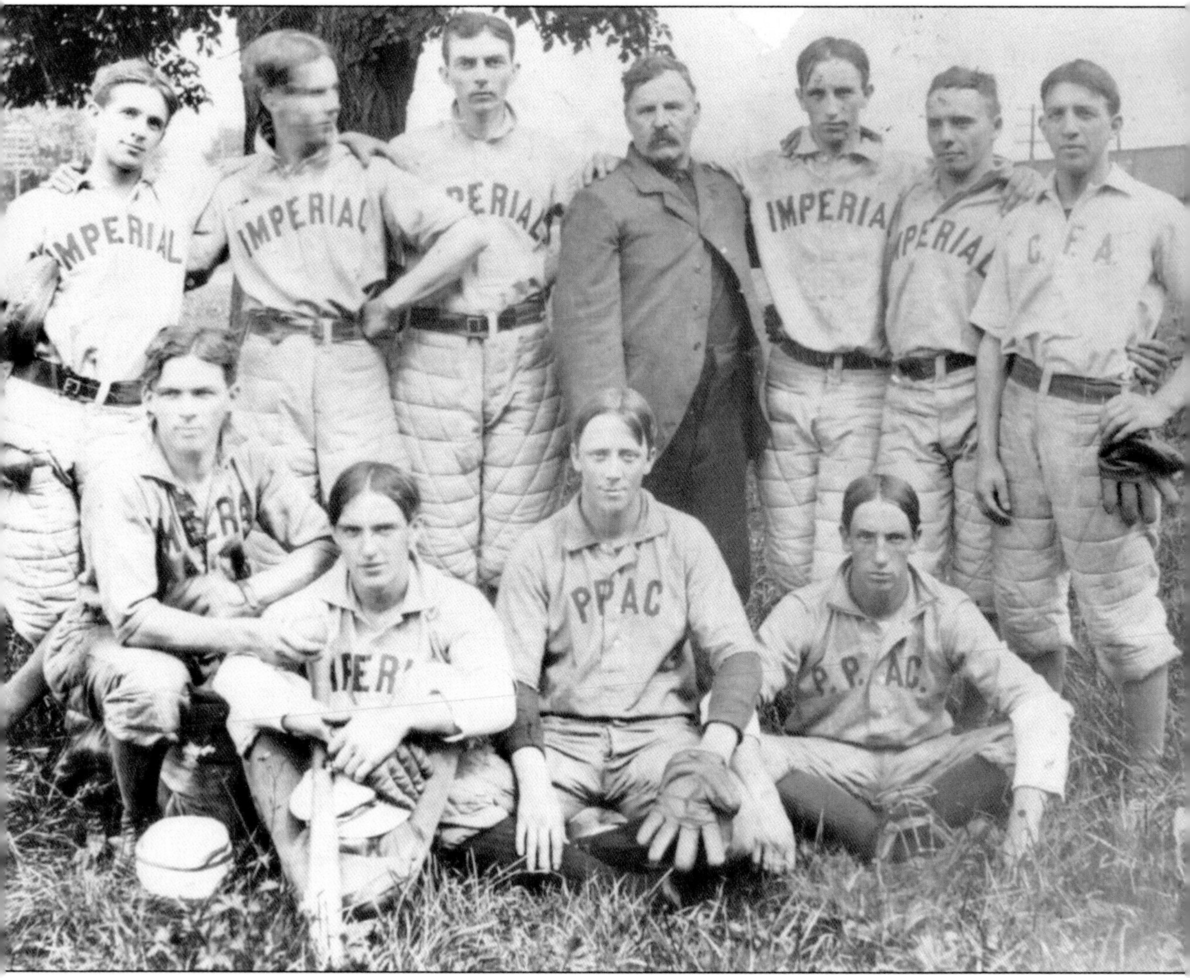

Imperial Engineering also lent its name to the company ball team, though some of these fellows are wearing uniforms for Painted Post Athletic Club and Corning Free Academy. Note the quilted knickers and the gloves with separated fingers. In this c. 1904 photograph are, from left to right, (first row) Fred Barclay, Nicholas Hitchcock, "Red" Covert, and Archie Hamilton; (second row) Clarence Nichols, Martin Mulverhill, Fred Brace, W.B. Dunham, Tom Hart, Chester Smith, and Doug Bonham.

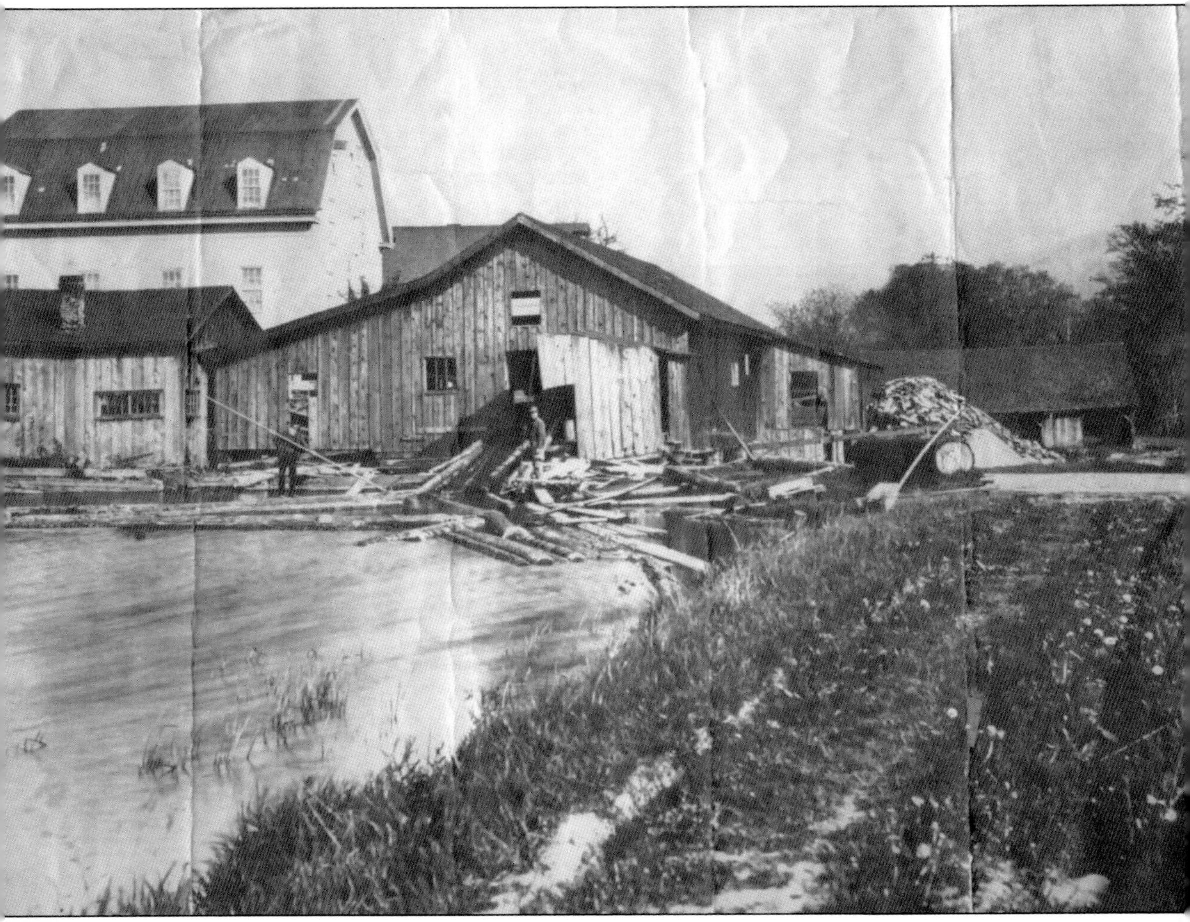

Much of the early industry in the area involved wood. A.E. Hubbard operated a 19th-century lumber mill at Painted Post.

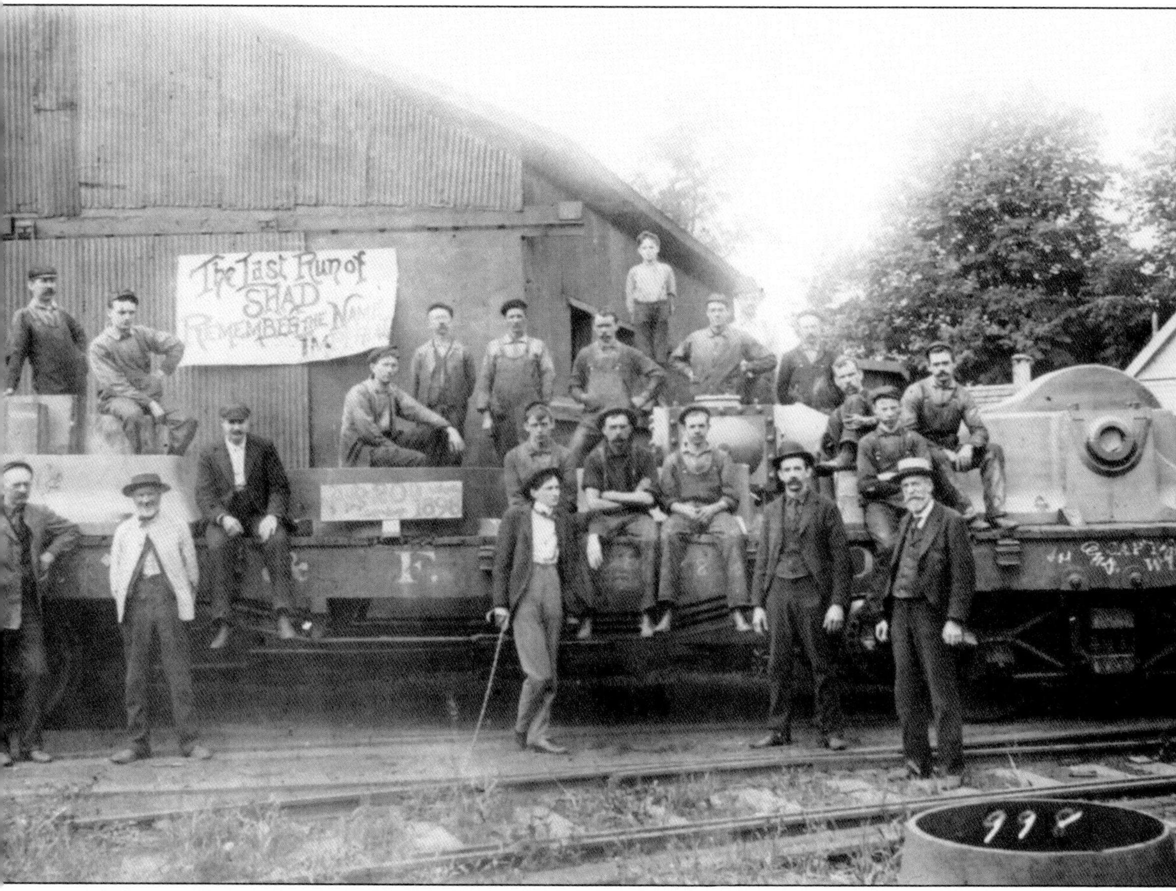

Weston Engine Company employees celebrate their final job before the company closed in 1898.

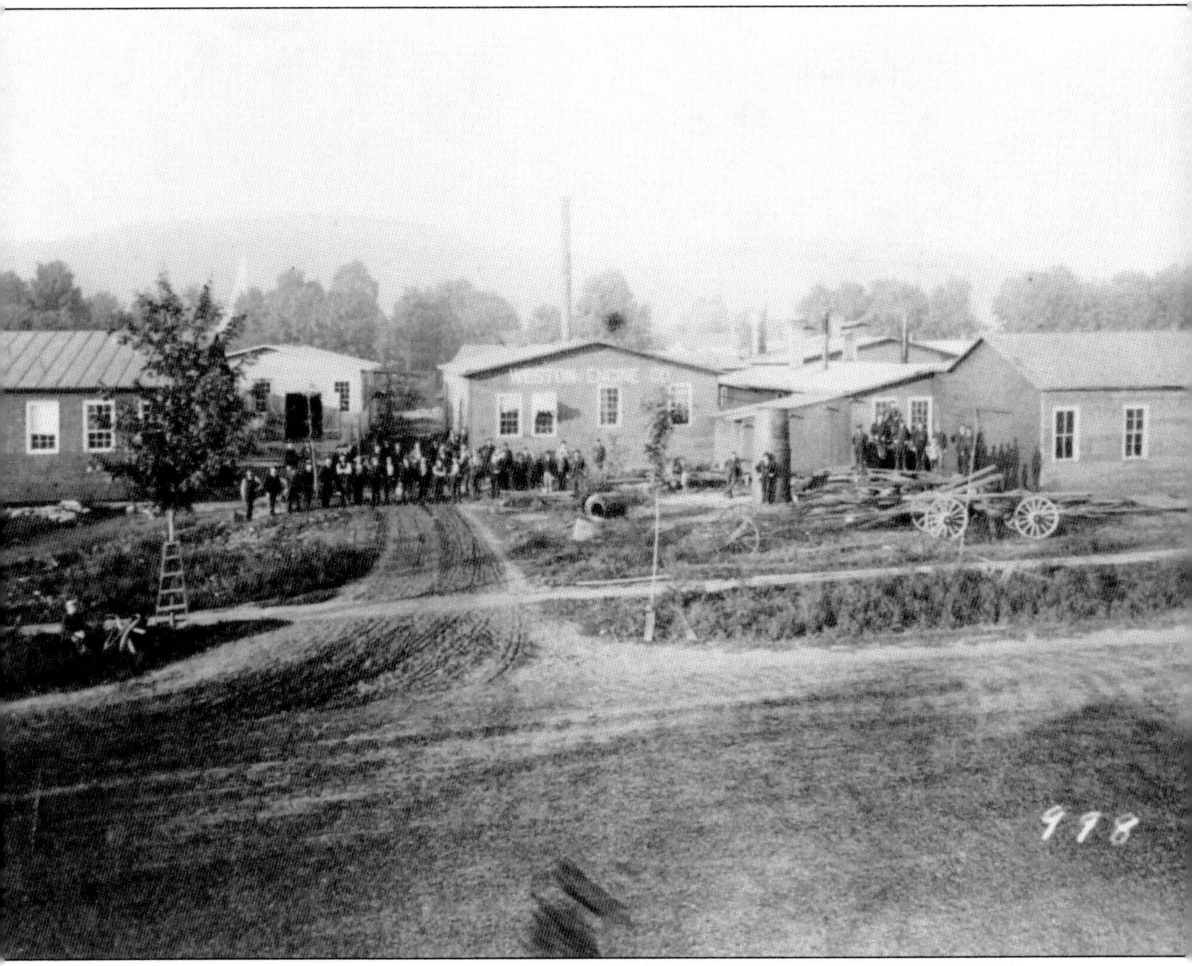

Weston, another predecessor of the Rand, experienced happier days in 1883. Located at this time on East Water Street, the company started with Abijah Weston's foundry and machine shop in 1848. Weston products included steam engines and iron bridges.

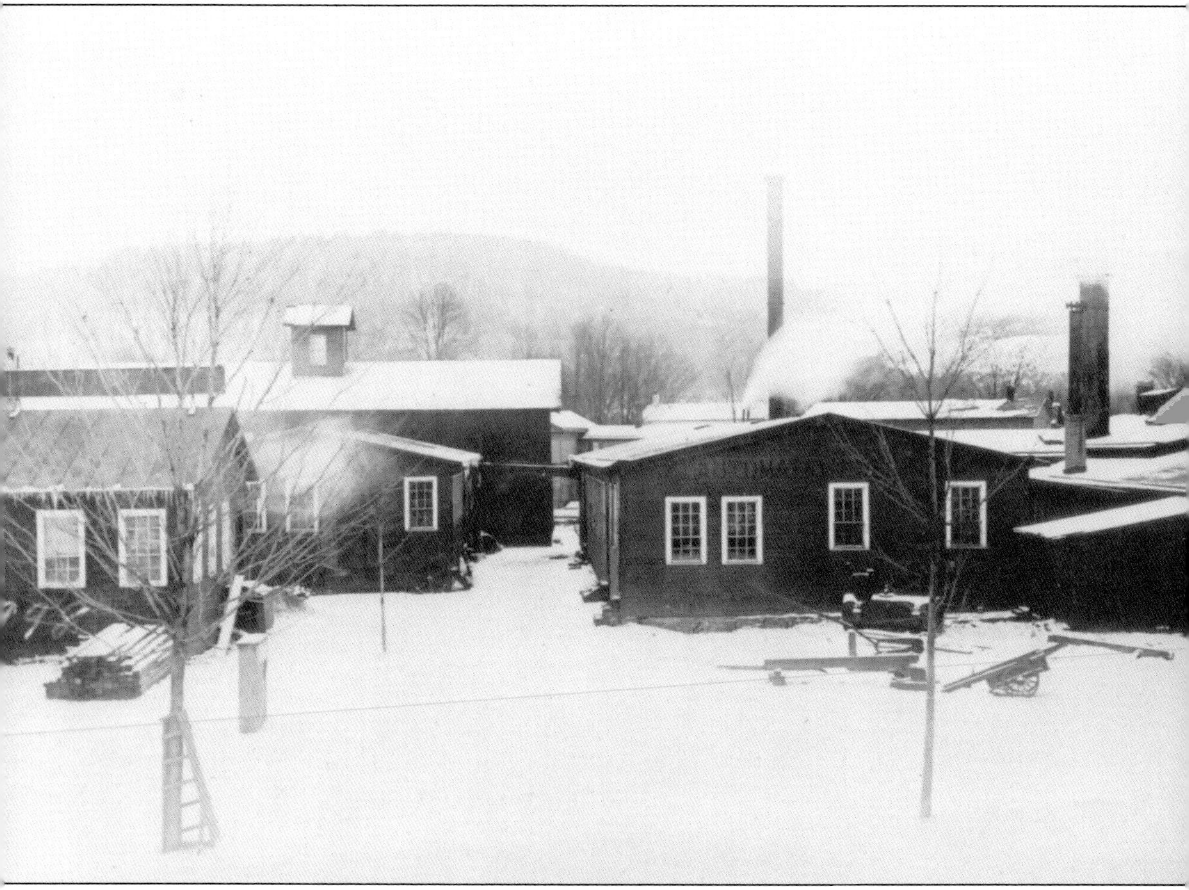

Wintry weather in 1889 brought hanging icicles and a blanket of snow. But, to judge by the smoke from the stacks, Weston kept on working. Notice that this photograph and the one on the previous page were taken from almost the same vantage point. There has been some painting, shingling, or tarpapering in the intervening six years, and a barnlike building with a cupola has been added in the back at left.

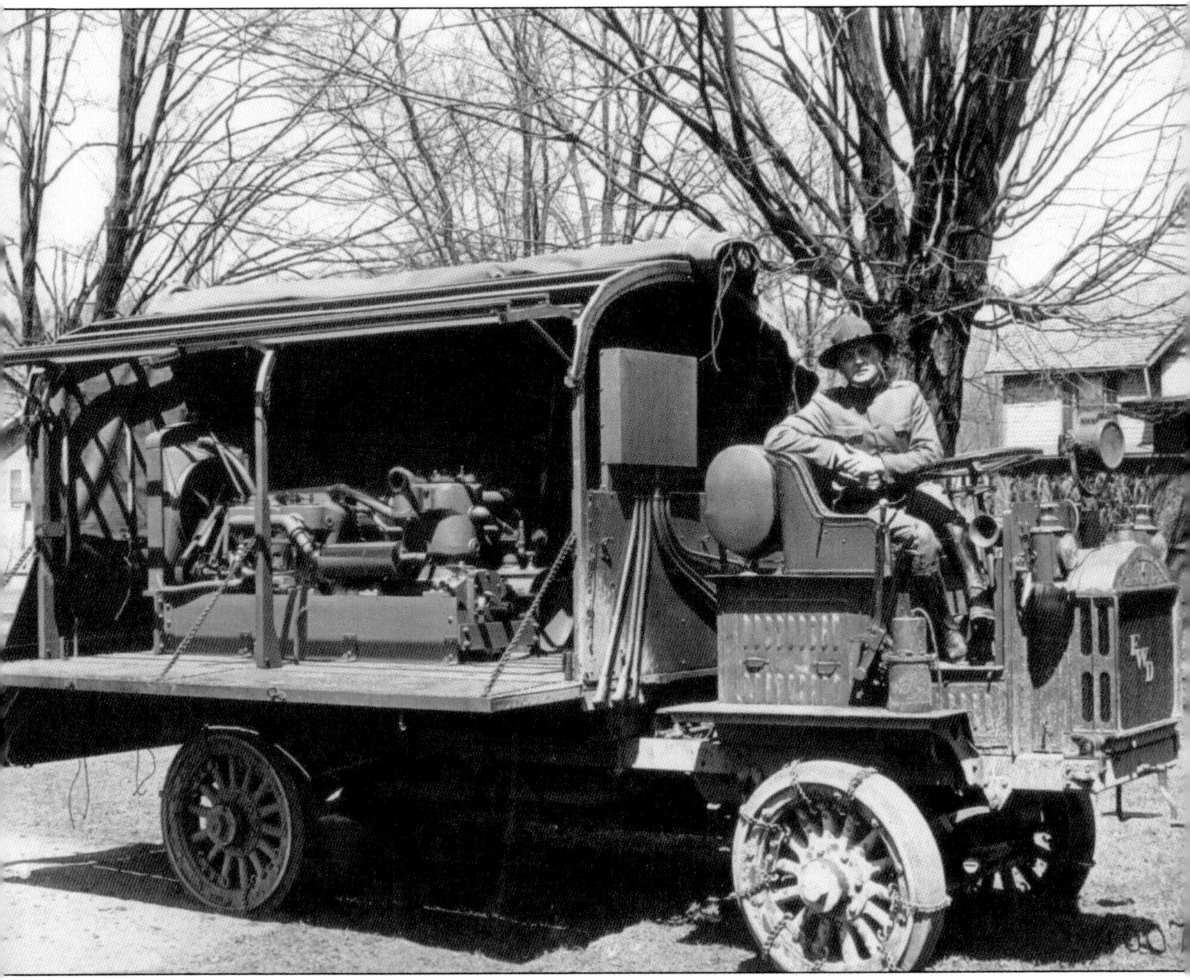

Around 1920, Ingersoll-Rand's Painted Post plant experimented with what was described as a six-by-six (six-wheel drive) semiportable Army truck. Note the fuel tank behind the driver, the horn and spotlight in front of him, and the hand crank under the radiator. All visible tires have chains.

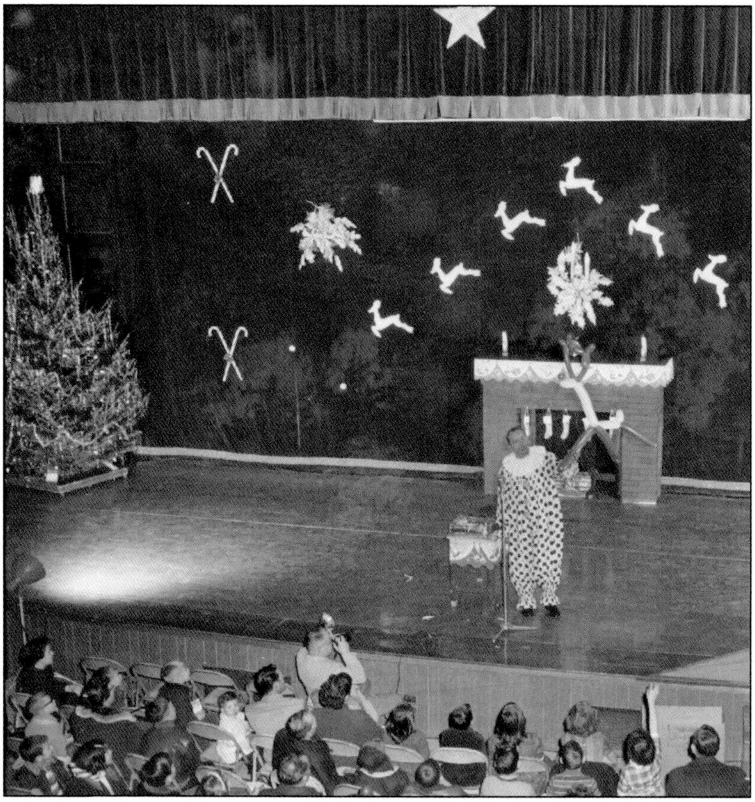

This Christmas celebration for Ingersoll-Rand employee families appears to have taken place in the 1950s.

The 1934 Ingersoll-Rand company Christmas party must have been an elaborate affair.

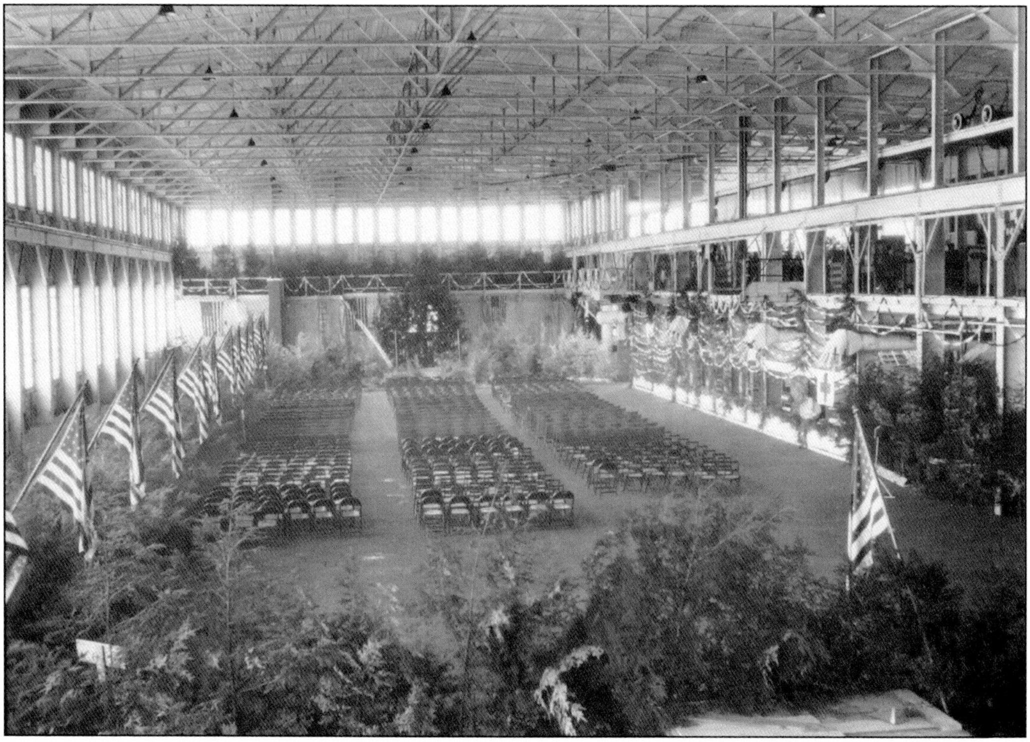

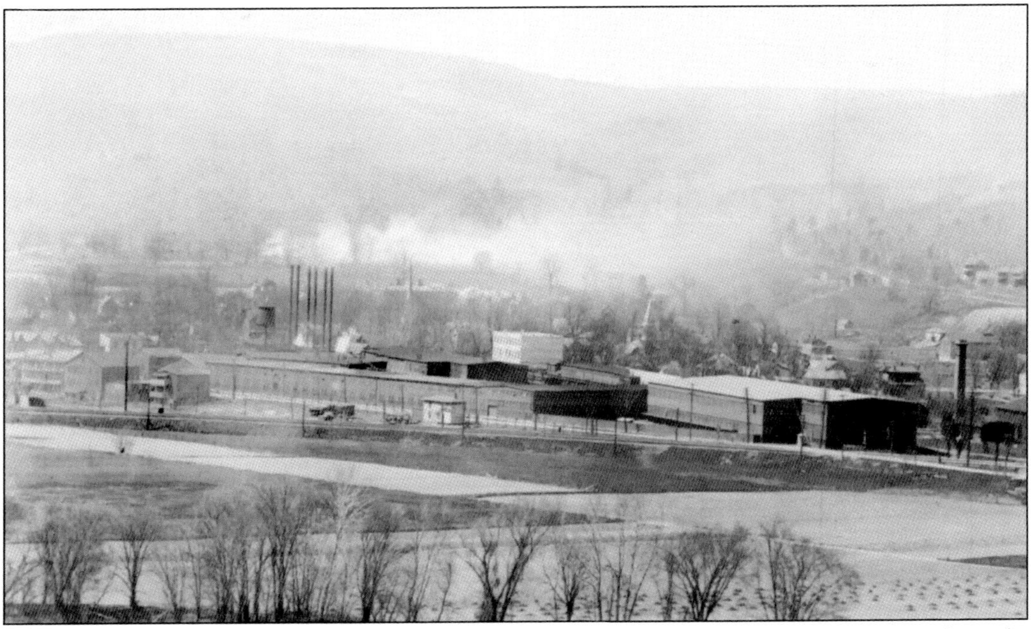

All that smoke was once a very welcome sight for residents and newcomers, as it meant that jobs were available. While the work is still welcome, residents today appreciate the health hazards a little better. This October 6, 1987, photograph shows the engineering department, the three-story white structure at center.

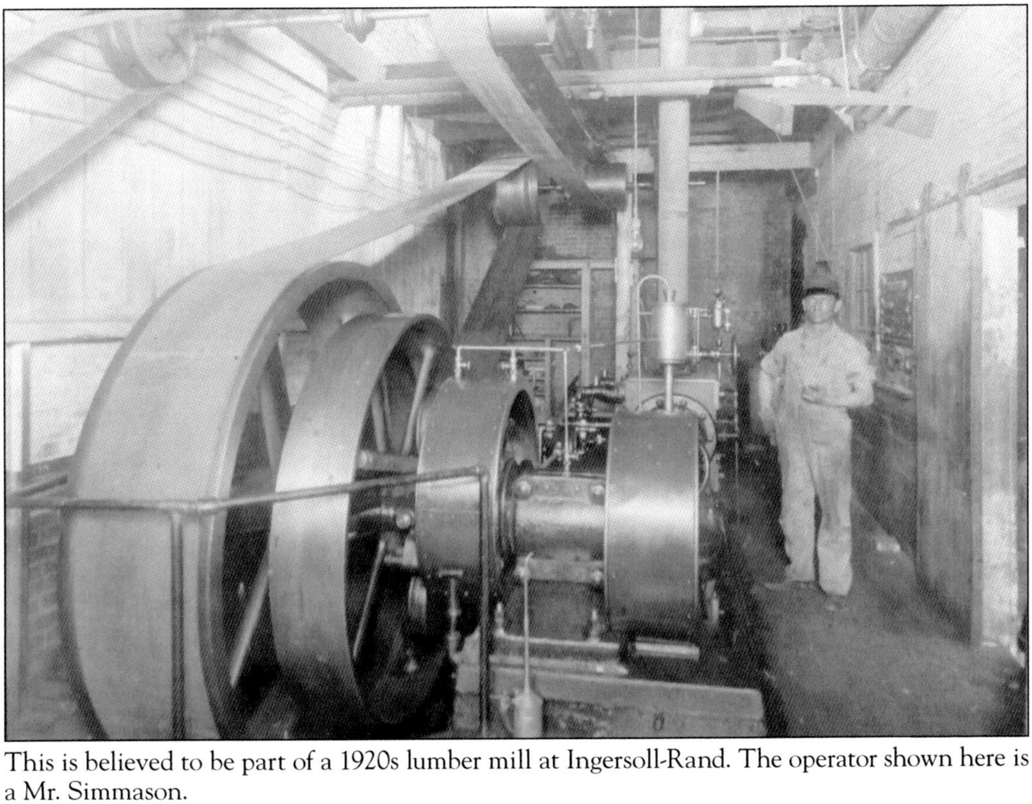

This is believed to be part of a 1920s lumber mill at Ingersoll-Rand. The operator shown here is a Mr. Simmason.

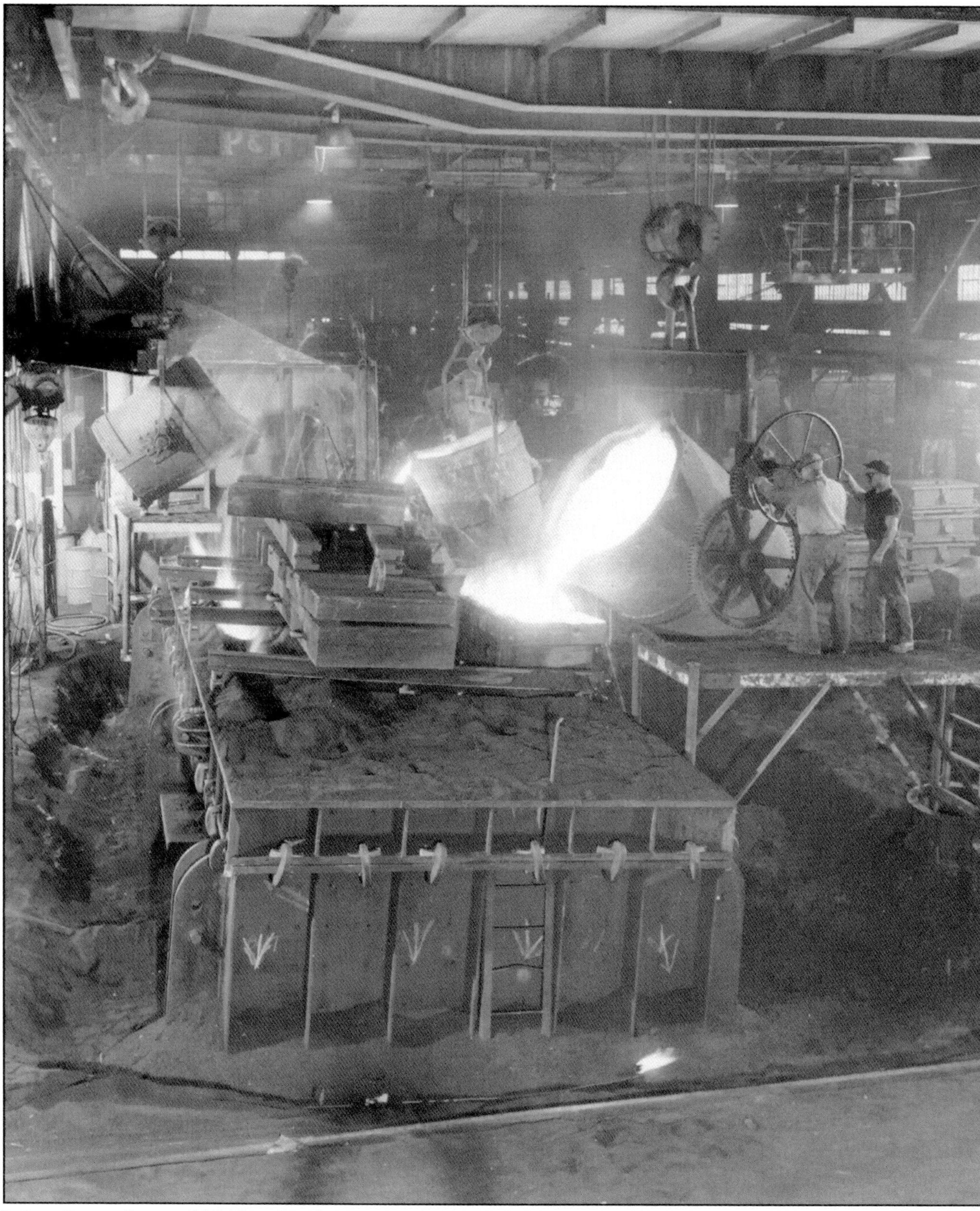

John Sapinsky and Eddie Cord are pouring steel in the main bay at Ingersoll-Rand on January 25, 1962.

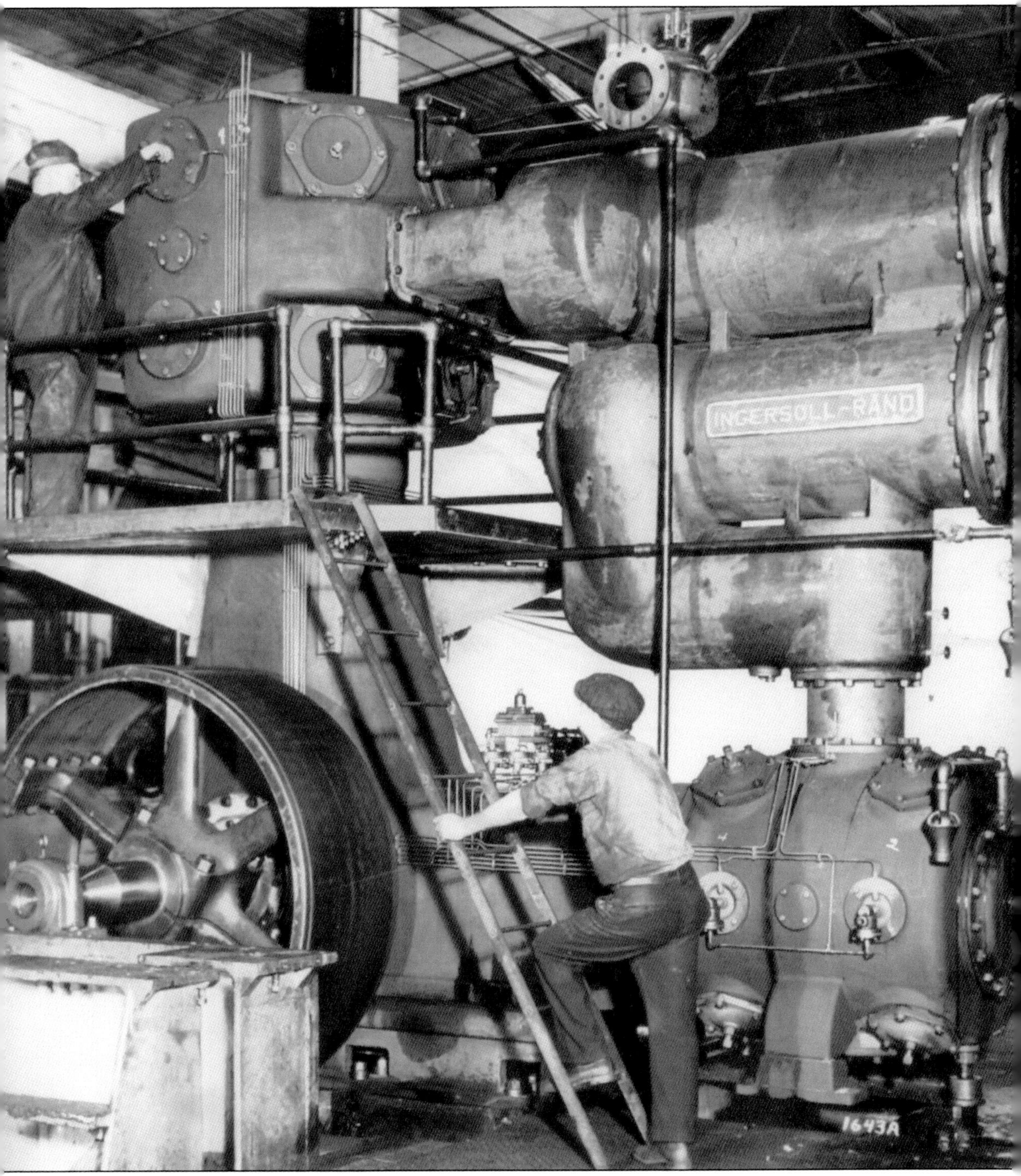

A compressor is being assembled in Ingersoll-Rand's Plant 3.

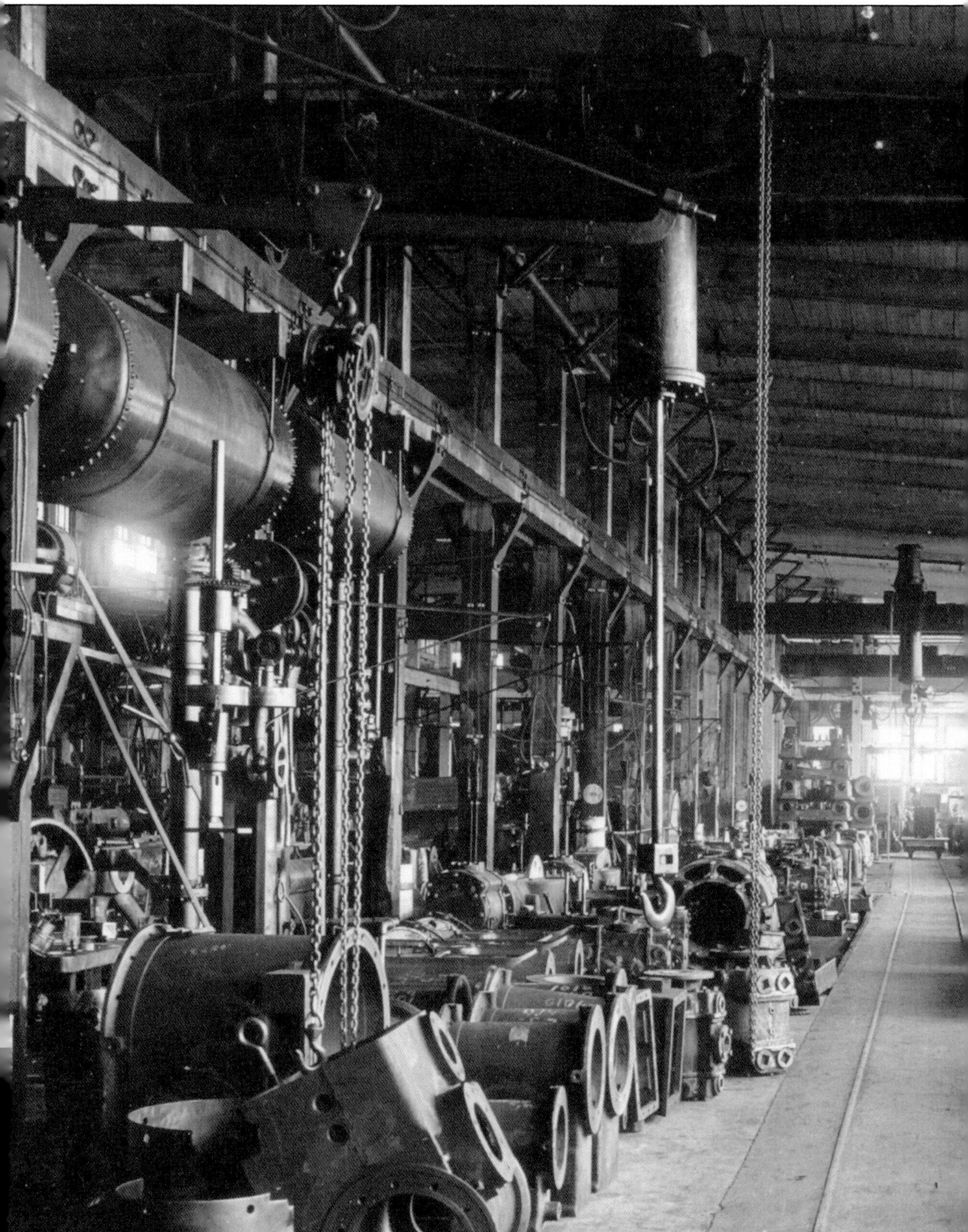

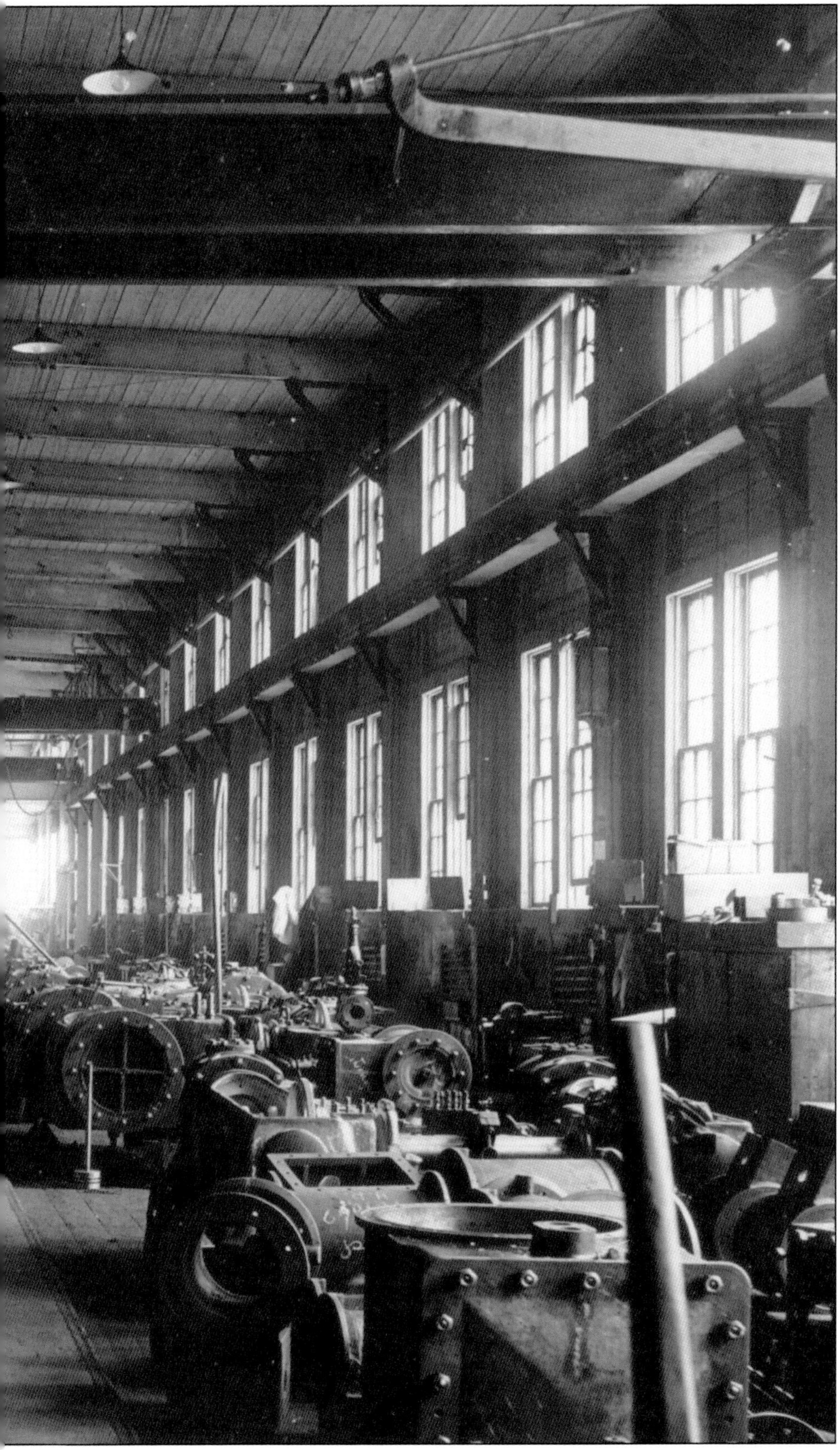

This 1912 photograph of Ingersoll-Rand shows a row of overhead electric lights. Clearly, though, most of the light in this space comes via sunlight through the windows.

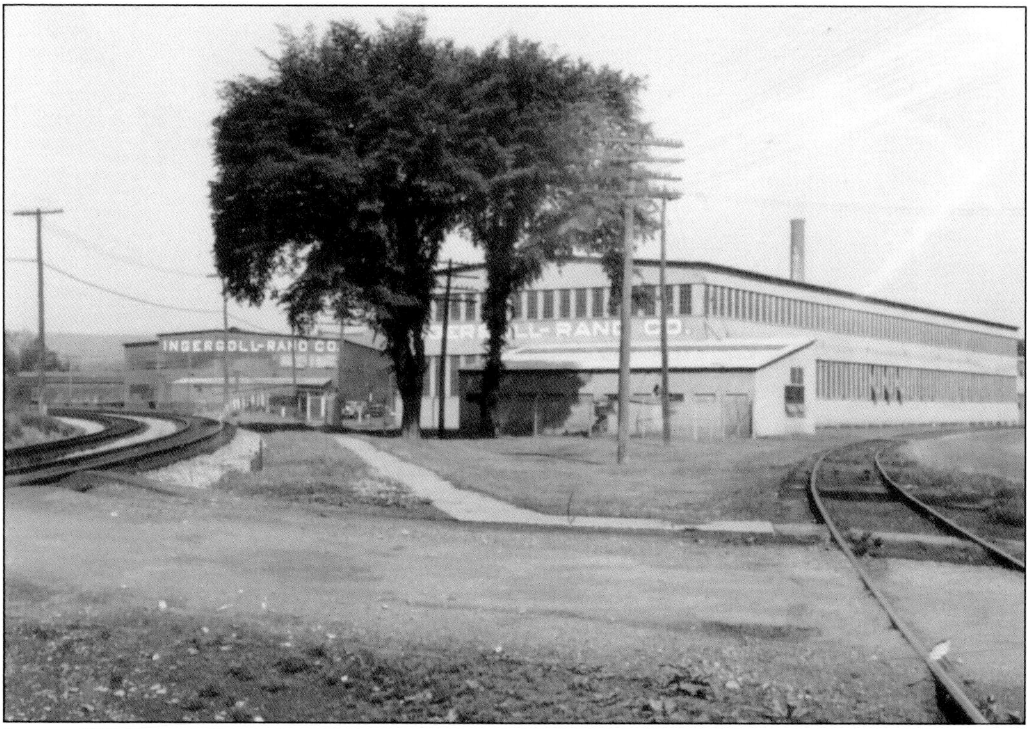

Ingersoll-Rand was formed in 1905. Dresser-Rand (of which the Erwin plant became a part) was created in 1986, originally in partnership with Dresser Industries. Dresser-Rand is traded on the New York Stock Exchange. This view is from First Street.

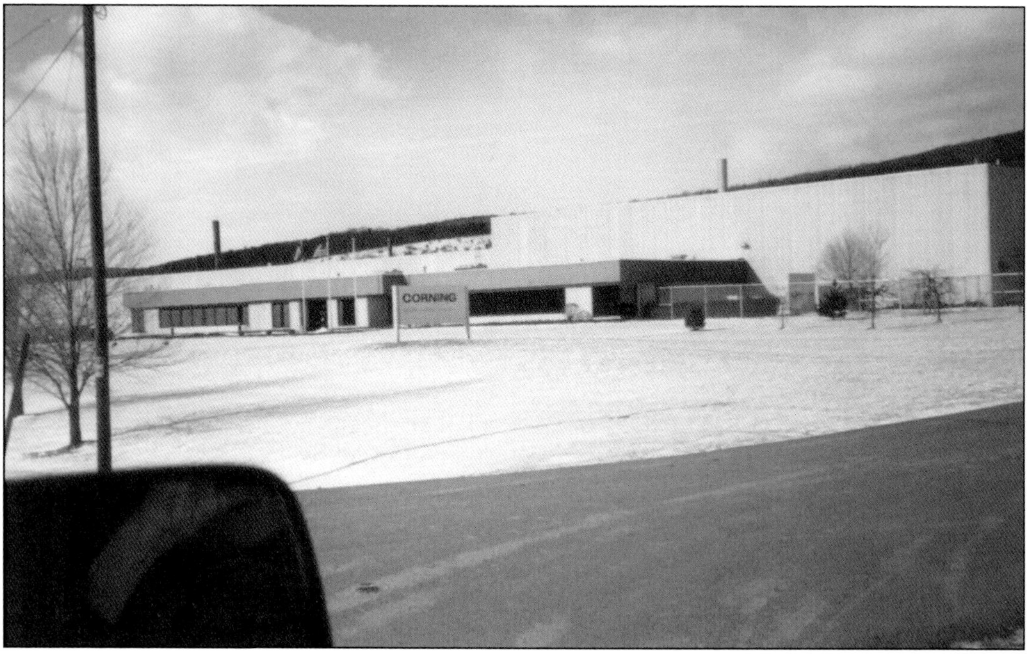

Corning Incorporated (formerly Corning Glass Works) also maintains extensive facilities in Erwin, in the Sullivan Research Park area in Gang Mills, and at I-99, exit 2, near Erwins. (SCH.)

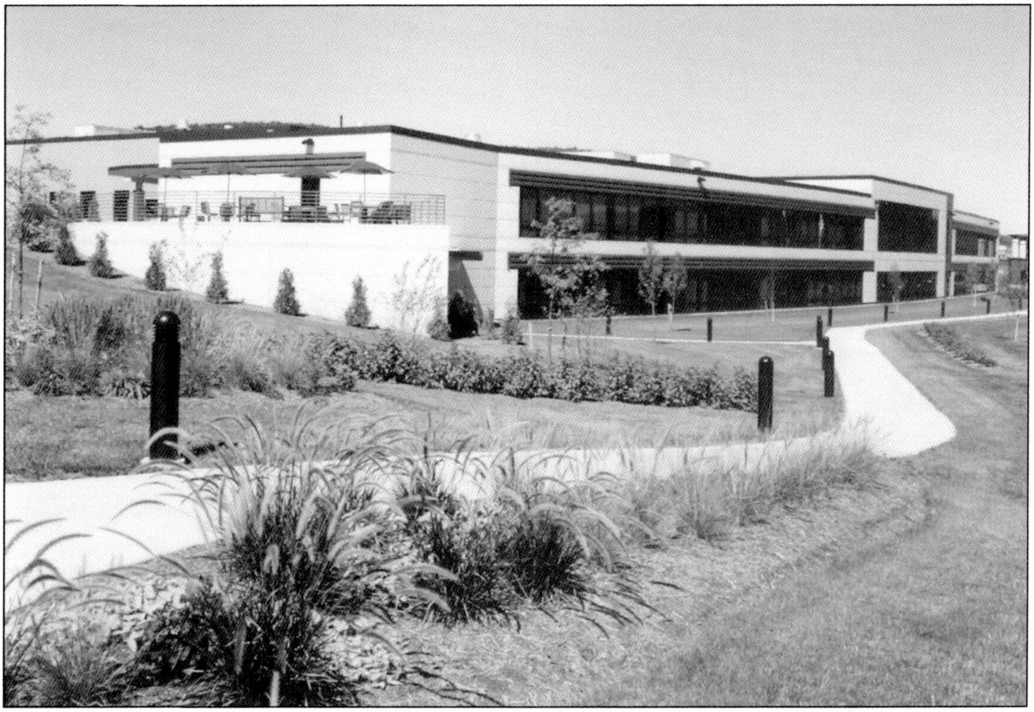

This Corning Incorporated office building was once the Photonics Plant. (CI.)

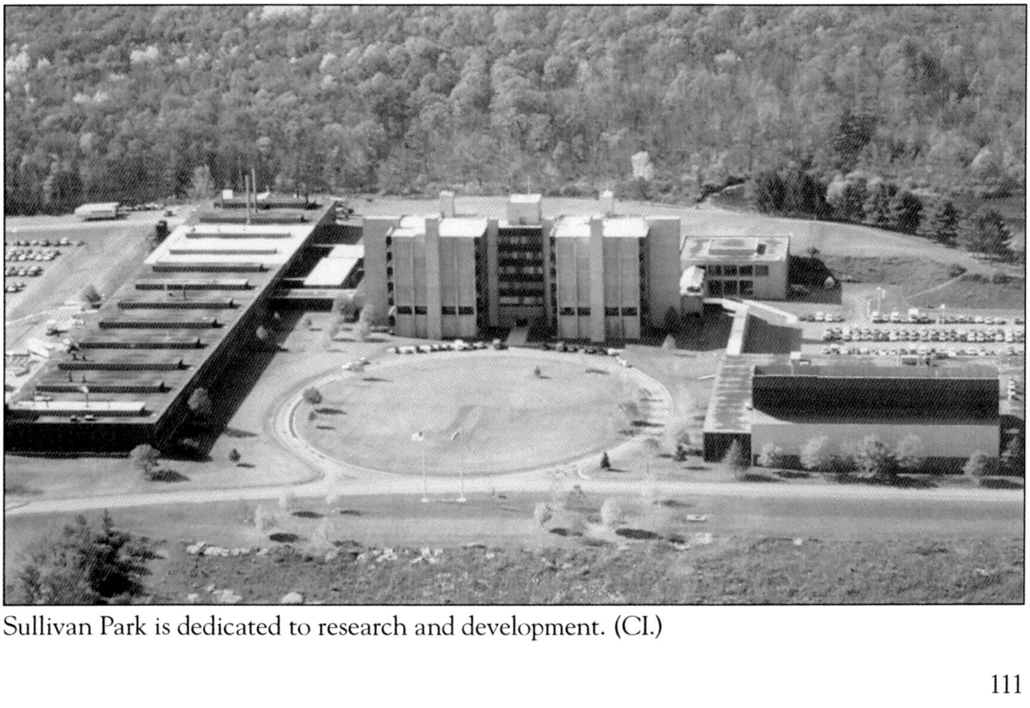

Sullivan Park is dedicated to research and development. (CI.)

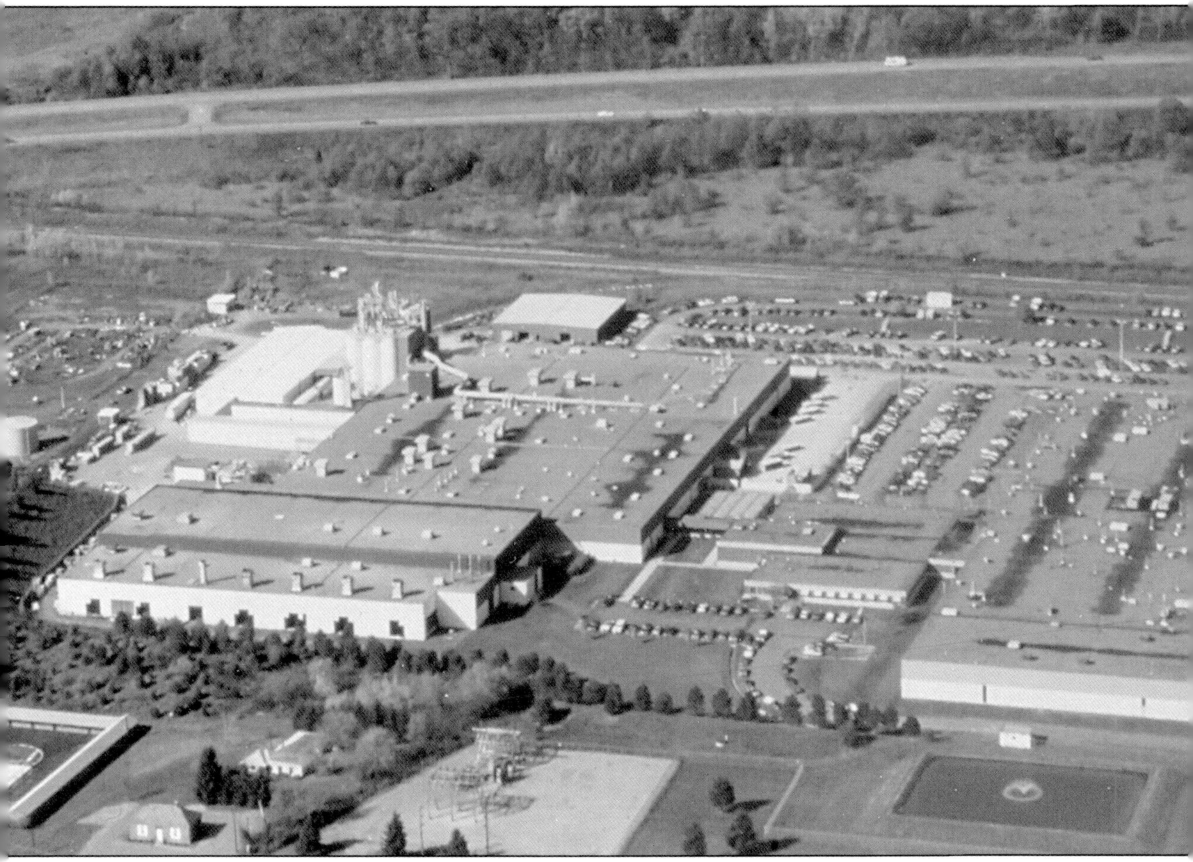

When the Brooklyn Flint Glass Works moved to Corning in 1868, its leaders could never have foreseen the size the company would attain. Also unanticipated would have been the fiber optics and other high-tech applications the firm specializes in. Even the ability to take this aerial photograph of the Erwin plant would have been beyond their vision. (CI.)

Five

The People

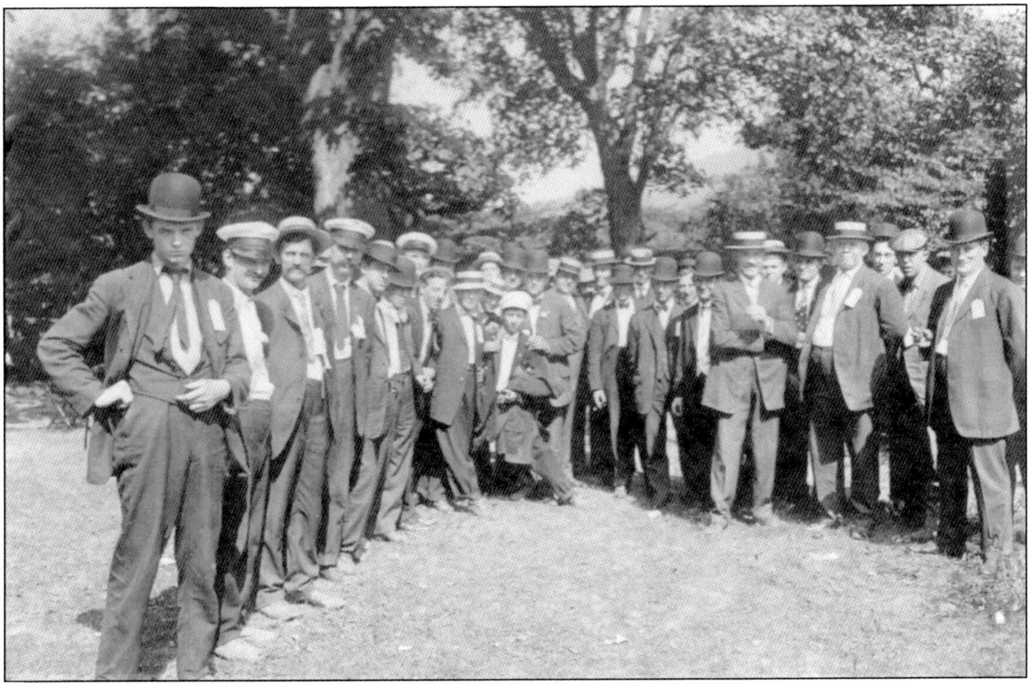

Housing, industry, amenities, population concentrations, even landscape and natural resources—these are just the stage on which the play of Erwin and Painted Post is presented. Just as a play is about the characters, a town is about its people. In Erwin's play, the performance has run for over two centuries, and it shows no sign of closing. Many of the actors have "retired," but, thanks to photography, they can be known even now.

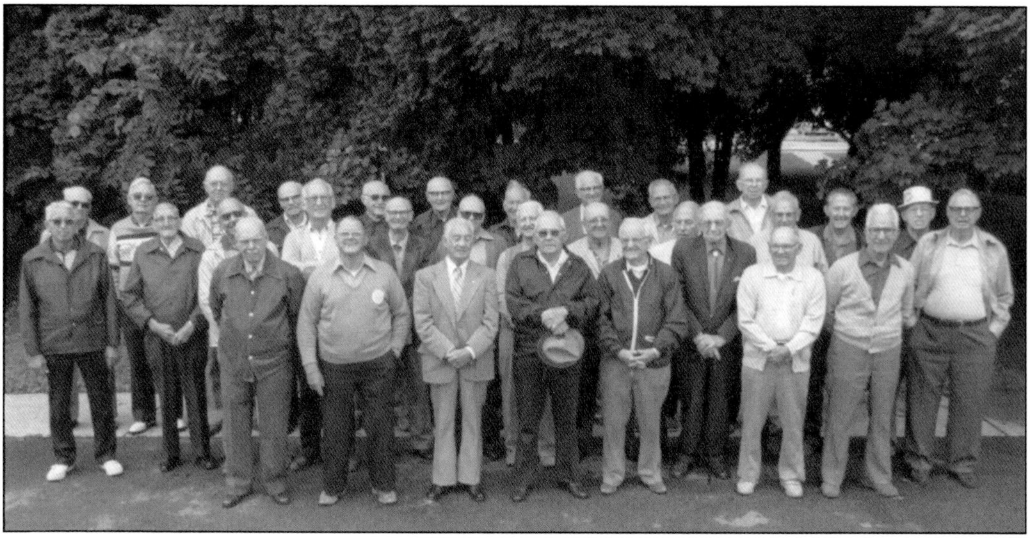

The Corning–Painted Post Men's Senior Citizens Club gathered for its annual picnic at Cowanesque Lake in 1985. Even though it was mid-June, cold weather forced the cancellation of the trip, and the men held their picnic in the Methodist-Presbyterian Church.

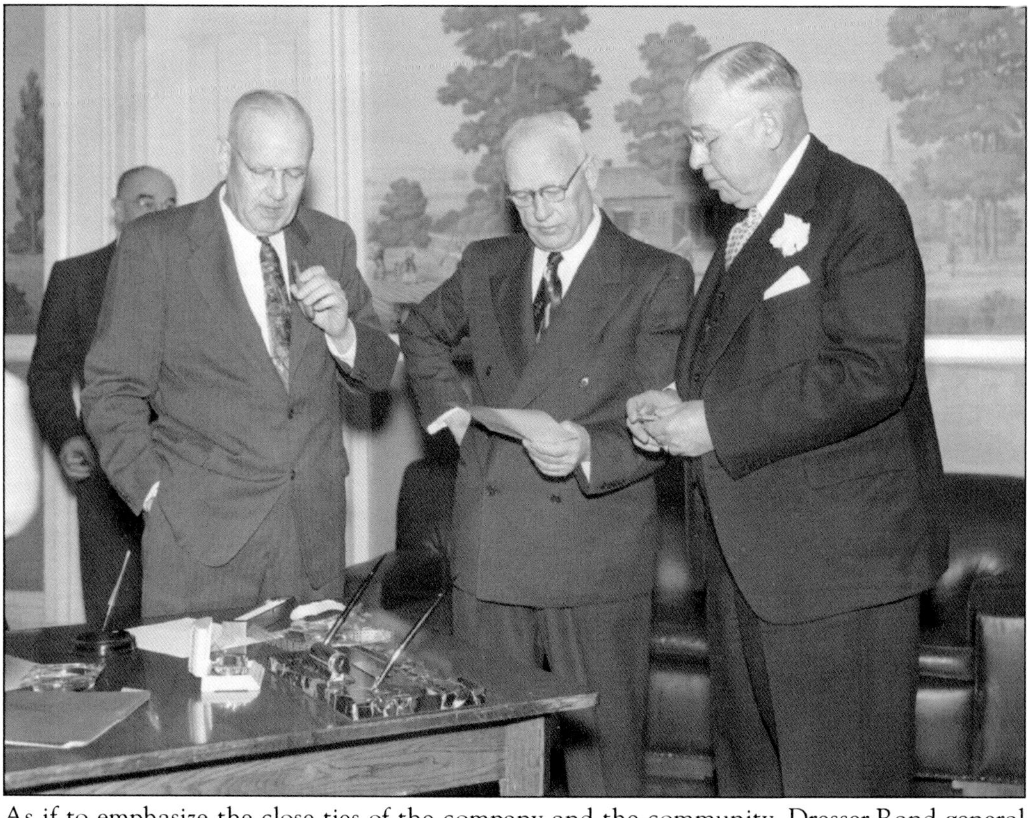

As if to emphasize the close ties of the company and the community, Dresser-Rand general manager E.J. "Edward" Smith (right) was elected mayor of Painted Post. He served from 1929 to 1935. Seen here with former mayor Smith on February 6, 1955, are Frank Love and an unidentified gentleman. This scene may have taken place in the Imperial Club.

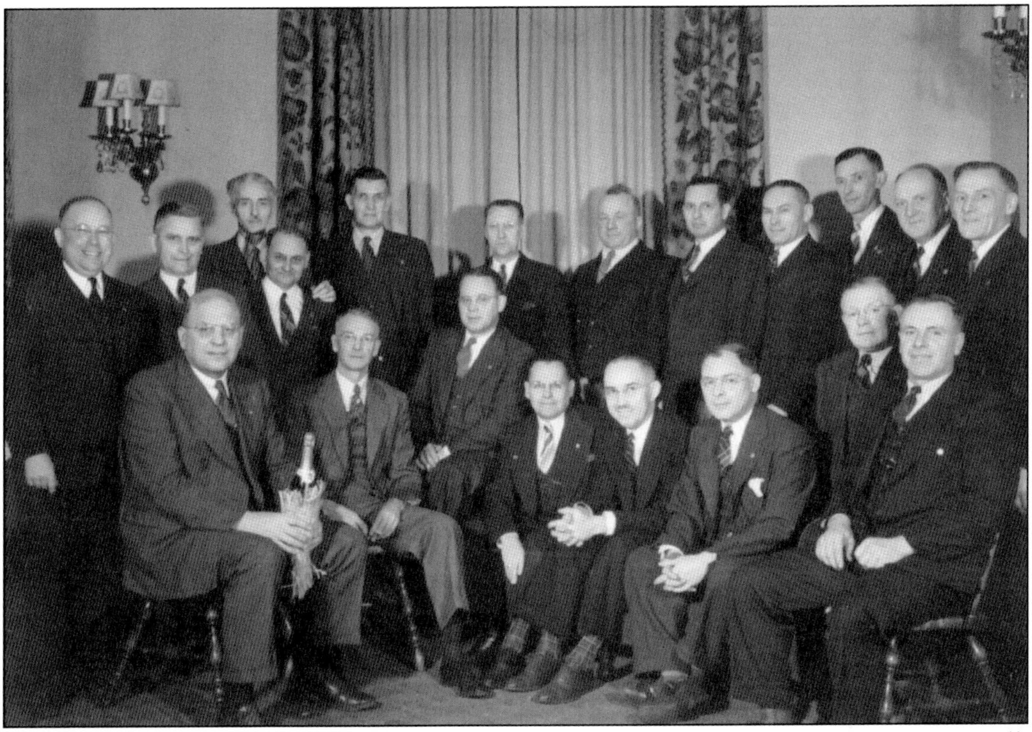

A.J. Carlton American Legion Post No. 922 met in Legion rooms at the Erwin Town Hall. Members formed a Last Man's Club in 1941. As of October 11, 1989, Mason Bower was the last man living. Presumably, he got the bottle of wine shown here. The post itself has since gone out of existence.

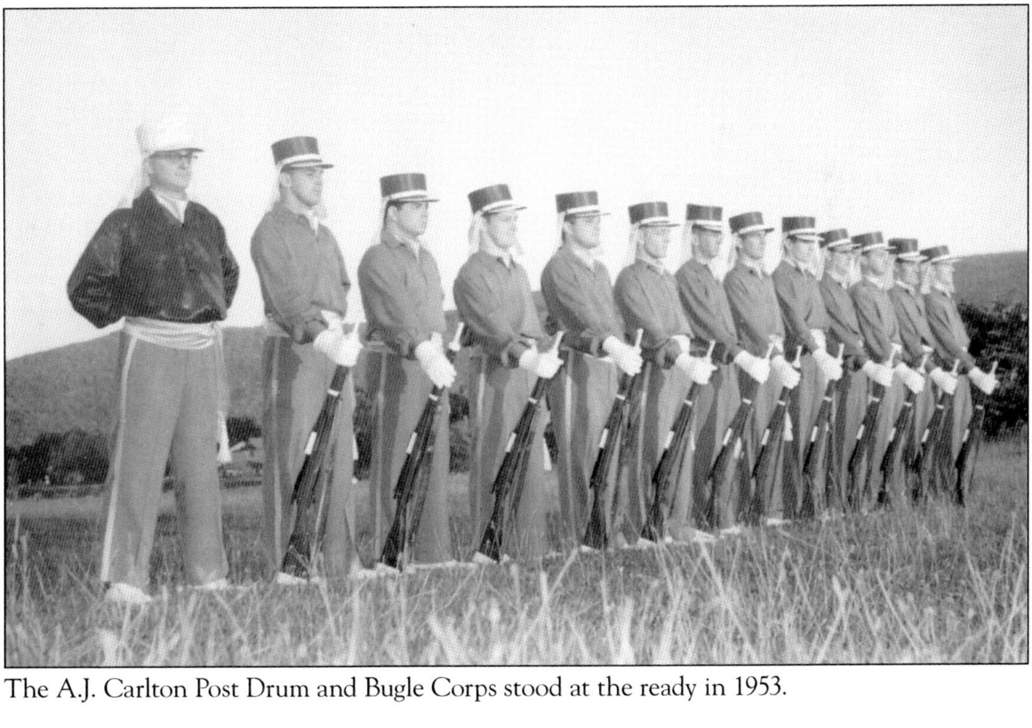

The A.J. Carlton Post Drum and Bugle Corps stood at the ready in 1953.

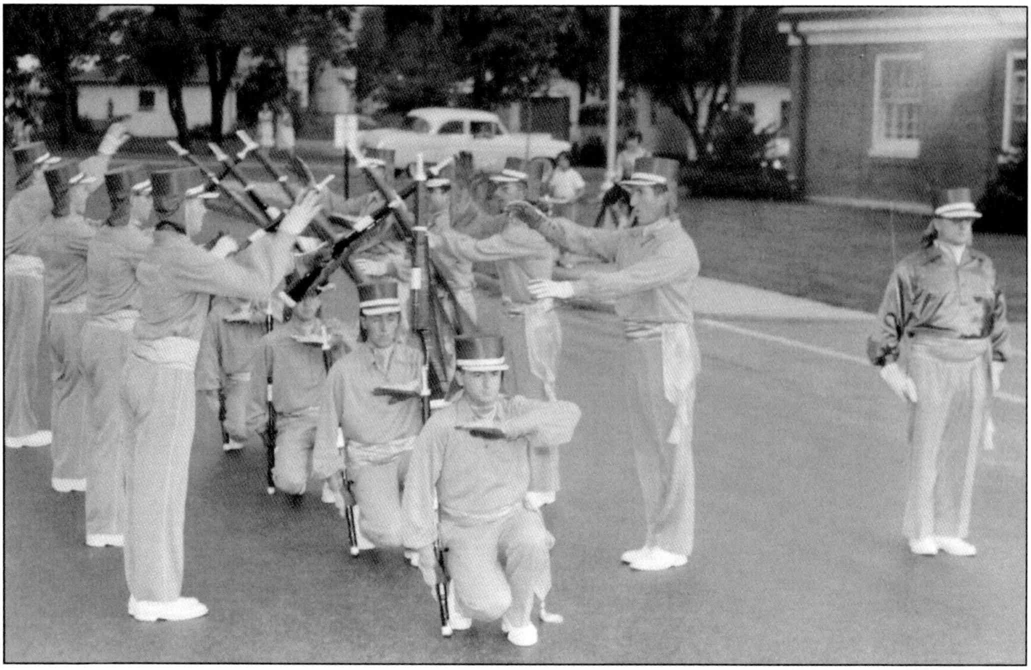

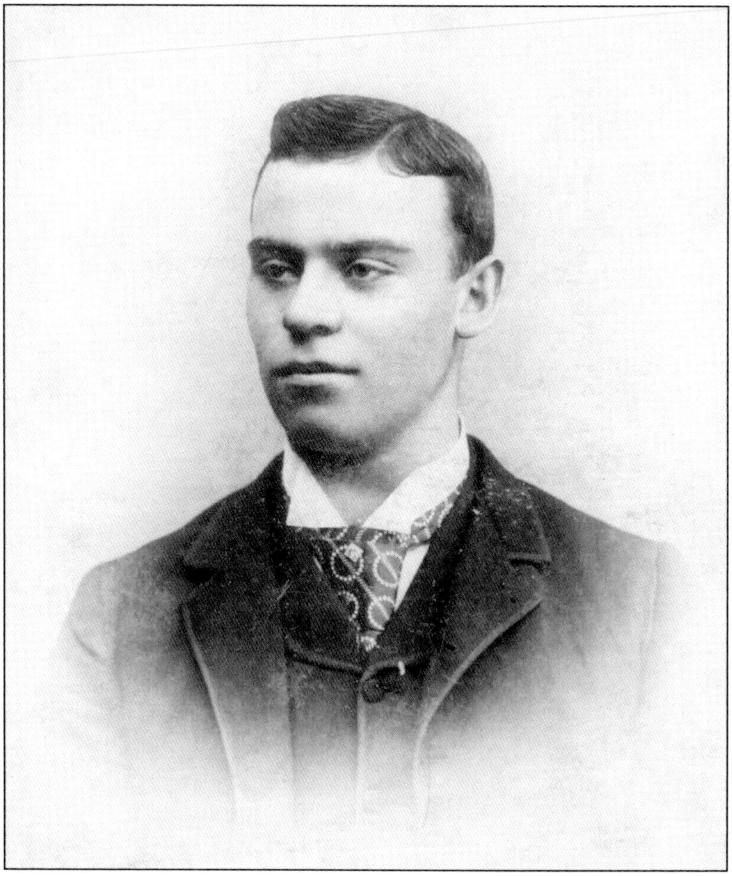

Performances for the A.J. Carlton American Legion Post Drum and Bugle Corps required hours of painstaking practice.

This photograph from a Painted Post file is labeled "Uncle Ed Clark," but, unfortunately, nothing else is known about him. The design on his cravat is impressive, though.

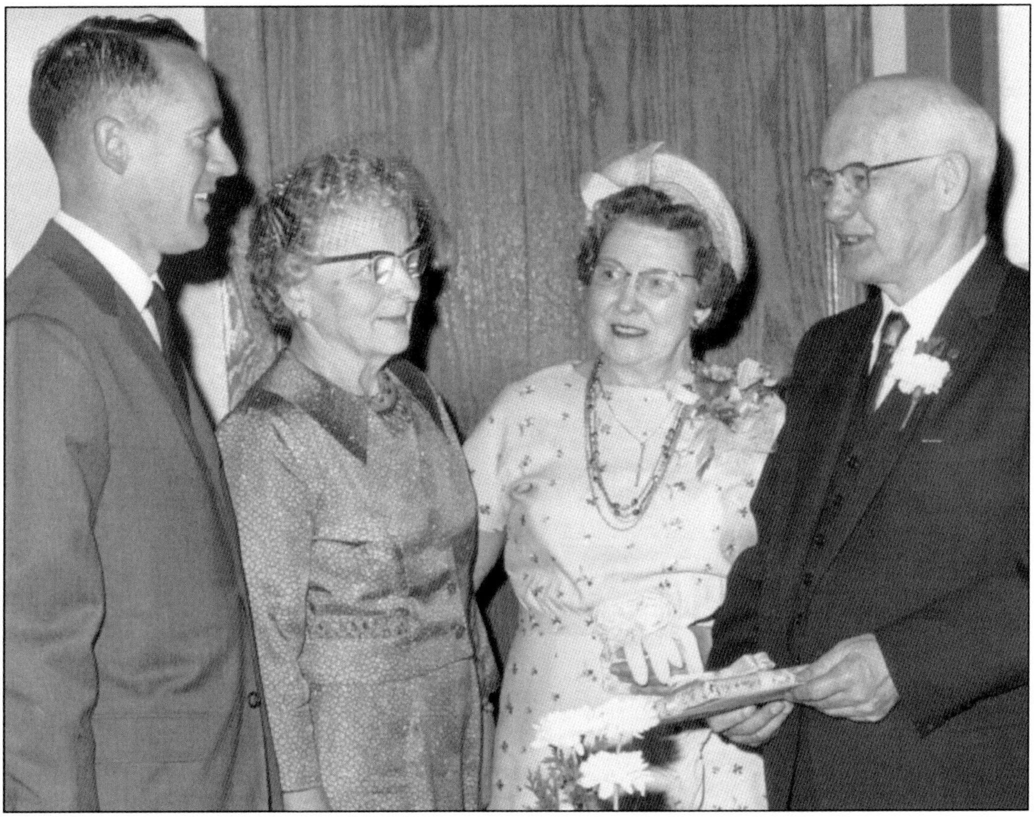

Painted Post resident Calvin U. Smith was superintendent for numerous rural school districts, including those in Erwin. When Corning–Painted Post School District was fully implemented in 1957, one of the new elementary schools was named for Smith. Here, Smith (right) visits the school. The other persons in the photograph have yet to be identified. He is buried in Coopers Plains Cemetery. (SCH.)

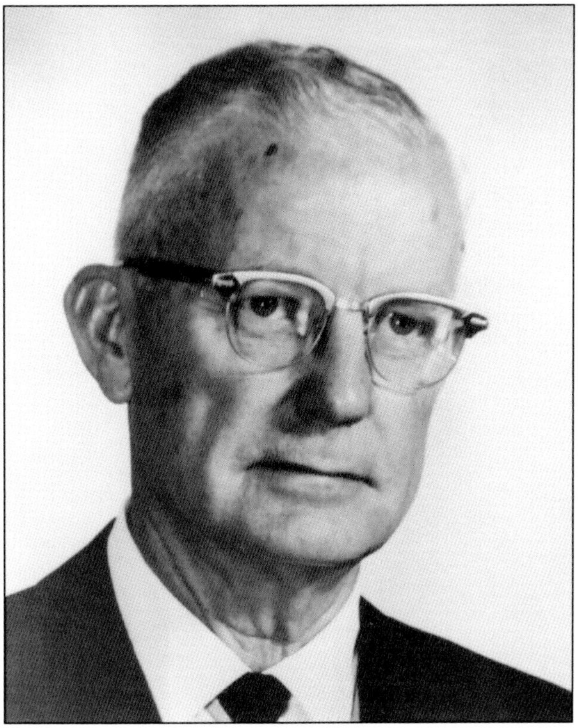

Ellsworth C. Cowles was chief design engineer for portable compressors at Dresser Rand. He also opened the Erwin Museum in 1934, operating it until 1973. Cowles was Town of Erwin historian. As an archeologist, he helped describe the Lamoka culture, whose people lived in the region during the Late Archaic period, about 4,500 years ago. (SCH.)

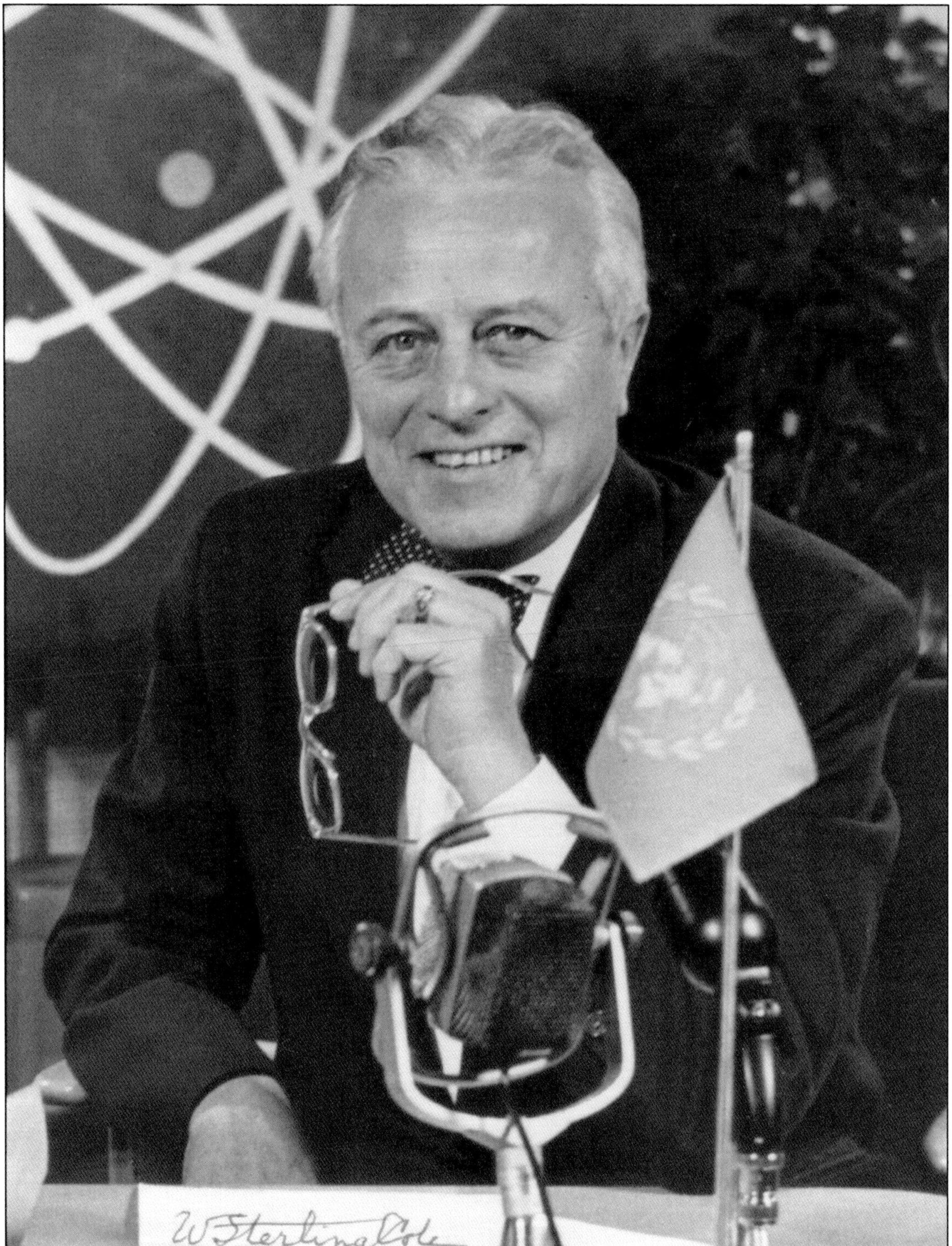

W. Sterling Cole, who was born in Painted Post, served the district as US Representative for 22 years. He was director-general of the International Atomic Energy Commission from 1957 to 1962. Cole, Ellsworth Cowles, and Calvin Smith have all been inducted into the Steuben County Hall of Fame, along with Joe Costa and E.J. Smith. (SCH.)

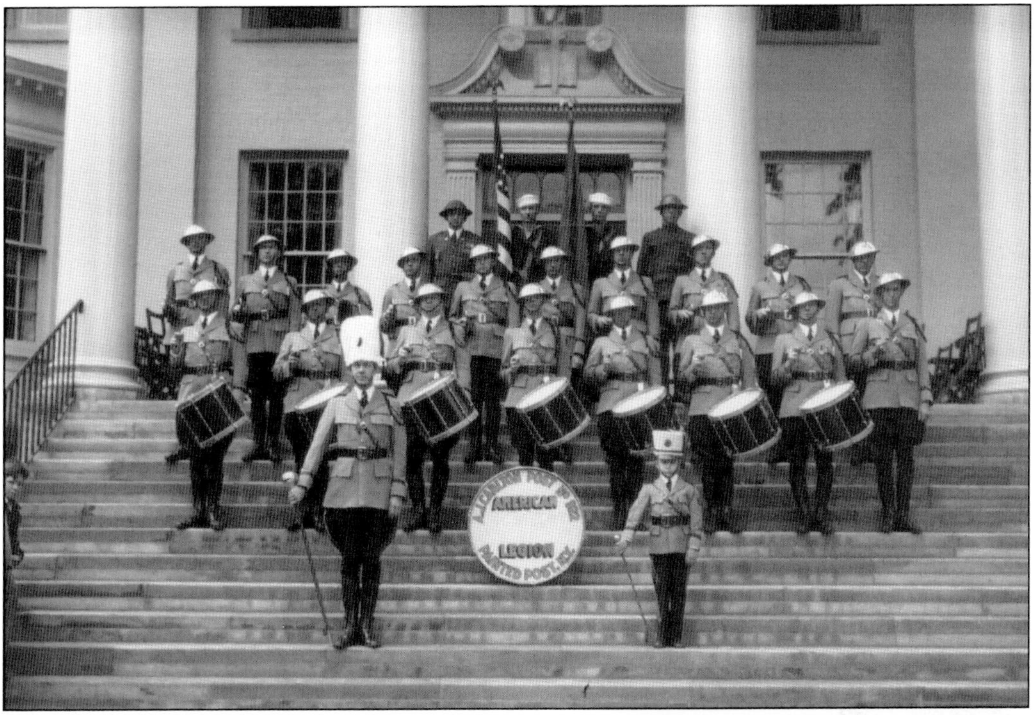

The Legion band (heavy on drums, but doing pretty well on brass, too), formed up on the steps of the high school. Note the tiny drum major in his snappy uniform.

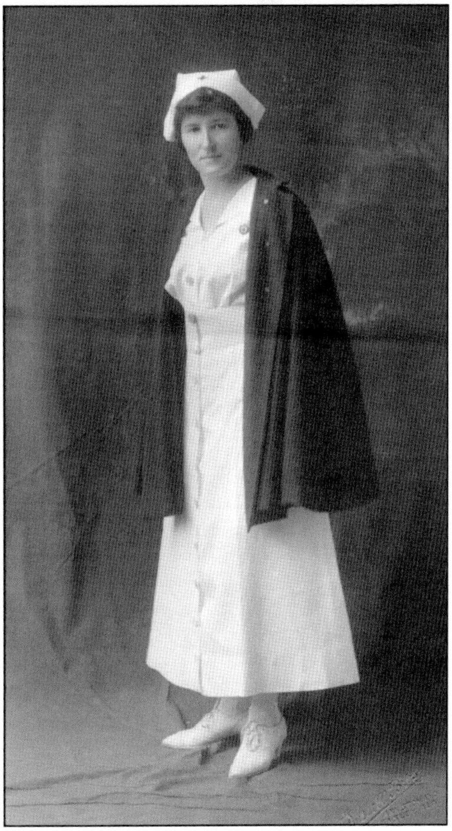

Sal Rush was a local nurse.

Rachel Erwin Birdsall was sister to Samuel C. Erwin.

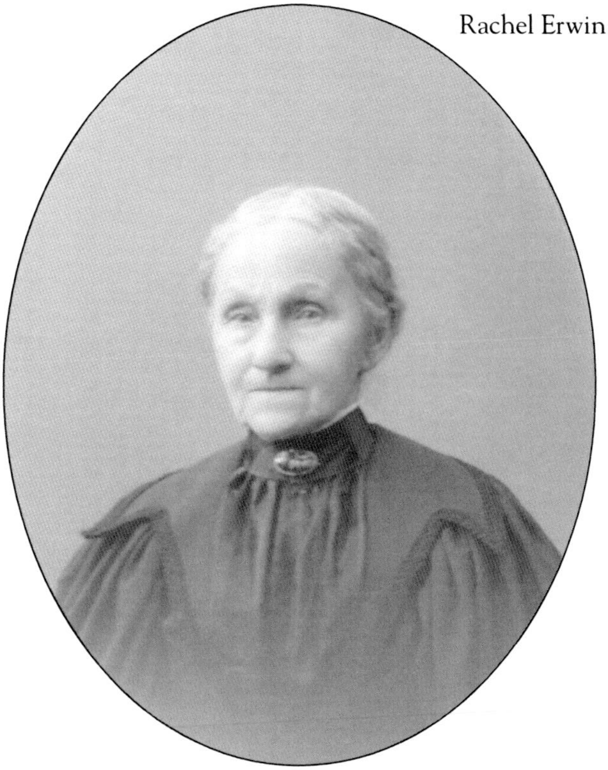

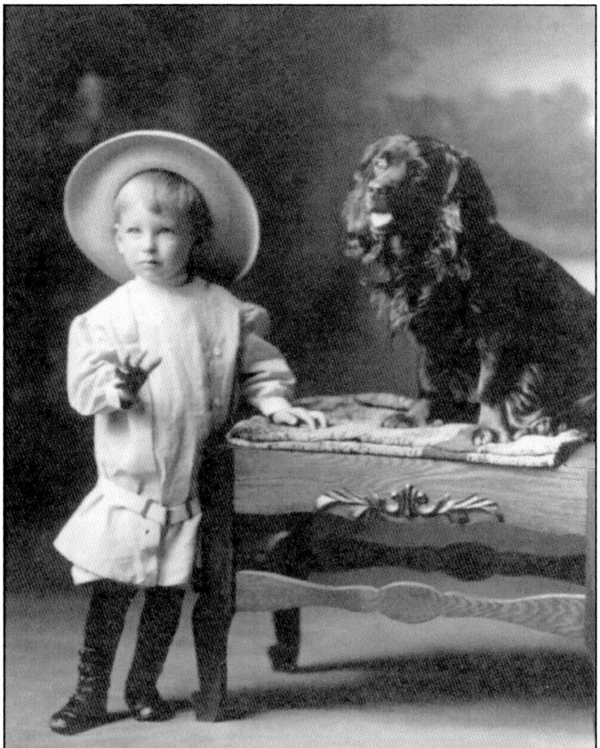

This wonderful photograph has been preserved, but, sad to say, the identity of the boy and the dog have not.

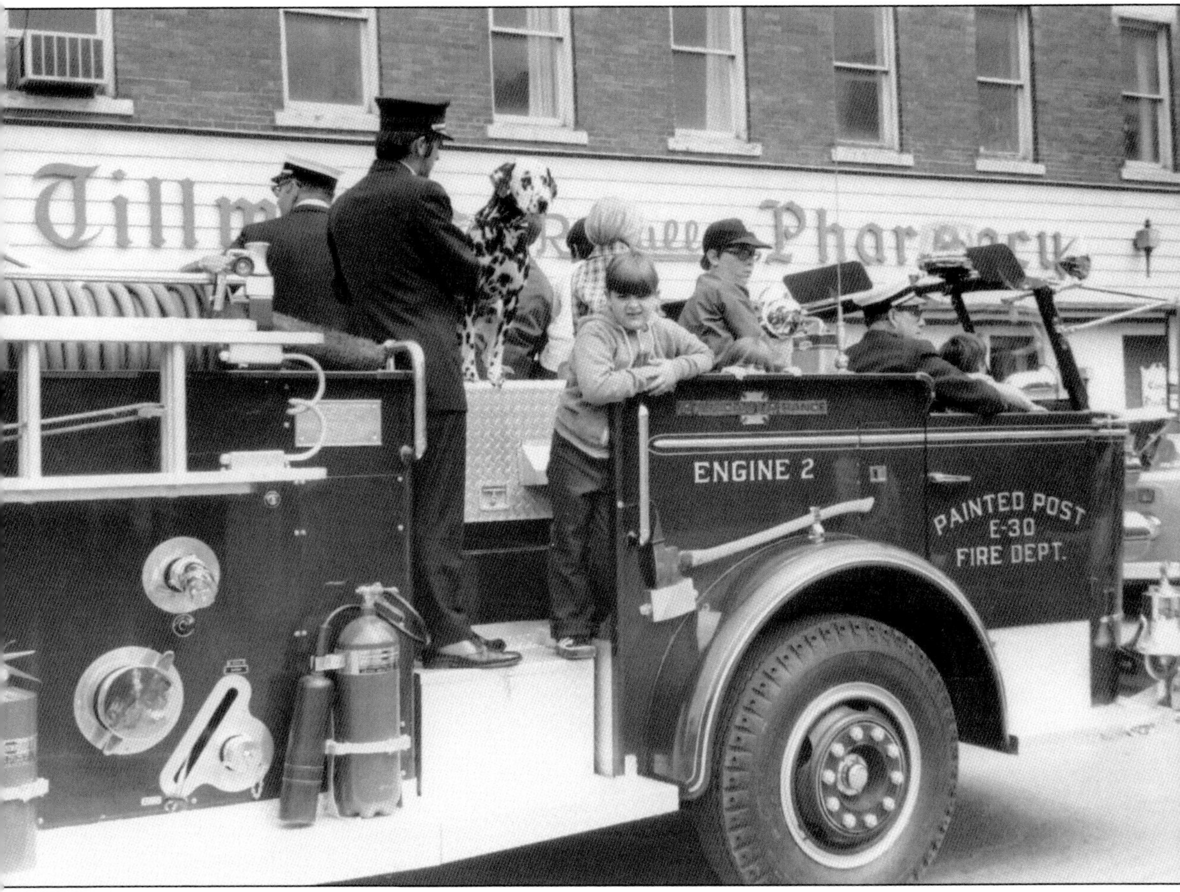

This parade, complete with a fire engine and its dalmatian and "littlest firefighter," probably took place before the 1972 flood. Note the Volkswagen "bus" in the background.

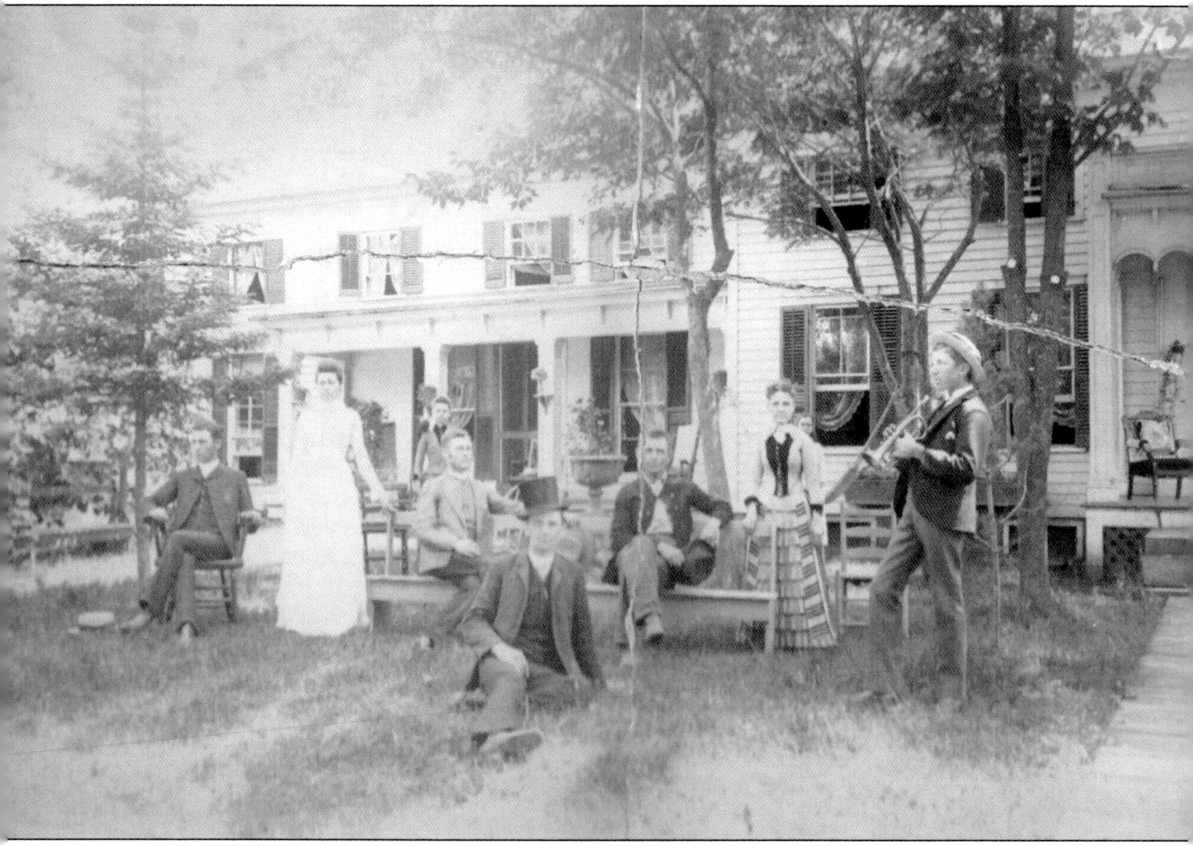

Abraham and Mollie Burt enjoyed a fine, large home, built around 1890. The man seated in front, with a top hat worthy of Abraham Lincoln, is Sam Hewlett. Shown in the row behind Hewlett are, from left to right, Ambrose Hewlett, Mabel Adams, John Adams, Abraham Burt, Mollie Burt, and Belden Burt. Standing behind John Adams is Mamie Erskine, and behind Mollie Burt is Erskine Sanders. Belden Burt appears ready to play a trumpet fanfare for the occasion.

Pat Monahan and Nike played major roles in creating the Crystal Hills Trail. Monahan, who was president of the Finger Lakes Trail Conference, is the one on the left. (FLTC.)

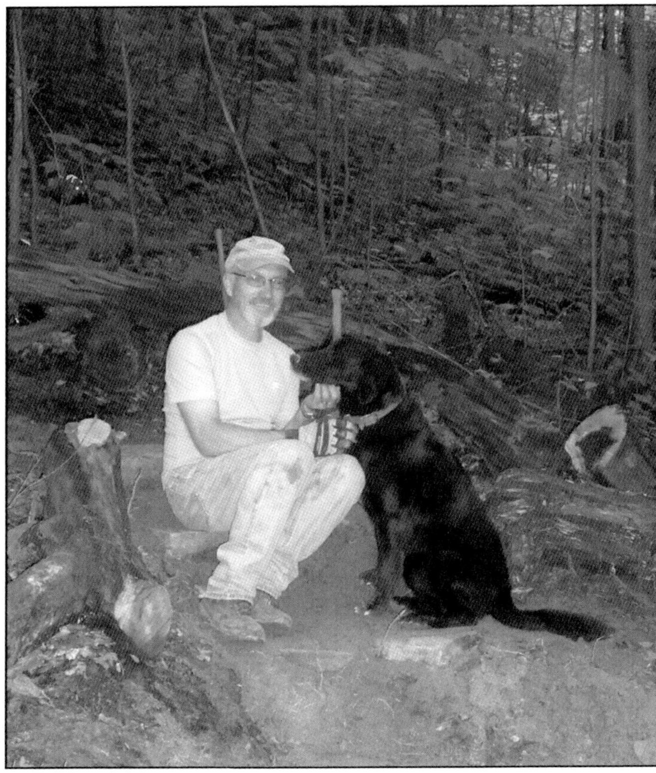

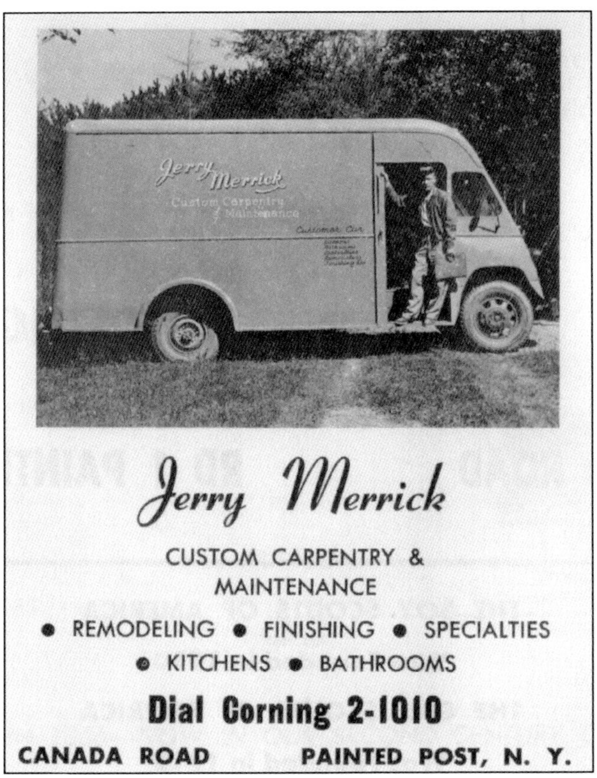

Jerry Merrick operated his business from Canada Road. Why does it say "Customer Car" on the side of the van? Perhaps it was meant to read "Customer Care"? (SCHS.)

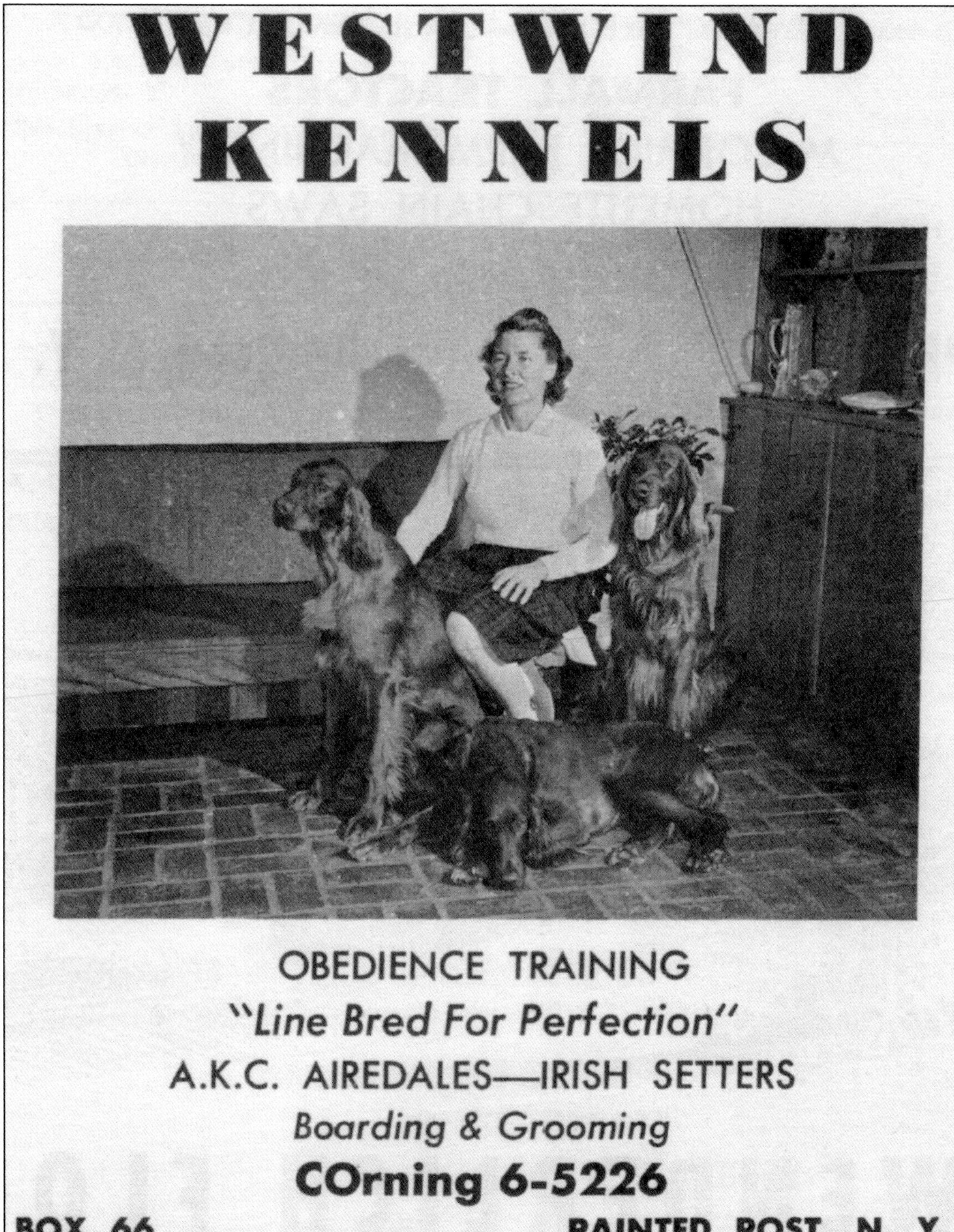

People, pets, wildlife, and livestock have all been part of the Erwin story. (SCHS.)

The J and J store catered to home needs and home extras. (SCHS.)

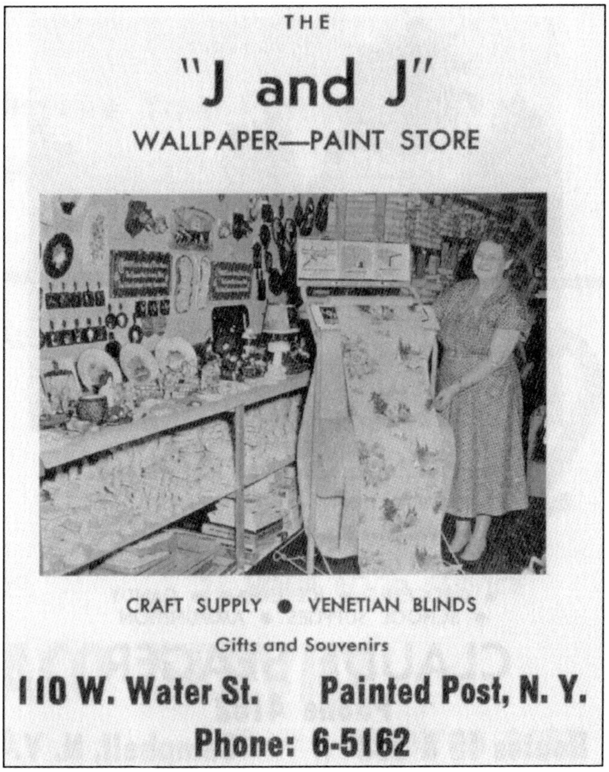

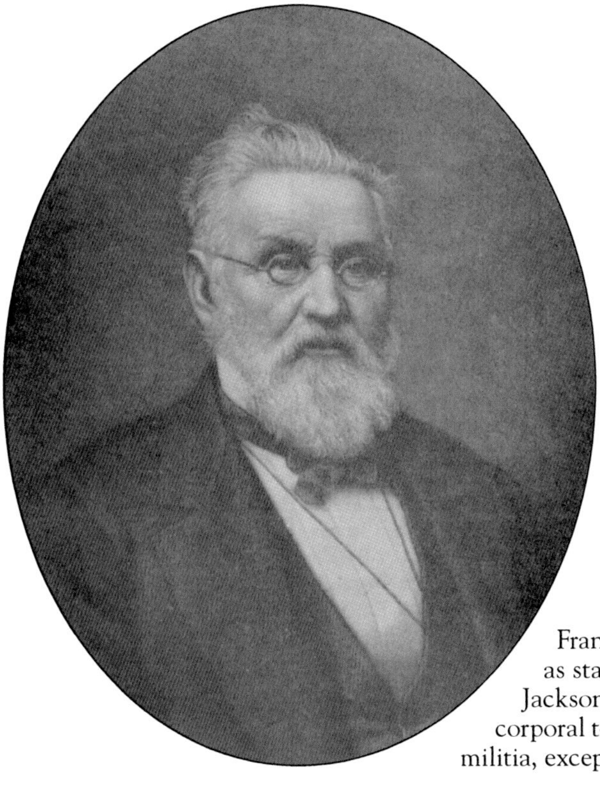

Francis E. Erwin served as town supervisor and as state legislator, championing Jeffersonian/ Jacksonian Democratic Party positions. From corporal to general, he held every rank in the state militia, except captain. (SCH.)

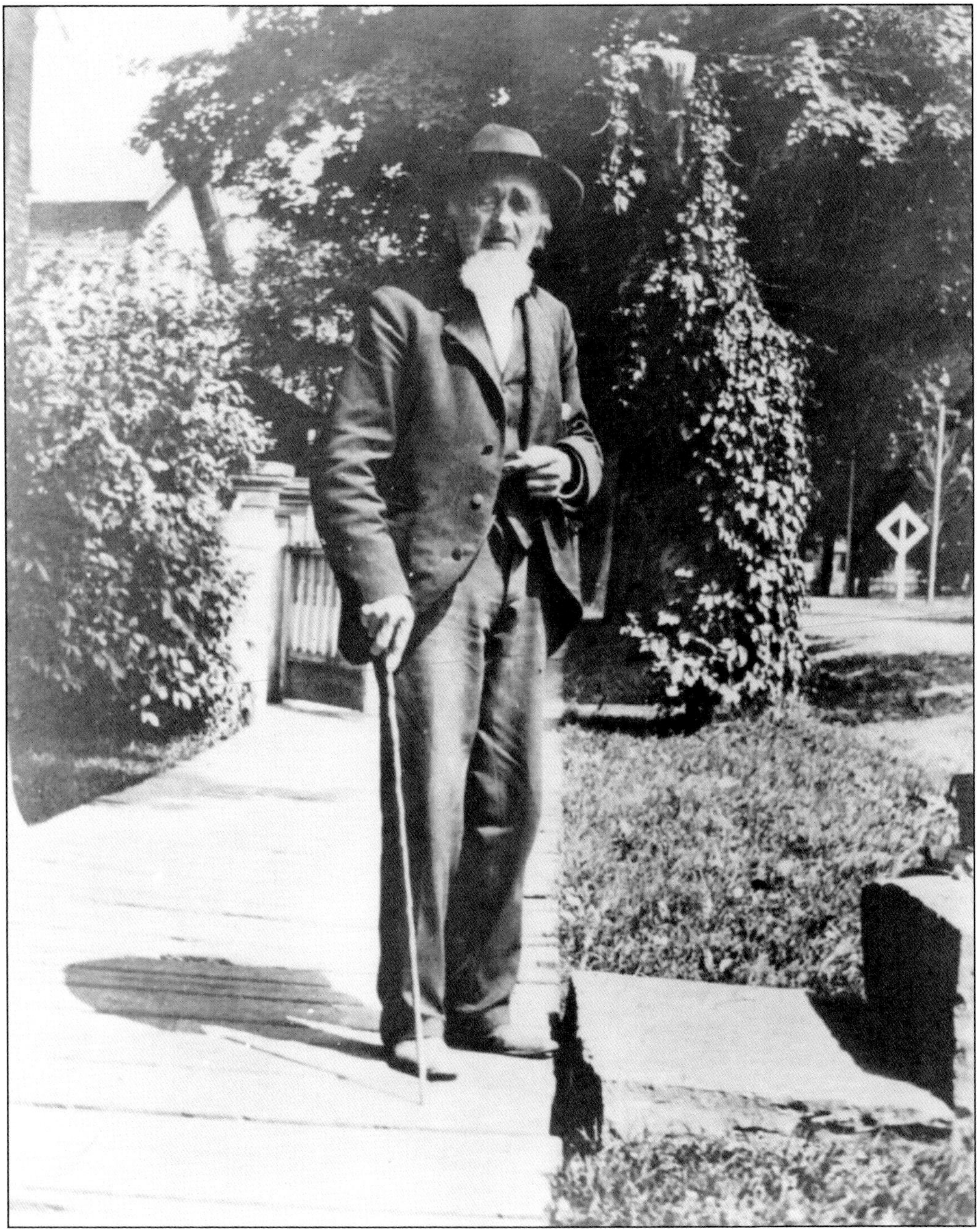

Berry Wood (1817–1902) was a gunsmith in Painted Post. Note the carriage block on the right, and the diamond-shaped railroad crossing sign in the background.

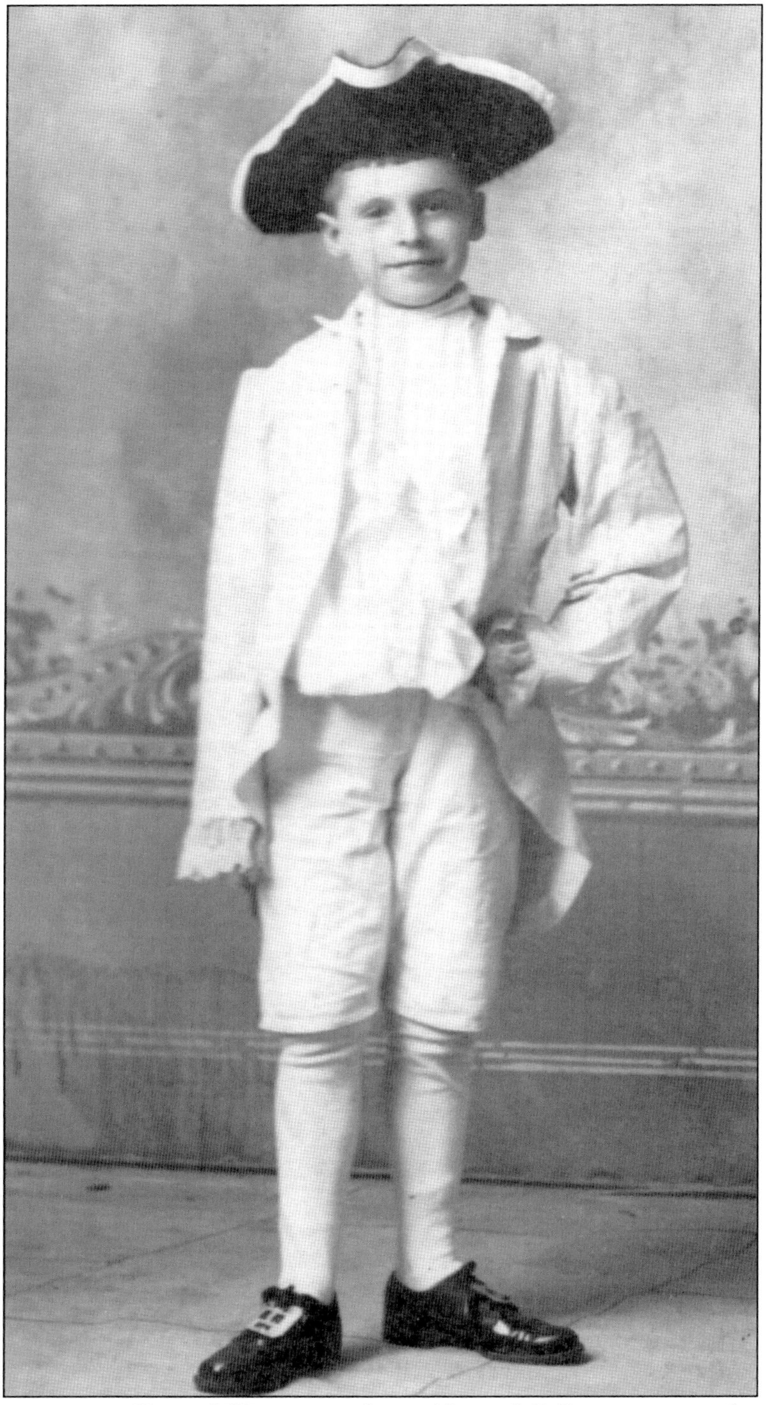

Just about a century ago, Kenneth Erwin, grandson of Samuel C. Erwin, memorialized the town's early days. To him, Erwin's beginnings must have seemed as far back as ancient Egypt. He surely could not have foreseen the 21st century, with its worldwide Internet and interstate highways. When Erwin folks look back a century hence, we will be ancient history to them. As for what marvels will fill their lives, we can only dream, and we wish them well.